D0820686

COMMUNITY ORGANIZERS

COMMUNITY ORGANIZERS

SECOND EDITION

Joan Ecklein
University of Massachusetts

John Wiley & Sons
New York • Chichester • Brisbane • Toronto • Singapore

Library of Congress Cataloging in Publication Data

Ecklein, Joan Levin.
    Community organizers.

    Rev. ed. of: Community organizers and social planners.
1971, c1972.
    Includes index.
    1. Community organization—Case studies.   2. Community
development—United States—Case studies.   I. Ecklein,
Joan Levin. Community organizers and social planners.
II. Title.
HV91.E24   1984   361.8   83-25899
ISBN 0-471-08922-2

Printed in the United States of America

10 9 8 7 6 5 4 3 2 1

To my daughter, Ingrid

Preface

Although this book is a second edition, the field of community organizing has changed so markedly in recent years that I found it necessary to replace the great majority of the material in the first (1972) edition with new cases. The differences between the first and second editions are worth noting because they reflect the way in which community organizing itself has evolved.

In the first place, the fact that this edition is entirely concerned with community organizers—where the first edition was divided between community organizers and social planners—is a tribute to the fact that community organizing during the past decade has become an enormously complex and often sophisticated phenomenon. More than ever before, organizers and planners work in different spheres. A book trying to cover both kinds of activity, which made perfectly good sense in 1972, would today seem an unnatural hybrid.

Of the 44 cases in this edition, all but 10 are new. The reasons for this wholesale turnover in the contents of the book have partly to do with a changing context—the expanding American economy of the 1960s has given way to chronic recession, and social programs are under constant attack—but they also reflect changes in the understanding and practice of community organizers.

Most noticeably, perhaps, Chapter 7, "Women and Organizing" is a reflection of the way in which the women's movement has exploded onto the American political stage since the late 1960s. Although feminism is not usually thought of in the context of community organizing, there have been a growing number of organizing projects dealing specifically with issues that are important to women. For example, shelters for battered women have been set up in hundreds of cities. The reading "Take Back the Night" discussed marches that protest violence against women, another recent form of organizing.

Throughout the book, most notably in Chapter 4, there is a stress on the importance of dealing with racial issues in community organizing. The first edition of the book had plenty of case histories of organizing among nonwhite as well as white people, but at that time there had been little experience in working with *both* whites and nonwhites. The importance of overcoming racial barriers has become more widely understood among organizers in the intervening years. As far as I know, however, the issue has not been extensively discussed in other books on organizing.

Chapter 9, another new chapter "Organizing for the Long Haul," makes explicit an issue that organizers themselves rarely address. In this chapter I juxtapose cases in which the organizers have three distinctive ideological orientations: populism, socialism, and what can be called a community-development approach. The overall political framework in which an organizer sees his or her work can have a marked effect on the day-to-day practical work of organizing. A self-conscious clarity about one's political assumptions can often be very helpful to an organizer.

Although the first edition of this book grew out of a curriculum development project within the field of social work, it was geared to a wider audience, and this is true of the second edition as well. Most of the case histories presented here are taken from interviews rather than being reprints of articles. I interviewed organizers who, in many instances, are accustomed to getting their ideas across in one-on-one conversations more than in written position papers. The book provides a medium in which these people's reflections on their organizing experience can be made available to other community organizers, to other political activists, and to students seeking an inside view of what community organizing is about.

Some of the cases that are carried over from the first edition have been retained because they are still highly relevant—in the issues they confront and in the organizing tactics they describe. Others are included for their historical significance. For example, "Alinsky starts a Fight" describes classic 1960s-style organizing undertaken by the late Saul Alinsky. The two cases that follow illustrate how the "Alinsky approach" has evolved over the past decade. It is important for readers to see graphically that community organizing is still in its formative stages and that it has been changing rapidly.

My acknowledgments start with Armand Lauffer, co-editor of the first edition. The 10 cases that are retained from the first edition are our joint responsibility. (These cases include all of Chapter 5 plus the cases by Cesar Chavez and Robert Perlman in Chapter 2, by Lawrence Grossman in Chapter 6, Anne Braden's "SCEF Responds to a Crisis" in Chapter 4, and "Hollow Hope" in Chapter 9.)

I thank all the people who gave so unselfishly of their time, insights, and expertise in helping put this edition together. Betty Mandell encouraged me to undertake the work, consulted about every aspect of the book, and gave many suggestions for people to interview. I also benefited from the wisdom and insight of colleagues at the College of Public and Community Service: Elaine Werby, Ann Withorn, Michel Stone, and Charlotte Ryan. Marie Weil and Dorothy Markey gave me their enthusiastic support as well as arranging interviews for me in Los Angeles and Yonkers, New York, respectively. Michael Kane, a housing organizer in Boston, gave me very useful insights into the "new populism" that guides much present-day community organizing. Cindy Kulp helped me by providing insights about Freire.

Donna Nelson was a most patient, cheerful, and efficient typist. It was her onerous task to type the interviews from the cassettes. Susan Scheinfeldt and Ruth Anderson also typed portions of the book. I appreciate their thoughtfulness as well as their speed and accuracy. Jim O'Brien was absolutely invaluable in helping me put the book together. His expertise in editing, knowledge of social movements, and droll sense of humor enabled me to finish the book.

I have the most profound respect for the organizers that I interviewed. They are working for social justice for very little or no money and their hours run literally around the clock. With that in mind, I feel very apologetic toward the people whom I interviewed but whose stories I was not able to include in the book, either because of limited space or because of the need to group the cases around particular themes. These people are Frank Wilkinson, Wayne Crosby, Meg Campbell, Stephen Holt, Ramon Salcido, Nancy Andrews, Louis Finfer, Royal Morales, Phyllis Silverman, Sang Quy Do, Nancy Evans, Patricia Mazur, Kathy Weremiuk, Pat McCoy, James Hooley, Dorothy Markey, Alma Woodlan, Fred Danback, Harry Firstenburg, Rick Nestler, and William Tamraz. (The latter six were all active in a community group working to clean up the Hudson River in Yonkers, New York.) I am indebted to them for their time and insights, which helped shape the book.

In the most profound sense I owe thanks to my parents, Isadore and Miriam Levin, and to my uncle Julius Kaplan, for nurturing in me an appreciation of history and a keen sense of social justice. My daughter, Ingrid, patiently accompanied me to many of the interviews or suffered my absence when it wasn't possible for her to come along. There were also many times over the past three years that I had to work on the book when we could have been spending time together.

Joan Ecklein

Contents

CHAPTER 1

Introduction

This book is about a relatively new occupational grouping of people who intervene, organize, and plan with and on behalf of others. It is a book about, by, and for community organizers. Their activities are not by any means new, but it is only during the past two decades that community organizers have emerged as a distinct grouping of people, many of whom have professional training for their work.

American history is studded with the growth and decay, accomplishments, and failures of voluntary associations. Despite the ideology of rugged individualism, and of individual advancement along the lines of the Horatio Alger stories, much of America's social progress has been based on the emergence of social movements, trade unions, and self-help associations. Collective rather than individual action has most frequently led to reform and the reallocation of resources. And at every stage the role of organizers—people who have worked to build groupings of people aimed at bringing about social change—has been crucial.

Yet the history of organizing for social reform in America has been fragmentary. Until very recently, organizers of one generation were frequently unaware of the contributions of their predecessors. Traditions, techniques, and strategies were not passed down or built on. Most recently, the repression of the McCarthy era of the 1950s helped to seal younger people off from the rich experiences of union and community organizing during the Great Depression of the 1930s.

During the 1960s, however, there took place a proliferation of popular movements—a massive civil rights movement initiated by blacks in the late 1950s was followed later in the decade by popular protest against the Vietnam war—a protest that involved unprecedented numbers of people. A generalized youth rebellion, touched off largely by issues of racism and the war but encompassing a whole range of grievances against "the system," flared briefly in the late 1960s and early 1970s. The late 1960s saw the beginnings of the present-day women's movement. At the same time, from the mid-1960s on, as an offshoot of the civil rights movement, there were a host of organizing efforts aimed at giving poor people a voice in the political decisions that helped to shape their lives; welfare-rights organizing was one example of this kind of activism.

New governmental programs were a part of this upsurge: they were a response to the civil rights movement and at times they helped to encourage new activism. Programs like the Office of Economic Opportunity and Model Cities opened up professional-level jobs for people with skills in community organizing. And within related professions like social work, community organizing became acknowledged as an important skill. It was formally recognized as a distinct field within social work in 1962, a field paralleled to others like case work and group work. As time went on, social work schools offered more classes in community organization so that students would have the credentials needed to get the new jobs that were opening up in the new government programs. There was also an increased recognition that organizing skills were necessary in traditional service agencies if the clients were to be properly served. In other words, community organizing was becoming a self-conscious occupation, with skills that could be transmitted from one person to another.

This book is actually a product of the ferment of the 1960s. The first edition (published in 1972) came out of a curriculum development project aimed at developing teaching materials to help train people obtaining master of social work degrees with specialties in community organizing. (The first edition included cases on social planning as well as community organization; it was coedited by Armand A. Lauffer, and it also reflected the work of our colleagues in the curriculum development project, Arnold Gurin, Robert Perlman, and Wyatt Jones.) The cases in the book vibrated with the new activism of the 1960s as the book shared with students the reflections that community organizers were making on their successes and failures.

Now it is a different decade and a lot has changed about American society. Most noticeably, economic expansion has given way to a series of protracted recessions. The political climate is far more conservative. There is less government funding for the participation of people in developing or overseeing human service programs. "Maximum feasible participation of the poor," it was once called. Indeed, many of the programs themselves are in the process of being dismantled. Correspondingly, there has been a deemphasis in schools of social work on community organization as a field of specialization. The cost of a graduate school education is enormous and the jobs with professional-level salaries are becoming more and more scarce. Consequently, there have even been predictions of the "death of community organization."

Paradoxically, throughout the country there is actually a tremendous amount of community organizing going on. Most of the people who are doing it full time are working for poverty-level wages, out of a profound commitment to social change and social justice. Many people who have other jobs in order to make a living and support families still consider organizing work as their primary commitment. Moreover, even when we look at the cutback in jobs for organizers working for governmental and private agencies, we can see that the present situation is by no means a static one. Individuals being trained in schools of social work still very much need these skills, and funding for community organizing is likely to increase again in the future. Finally, the very existence of the cutbacks means that workers in direct-service agencies need to have an organizer's perspective if they are to avoid burnout. They are facing clients in desperate situations when they themselves are overworked. Unless these workers have an organizer's understanding of power relationships and how to organize for increased resources, they will not only be unable to service their clients' needs but will be in danger of losing their own jobs through continued cutbacks.

Thus, an organizer's skills are needed now more than ever, and there is an immense array of situations in which individuals who know something about organizing can make an impact. And today, much more than when the first edition of this book was put together, there exists a systematic body of knowledge and experience about what organizing involves. Community organizers today are far more self-conscious and less intuitive about what they are doing. The statement in the first edition that organizers are "operating with rudimentary skills, little practice theory, and fragmentary knowledge in a field of practice of unknown complexity" is much less true today than when it was written. According to one estimate, for example, there are now more than a dozen organizer-training centers connected to various networks of citizens' organizations. The very existence of such networks, which have expanded the concept of "community" to encompass statewide and even nationwide organizing, marks a major difference between organizing in the 1960s and in the 1980s.

In this book, nearly all the case materials are presented in the first person. The organizers speak for themselves, describing and analyzing particular aspects of their work. Almost all the cases were edited from taped interviews. The objective is to depict how community organizers go about their work. Sometimes, what is described in the book is spectacular and inspirational, and sometimes it is depressing and insipid. Illustrations of both good and bad practice are included, in order to make the book as close to the realities of practice as possible. Each organizer naturally has her or his own biases, and the cases might be told in slightly different ways by other people involved in them. The cases are of varying lengths, and only material that is useful for teaching and learning is included.

The great majority of cases in this book concern organizing among low-income urban residents around various issues of concern to them. But the cases are chosen for their usefulness for teaching purposes, rather than because of the particular constituencies they represent. That is, the cases seek to represent general principles of community organizing, not primarily the specific problems of particular groups. It can readily be seen that some constituencies important in the 1970s, such as senior citizens, gays and lesbians, and Native Americans, were not represented or were underrepresented in the book, but the overall principles of organizing are largely the same for different constituencies. The omission of cases from rural and small-town areas was more of a deliberate matter of choice. I felt that the problems of organizing in these settings are sufficiently different from those in urban areas that they would really warrant a separate treatment altogether.

Two final points should be made concerning the scope of the book. First, it focuses on the activities of people who in some respect can be called professional organizers. They may be paid very little, or they may hold other full-time jobs, but they are professional organizers in the sense that they see organizing, in and of itself, as their role. When one campaign has played itself out, or has succeeded, they will move on to another. In this respect they are unlike people who may be called community leaders, whose role in a particular campaign may be no less important than the organizer's, but who are primarily interested in a particular issue and a particular constituency. Second, it should be made clear that this is not a how-to-do-it book. Clearly an organizer should bring a range of skills into a campaign—from writing leaflets to doing layout to making use of the opportunities for free publicity offered by the local media. But it is not the purpose of this book to teach these or other specific skills. The cases in the book are selected because they give the feel of an organizer's work and a sense of the political questions that an organizer is faced with.

SOME THEMES

Community organizers are concerned with advancing the interests of disadvantaged groups, with improving social conditions, with the delivery of needed services, with redistribution of power and influence, with enhancement of the coping mechanisms of target populations, and with strengthening community participation and integration. These objectives, however, are frequently in conflict with each other. The establishment of a multiservice center, for example, may be achieved much more effectively by some standards without resorting to broad community involvement. Organizers may represent different constituencies, each struggling for the same objectives in opposition to each other. A focus on delivery of a service may, in reality, do little about the redistribution of power. It may even consolidate it unevenly.

There is an underlying tension between a service-oriented approach and a social-action orientation. Services focus on individual need, whereas organizing focuses on the location of common problems and joint efforts at their solution. In a sense, each may be considered a correction of the other. Social action may ignore the needs of individuals, where service orientation may ignore the impact of social conditions on the problem of concern. Some action-oriented organizations, like the Massachusetts Advocacy Center described in Chapter 8, have added services as a support to their action platforms. Other organizations have built their action platforms on the foundation of earlier focus on service—Caesar Chavez's community union is an example as is the Rhode Island Workers Union, which is modeled after Chavez's organizing strategies; both are described in Chapter 2. Still other action organizations refuse to deal with service needs during certain phases of the organizing process for fear that these might dilute the organization's purposes. Other agencies have attempted service and action simultaneously only to find that the pursuit of one was detrimental to the other.

The question of goals and goal displacement enters here. Every organizing decision, and every action taken, is complemented by a set of alternative decisions not made and actions not taken. Actions and decisions represent commitments in directions that may not easily be reversed. An early focus on service, for example, makes it exceedingly difficult to reorient an organization towards action at a later date. A focus on ethnic or neighborhood solidarity at one stage may make it impossible to progress to a community orientation at another. Goals may be continually displaced as day-to-day activities set precedents for future directions. The relationship between service and action is a case in point. At times, an action program is initiated in order to effectuate changes in a service system, only to become an arm of that system or to perpetuate it once a particular concession is won.

Reform-oriented associations frequently disintegrate or disappear once their reform efforts are satisfied, if only partially. As reforms become institutionalized, or as an action organization assumes responsibility for the delivery of services or the monitoring of service delivery, the focus of membership concern frequently shifts to maintaining the service and its efficient delivery. Thus, reform efforts become bureaucratized and institutionalized, the new institutions developing lives of their own. These, in turn, may become unresponsive to further change.

A further tension exists in the fact that organizers must concern themselves simultaneously with the achievement of specific changes and the accomplishment of visible victories, while building a network of relationships that make and maintain the voluntary association. How is success to be measured? By achievement of specific reforms, or by longevity of organization? By the establishment of a new network of relationships and a sense of community or by a visual accomplishment?

The roles an organizer plays and how he or she plays them is very much a matter of skill, style, and experience. The timidity or the brashness of individual organizers—their personal style—may be due to a variety of factors. Organizers must be wary of many pitfalls. Organizers may be overtly manipulative, or they may be afraid to manipulate and exploit people. They may perceive themselves as meddlers or intruders in the lives of others, while simultaneously being unable to commit themselves to prolonged involvement with those whom they organize. They may, conversely, work so hard and become so committed as to lose their perspective and burn themselves out in a year or two. Organizers may be so personally unable to make decisions or so ideologically committed to "letting the people decide" that they throw responsibility for complex decisions into the laps of those unprepared. They may become depressed by frequent defeats or elated by small victories. They may put too much or too little faith in those with whom they work.

In the political atmosphere of the 1980s, the dangers of absorption through partial victories do not loom as large as in the 1960s. The opposite kind of danger, however—the danger of repression—is no less a problem than it was earlier. Organizers are frequently unprepared to recognize repressive measures when confronted with them. Yet as the long-term activist Sam Abbott argues in Chapter 2, organizers must be ready to recognize surveillance, provocation, and other deliberately disruptive activity for what it is. Beyond that, they should be ready to deal with it constructively so as not to be deflected from the goals the group has set for itself. At worst, repression can include criminal charges and even assassinations. A good example is the Black Panther Party, which was unprepared for the sometimes murderous repression it encountered in the late 1960s, and was subsequently destroyed as an organization.

Organizers are rarely free agents. Regardless of value and ideological commitments, or of skill and expertise, much of their work is determined by the contexts within which they practice. Contextual components include (1) the auspices under which they operate—the legitimating and sponsoring body, (2) the source of financial and other support, (3) the purpose of the organization for whom or on whose behalf they act, (4) the target of their intervention, whether a population group, organization, or service network, (5) the internal structure of the organization within which they work, and finally, (6) the locus at which their intervention is pitched—the neighborhood, the local community, the state, and the like. Together, these components constrain and limit the scope of their activities, and give them the mandate for their actions. It is very important that these aspects of the organizing context be in harmony with one another. If the sponsoring agency has one set of goals in mind, and the community residents with whom the organizer is working have an entirely different set of goals, the organizer's position is likely sooner or later to become untenable.

Since the 1960s, some lessons have been learned about sponsorship. To take one example, there had been a heady feeling that government funds once available for organizing people at the local level would always be there. The lesson that there are powerful forces within and outside government who see their interests threatened by local organizing—and who have the power to curtail these funds when the organizing is most effective—was learned the hard way in many instances. Today imaginative strategies are being developed to stay clear of funding sources that would in any way compromise the goals the people in the organization have set for themselves. An example is the canvassing technique that has been developed by a number of organizations, often on a statewide level. Canvassers seek small individual contributions, often on the basis of the group's public identification with certain visible issues. This is a tremendously more sophisticated approach than the one that was common at the time the first edition of this book was published. In general, while the first edition had a chapter on "The Organizer as Man in the Middle," I felt that such a chapter was simply not needed in this edition.

Organizers are frequently caught in a bind between their professional and ideological commitments to long-range goals and the need to achieve immediate objectives, between their espousal of utopian objectives and the need to achieve feasible goals. Most organizing efforts are aimed at the secondary manifestation of social problems. Most organizing, whatever the rhetoric behind it, is in practice aimed at piecemeal adjustments of the machinery of society. Many organizers, we know, have been accused of applying Band-Aid therapy. We feel this an unfortunate analogy and offers little understanding of a complex set of phenomena. The magnitude and direction of any social changes may be determined by forces out of the reach of most organizers and their constituencies. Nevertheless, the only way to begin to get leverage is to combat the powerlessness of people who are dealt with unfairly by the society.

The Brazilian educator Paulo Freire has articulated a concept that many organizers today have found crucial to their work in seeking to develop indigenous leadership in the groups they work with. This is the concept of "critical consciousness," a process in which individuals see their world in different ways and gain both the motivation and the self-confidence to change it. Whether seen in Freire's theoretical framework or not, the need to develop leadership is central to virtually every community organizing effort. Today's best organizers see their relationship to community people as one of profound mutual respect in which personal relationships develop that allow both of them to change, grow, and develop. Perhaps the ultimate goal may be the breakdown of the distinction between organizer and leader.

It is certainly not a new insight that in order for people to organize successfully they must have an understanding of how their society is put together. In Europe, where there is far less of an opportunity for working-class people to obtain formal higher education, worker's education has traditionally been viewed as an important aspect of any organizing effort. We have no such tradition in this country. Ideas like Freire's are sensitizing organizers to the need for systematically educating community people about the complex problems in our society, and the need for very fundamental changes.

COMMUNITY ORGANIZING IN THE 1980S

During the 1960s there were three major organizing traditions at the community level. First, there was community organizing as an adjunct to established service agencies or, increasingly, to governmental programs spawned by the Johnson administration's War on Poverty. Second, there was community organizing coming out of particular social movements, such as the civil rights movement. Third, there was community organizing in the tradition developed by Saul Alinsky in the 1930s. Of the three, Alinsky's approach is the most prominent today. There are many variations on the Alinsky style of organizing and as we show in Chapter 2, the style has evolved: rather than just individual neighborhoods being organized, groups are typically organized on a citywide and statewide as well as neighborhood basis. Some of the groups have national linkages as well. This type of organizing also has a new name: it is generally referred to as "the new populism."

There has been a lot of experimentation, and these groups have grown and changed over the years. While the exact significance of these groups and their potential for basic social change are in some dispute, it is clear that they represent a very significant form by which blue-collar and white-collar working-class people are organizing defensively in the economic and political context of the early 1980s.

In the Alinksy tradition, the new populist organizations are very result oriented, they focus on specific issues and they use professional organizers who have technical competence in research, use of media, and so forth. These organizations have spawned training centers of their own for their organizing staffs. At the same time, they are mindful of the criticism that too elaborate an organizational structure can make them bureaucratized and ossified to the point of stifling their militancy. The new populist organizers are trying to prevent this from happening; at the same time, they see a necessity for stable organization that will take on varied fights in protection of the people's interests.

The distinction between community leaders and staff (organizers) in these organizations has been viewed as a serious drawback to the organizing efforts. The distinction is very clearly drawn. Organizers come from outside the communities in which they work and for the most part receive training through the staff of the organization. In a situation like this, there is inevitably a serious question about the organizer's commitment to the neighborhood. Community people may be suspicious of outsiders who are only going to be there for a short time and then move on to something else. The organizers tend to be more highly educated than community people and they are looked on as transients who will do their life's work elsewhere while they fill in a gap after college. What this means in practice is that the organizers, while able to provide skills that community leaders may not have, also call the shots on tactics and strategy. A very studious effort is generally made to have only community leaders conduct press conferences, chair meetings, and act as spokespeople, while the organizer stays in the background. However, if the organizer is actually making most of the decisions this arrangement is demeaning to everyone. Also, community people can become too dependent on professional organizers. The goal of an organizer ideally is to work himself, or herself, out of a job. There are no easy answers to these issues, but it seems clear that there has to be a conscious effort to train community leaders, not only in the specific skills necessary to organizing, but in analysis of the American corporate structure and all its ramifications.

An organization's commitment to quick victories on very specific issues may also have unintended consequences. Perhaps the most important of these is that a community group organized in a white neighborhood may be unwilling to deal with issues of racial equality. In Chapter 4 the case "Going Slow Against Racism in White Neighborhoods" illustrates some of the dilemmas involved. Here a young organizer was told by his trainer that he should stay away from a race issue in a racist white neighborhood, as it would prevent them from getting a foothold in that community. One problem with this approach is that, if race issues are excluded at the outset in order to get a group started, it may be very difficult to take up the issue at a later date—especially if people with deeply ingrained racism as part of their basic ideology become leaders in the organization.

Another consequence of the focus on quick victories, and inattention to education, may be a heavy turnover in membership. This is difficult to document, but new populist organizers have told me about problems stemming from high membership turnover. Community people come and go, and so do the leaders. One organizer stated that every several years he has to train people anew in dealing with various community issues. Thus, while the organization may be a stable presence in a community, if the membership is unstable this poses problems. If people had a broader perspective on the problems faced by their community, they might be more likely to stick with the organization over the long haul.

As a final note, I have acquired a profound appreciation for organizers. They are on the line in a very public way, and their successes are very difficult to measure. They must often be satisfied with tentative accomplishments. Even the best organizers may be plagued with the feeling that they have not done the best possible job, that alternative choices of action might have led to a closer approximation of the original goal. There are no easy solutions to complex problems. Yet these men and women know that their day is short. Their work is great and they do not desist.

HOW TO READ THIS VOLUME

With these cautions in mind, we invite the reader to examine the assumptions and the practices of the community organizers whose work is described in the following pages. To what extent have these organizers actually accomplished what they set out to do? Were their objectives clear from the start? Were their objectives appropriate to the situations in which they found themselves? Were they sufficiently cognizant of alternative tactics? Were their tactics informed by strategy or conscious design? What might be some of the unintended consequences of their actions? The cases, vignettes, and illustrative materials that follow should not be used indiscriminately as guides for action. Their value is more for the questions they raise than in the answers they provide.

CHAPTER 2

Community Development, Social Action, and Social Movements

These cases illustrate both the differences and the similarities in the community-development and social-action approaches. Two of the authors, Cesar Chavez and the late Saul Alinsky, have been extremely influential figures, and their organizing techniques are spelled out in the cases "La Causa and La Huelga" and "Alinsky Starts a Fight." Chavez, committed to very long-term organizing, is still doing the same kind of organizing today. George Nee's case, "Chavez Is Right," shows an application of Chavez's approach in an urban context. The Alinsky case, set in Rochester, New York, is a classic case from the 1960s. Even though he died his methodology has been adapted and improved on by contemporary organizers. "The Boston Model" and "After Alinsky" both show his continuing influence. The other two cases in this chapter are by long-time social activists who illustrate how it is possible to fight against illegal repression of social movement organizations.

What comes through so forcefully in the Chavez material is his enormous stress on human dignity and self-respect. Chavez epitomizes a personal style. Quiet, unassuming, and modest, he nevertheless builds on personal charisma. He puts great stress on the role of leadership, in particular the need to lead by example, to

11

have great patience, and to give wholly of one's time and energy to the "cause." Chavez takes the reader all the way through the organizing process, showing that organizing can be a rational and self-conscious activity. He also shows how difficult and slow-moving it can be.

Chavez built his movement around the development of mutual obligations—to himself, to the organization, and to other workers. He made certain that members would have a deep stake in the organization before he even began to speak about becoming a union or going on strike. He was not willing to risk failure until he felt that the organization's membership was ready. He refused outside help during his early organizing efforts for fear that reliance on the outside would sap him and the membership of the self-reliance needed to take control over their own actions. But he also shows great understanding of human failure and weakness, and the constant need for both organizers and organizational members to reevaluate their actions and to rededicate themselves to their tasks.

George Nee describes his long-time association with Chavez and the approach to organizing he learned from Chavez. Nee started out with a community organization of unskilled workers and transformed that into a community union with house meetings and a service orientation similar to the farm workers. He points out that the difficult transition to a union was very similar to that made by Chavez's organization. He discusses the patience an organizer must have, sometimes not even using direct-action tactics for four or five years.

The next two cases are from organizers who have worked at organizing since the 1930s and 1940s. They have a great deal to teach us from their many years' experience. They both have a commitment to mass participation and are concerned with basic structural changes in society. Note their commitment and deeply felt belief in the necessity of organizing black and white people together. Note also their awareness of the importance of maintaining communication with organizers in many different movements and in the case of Braden internationally also.

Sam Abbott,[1] who is currently the mayor of Takoma Park, Maryland, describes lessons to be drawn from a successful grass-roots campaign to stop the construction of freeways in the Washington, D.C., area. As the campaign grew, it encountered illegal harassment from local police and the FBI. Abbott documents four different types of such activity: undercover police assigned to watch the group, fake television cameras picking up dossiers on movement activists, provocateur activity leading into a brutal police ambush, fake letters used to inflame one group against another and prevent black and white unity. He suggests techniques to minimize the destructiveness of such activity. For example, he argues that the leadership of a group should acknowledge only among themselves that such activity is taking place, while concentrating all the group's efforts on the job they set out to do.

---

[1]Abbott started out during the Great Depression working on unemployed councils, for the Steelworkers, and in the Maritime Union.

The well-known southern organizer Anne Braden describes the spirited defense committee work in behalf of civil rights activists in North Carolina. The case spans 10 years because that is how long it took to win complete vindication for the defendants in the Wilmington 10 case. These people were convicted of very serious crimes stemming from work around integration in the late 1960s and early 1970s. According to Braden there was evidence that the federal, local, and state governments were determined to put the best of the civil rights activists in jail for most of their lives. The tactics used by the groups defending the activists consisted of massive mobilizing of people through using all channels of publicity available, picketing, rallies in Washington, D.C., petitions, pressure on the Congress of the United States and pressure from groups in other countries. Braden says that it was very important that people outside North Carolina were involved in the case because an outside catalyst was necessary to get justice. She also documents the persistence over a long period of time necessary to winning acquittals.

The Alinsky case illustrates the classic Alinsky technique as it had evolved by the 1960s. A great deal of the organizing going on today owes a tremendous debt to the methods Alinsky developed. The case is included here so that the reader may understand the origins of many of the present-day techniques. The case is issue specific and gives attention to the way in which Alinsky and other organizers from the Industrial Areas Foundation prepare a community for engaging in social action. The case of FIGHT in Rochester documents a conscious, well-thought-through strategy for building a people's organization. Alinsky is exceptionally cognizant of the need to select a cadre of qualified local people for leadership, of the need to deal with symbolic local issues in a creative and innovative manner, and of the possibility of using humor to throw the stupidity or intransigence of the "Establishment" back into its own face.

The case documents Alinsky's conviction that organizers must win specific victories of symbolic importance and that they must be prepared to exploit situations so as to help the organization perceive itself and be perceived as being more powerful. That perception alone may result in actual power redistribution.

The next case illustrates welfare rights organizing in Boston during the late 1960s and early 1970s. Many of the people who worked in the Welfare Rights movement had been trained by Alinsky organizers. Similarly, many of the people working in various community organizations today were in the Welfare Rights movement. The Welfare Rights movement has had a tremendous impact on organizing that is done today.

Unlike the Alinsky model, the Welfare Rights model and the Fair Share case that follow are membership organizations. The traditional Alinsky model featured an organization of organizations approach. People did not join the organization as individuals. In Welfare Rights people joined like they would a union. Because of that the methodology is different. Whereas the Alinsky organizer would traditionally make the rounds from church to church or club to club and talk to leaders and ask them to buy in, in the direct membership approach, organizers would go out and systematically knock on doors asking people to join as individuals. Alinsky organizers never door knocked.

In its heyday in the late 1960s and early 1970s the Welfare Rights organization in Massachusetts consisted of 55 local groups and 5000 members. It had a staff of 20 to 40 people, many of them VISTA volunteers. As can be seen from the case it was a militant, lively, direct-action organization. It could set up chapters quickly and get results for members quickly. As Staples points out, however, it was a single-issue, single-tactic organization whose narrow strategy may have led to its demise.

Staples helped to found Massachusetts Fair Share and now is associated with ACORN.[2] He has done a wide variety of other kinds of organizing including tenants, former mental patients, day care, employment issues, and labor unions. He now teaches community organization at Boston University. Fair Share is currently the largest citizen action group in the United States. It is a statewide organization that by 1982 had been in existence for 10 years. It has a dues-paying membership of 100,000 and employs a full-time staff of 65 professionals. It also has 200 canvassers who go door to door to raise money and build membership. It has an annual budget of $2 million.

Both ACORN and Fair Share have very strong parallels to the Welfare Rights organizing. The techniques used in setting up welfare rights chapters proved very effective and are currently being used in both Fair Share and ACORN, according to Staples. The initial phases of setting up chapters in neighborhoods is almost identical to that described in the welfare rights case. This includes the initial groundwork, home visits, organizing meetings, letters to neighbors, and a quick engagement in direct action leading to a quick success. The staff organizers play the same role in both organizations. The organizers don't hold leadership positions and are not spokespeople. The basic role of the organizer is to help the organization pull together and work with leadership in developing tactics and strategies that will win.

Stan Holt,[3] who narrates the Fair Share case, is a very experienced organizer

[2]Association of Community Organizations for Reform Now.

[3]It is worth describing Holt's career because it now spans three decades and illustrates some of the major changes that have taken place in organizing styles over the years. Holt is a Protestant minister who was active in CORE (Congress of Racial Equality), a civil rights organization active in the 1960s. He felt it was a flash-in-the-pan organization without real community roots although it had very dedicated, hardworking people. He felt he needed systematic training in grass-roots organizing techniques and went to Chicago and was trained by Tom Gaudet, an associate of Alinsky's. He learned from the Alinsky method to drop any pretense at ideology, to be very pragmatic and to work on specific, immediate, and realizable issues as a way of building power in a community. Holt feels that Alinsky neighborhood organizing methodology (illustrated in the Alinsky and Welfare Rights cases) "can't be improved upon."

Over the years Holt has worked as a community organizer in Chicago, Providence, Rhode Island, and Baltimore. In 1978 he came to work for Fair Share. When I interviewed him he was Fair Share's regional director in Fall River, Massachusetts. He sees Fair Share's strength as its ability to work simultaneously on neighborhood, citywide, and statewide issues.

who argues that the current Fair Share organizing is an improvement over the early Alinsky-style organizing. He feels that a centrally directed statewide organization has more power than neighborhood organizations. Fair Share with its enormous membership and large budget is no longer a movement but an institution with power.

As Holt describes Fair Share, note his sensitivity to the problems of developing indigenous leadership and membership control over decision making. What do you think of his distinction between systematically building for reform versus taking the issues as they present themselves and pragmatically building on them? What do you think about his ideas of organizers emphasizing working in Catholic parishes around family and neighborhood issues?

Unlike the membership in the Welfare Rights organization, the members of Fair Share and ACORN are not necessarily poor. They comprise mainly a stable, working-class population. They are populations that were not seen as targets of organizing efforts in the 1960s.

La Causa and La Huelga[1]

Cesar Chavez

A COMMUNITY UNION IS ORGANIZED

The strike and the boycott, they have cost us much. What they have not paid us in wages, better working conditions, and new contracts, they have paid us in self respect and human dignity.

Violence

If we had used violence we would have won contracts a long time ago but they wouldn't have been lasting because we wouldn't have won respect. Wages are not the main issue in the strike. If wages were the issue our organization would disappear after recognition and an increase in pay. No, what is at stake is human dignity. If a man is not accorded respect, he cannot respect himself and if he does not respect himself, he cannot demand it.

When workers fall back on violence, they are lost. Oh they might win some of their demands and might end a strike a little earlier, but they give up their imagina-

---

[1]This is a compilation of statements and observations on his own work by Cesar Chavez, director of the United Farm Workers Organizing Committee. They come from a variety of sources: personal interviews, newspaper and magazine articles, statements reported on T.V., and an earlier compilation from tapes made by Mr. Chavez in May 1967, while in Detroit. The tapes were edited by David Leonard Cohen in January 1969, when associated with the Institute of Labor and Industrial Relations.

tion, their creativity, their will to work hard enough and to suffer for what they believe is right.

Behaving violently is giving up the will to win. Some people just want to get knocked on the head, to be self-pitying. Violence just hurts those who are already hurt. Violence in the civil rights movement just makes black people suffer. Black homes are burned and black sons are killed. Instead of exposing the brutality of the oppressors, it justifies it.

There are many reasons for why a man does what he does. To be himself he must be able to give all. If a leader cannot give all he cannot expect his people to give anything. The violence upsets me. When I went on my fast, I told no one. I worked everyday as usual. But I could not keep it a secret long. Finally I knew I had to tell some that I would be going to our headquarters at Forty Acres. But I told only a few friends. It was a test, a dedication. It was not a hunger strike. I did not want publicity. I did not want the press to pick it up and to distort it. It was a personal thing. But the word did get out, and it was the best organizing I ever did. People came to me in lines for days. It was for all of us a religious experience. The fast gave lie to the grower's claim that we had no following. Some people came every night to attend Mass, eighty-five miles. We estimated ten thousand came during my fast. Everyone came, Mexicans, Filipinos, blacks—Robert Kennedy sent me a telegram. Then he came. Others came. They understood.

Friends swore to me they would never be violent again. Filipino women came and decorated the building at the Forty Acres, where I maintained my fast. It was beautiful art by people who are not artists. The fast brought the creativity out of people.

Mexican Catholics can be very discriminatory towards Mexican Protestants. But something beautiful happened during the fast. On the fifth day a Protestant preacher from Earlimart came. I asked him to preach to our Mass. At first he didn't believe it could be done. But I told him it was about time to repair some of the damage that had been done among our people. So he preached and there was a great spirit. A few days later I invited another Protestant to preach and then a Negro minister, and then the minister from Earlimart again. This time he brought his congregation to sing Protestant Mexican hymns. It was a beautiful thing. It has done much for our people.

When I finished my fast at the Mass of Thanksgiving, I was too weak to speak, but a friend explained for me what the purpose of the fast was. I have the paper in which some of my words were written and read.

"When we are really honest with ourselves, we must admit that our lives are all that really belong to us. So it is how we use our lives that determines what kind of men we are. It is my deepest belief that only by giving our lives do we find life. I am convinced that the truest act of courage, the strongest act of manliness, is to sacrifice ourself for others in a totally nonviolent struggle for justice. To be a man is to suffer for others. God help us be men."

On Being Able to Carry Your Own Weight

I started out working under Fred Ross, the organizer for the Community Service Organization, set up by Alinsky's Industrial Areas Foundation. I was his constant companion. I used to get home about 5:30 from work and Fred would pick me up and we would go from meeting to meeting. I observed how he did things and I learned from him. I had a need to learn. After a while I became a chairman of our local CSO group, then I became an organizer and staff person. Soon I was organizing in the whole state.

When I left CSO in April of 1962 I almost cried like a baby. CSO was the first organization to try to help Mexican Americans. I wanted CSO to organize farm workers. I thought the only way to really help Mexican Americans was on the farm fields. I offered to work for them for a year without pay. The organization did not agree, so I resigned. A week later I came to Delano. I turned down a union offer to organize for them. I didn't want outside support. If we were to have an organization, the members would have to support it. Outside offers of support were turned down, for we knew that if we became dependent early, we might not have the courage we needed later. Having studied the mistakes of CSO and other organizations, I did not want to repeat them. We wanted the workers to prove to us, and we wanted to prove to ourselves, that they really wanted what we were doing. The assurance came from monthly contributions of $3.50 in dues. It is true that some members came to meetings because they had an investment. If they had been active in the union for a year, they had $42 invested. They were there to see how their money was being spent and for no other reason. But as they came to meetings, we were trying to educate them, building the brotherhood and solidarity so necessary for the understanding needed to bring about a strong organization.

During the first winter of the organizing, I would go out to their homes and call on them to pay their dues if they were one or two months behind. I recall one particular incident that will remain with me for many, many years to come. I went to a home in McFarland, California, seven miles south of Delano. It was the evening of a very cold and rainy day. Because of the weather, there had been no work that day in the fields. I went to this home and knocked on the door. The union member was just getting ready to leave.

I told him that he was two months behind in his dues and that we would have to cancel his membership. He had $5.00 in his hand and he gave it to me. As I gave him back $1.50 in change, he told me that he was just on his way out to the store to buy food. I held the money in my hand for a few seconds trying to decide whether to take the money. If I refunded it, I would have to forget the idea of workers paying their own way while they were building a union. It was difficult. The man hadn't been working and had very little money. I took the money, and for the next week I felt very bad about it.

But something happened about three years later. The same man continued to pay his dues and became one of our best strikers. He also became one of the first workers to benefit from the Schenley contract when it was signed. Of course, there were still a lot of people who remained in between. Whenever a member would come to us for assistance, the first thing that we asked about and the thing we insisted upon was that his dues be paid up. They paid the dues and the services were theirs. Now in our Association the worker pays his union dues and in that way pays for his services. We tell them, "We want you to come and demand service, but first of all you have to pay your dues."

This is where we differ from other organizations, and from the poverty program. Helping people by providing services is not enough. Often people get some service and they ask you: "How much do I owe?" In the hand-out programs they say: "Nothing, it is your right, this is paid by the government."

We say: "Sure you owe something. You owe your participation and your responsibility to help other poor people." But that is not enough. Then you have to be completely ready to tell them exactly what they can do to help. You have to have an activity, a task, a job. And while they are doing it, you give them encouragement and you build them into real members. If a person asks what he can do to help it is because he does not know. You must tell him in clear language he can understand.

People do not know what to do. Do not romanticize the poor. The Mexican and the Negro are not some sort of noble innocent. We are all people, human beings subject to the same temptations and faults as all others. Our poverty *damages* our dignity.

Being disadvantaged is not romantic. It is tragic. We want to see ourselves and to be seen as human beings. We know the truth, even if some of the college people who come to help think we are the innocent and the growers are the devils. This is a very hard-nosed operation. Members who pay their dues get service; those who don't pay don't get any service.

Why Delano?

When I left CSO I knew it was to organize farm workers. I chose Delano as my target area for two reasons. First, my wife's family and my brother lived there. I knew there would be hard times ahead, and at least my eight children would not starve.

The second reason has to do with the composition of the work force in Delano. There are over 70 grape vineyards. Table grapes require tender handling. Laborers have to have some skill in leafing, spraying, binding, pruning. Workers here were the best paid in the industry and the most stable. The season lasts nine months. If you are going to organize and ask for commitment, you cannot go to the most desperately poor. They are not likely to take action. If you stand on a man's head and push it into the dirt, he may not even see the heel of your boot. But if his whole face is already above ground, he can see your heel and he can see freedom ahead.

Getting Started

People ask why we were so successful when other attempts to organize a union failed and when all other strike attempts killed union organizing. The reason is that we did not begin to organize a union. I never talked about a union and I never used the word strike. Instead of staying in one community and trying to organize workers against a background of repeated failures over the past forty years, I decided to visit as many communities as I could in the San Joaquin Valley.

I was counting on my past experience that no matter where you go, you will always find a few people who are ready to take up any cause you may have. This is not always so good. People join the wrong causes and some people join your cause for reasons that are not healthy. But what in poverty is healthy?

My family and I visited something like seventy-eight communities including small rural villages and large labor camps. I didn't go to people and say, "Look you're poor and I'm poor. Let's get together and take on the power structure." They would have looked at me as if I were crazy.

We distributed cards throughout the entire valley. Eight thousand of them were signed and returned. We walked through the fields, and door to door. We didn't ask all kinds of fancy questions. Just one. "How much do you think you deserve to earn for an hour's work?" At that time the average pay was 90¢ per hour. Almost everybody responded that they thought they should be getting a $1.00 or $1.10. Only a handful said $1.25, $1.50 or $2.00. I was dejected by their low aspirations and feelings of worth.

But some of the people wrote us notes of encouragement. We went and talked to each of these. We said, "If you and I get together, we can solve our problems. We have to help each other." And we tried to demonstrate what we meant. If a man was hurt, I would stay with him until I was sure we could get him medical services. If a man needed legal help, I might stay with him or travel to find it for four and five days. When I went out to visit those who had written the comments, with me I took things that I thought would be important for them to know—Social Security stuff and other useful material. On each piece was stamped the name and address of the Association in Delano. When they saw the name, they wondered about it and what was happening.

At first there weren't too many people to respond, but soon the word got around. Day and night people started coming to our house. We were building up a basic trust. We never talked about building a union, just an association of concerned people. But there were some, about twenty people, who went out and really did a job. They went out and took the time to sign people up. Thus our organization was created out of activity. When you go to talk you go to talk to everybody. The only place that I don't talk to people is at bars. I will talk to them at grocery stores, on the street, or anywhere I can. Your best means of contact in the community where you are organizing is simply to stop people on the street. The first reaction that you are likely to get when you stop someone to talk about organizing is that the person may think you are crazy. But because there is in most cases a natural reaction to pay attention to what you have to say, he listens.

The most important thing about signing up a member was that you made a friend. You visited a place, and they would later write to you. Then we would write back to them. If I would be in their neighborhood, I would try to stop in to visit. I visited them in their homes and ate with them. This I had to do because I didn't have any money. If you really want to make a friend, go to someone's home and eat with him. When you get to know people, their home's open to you. They gave me food and a place to sleep. Some gave me money for gas. They had begun to feel sorry for me because I was poorer than they were. Once we had become friends, they would tell me what they wanted. The people who give you their food give you their heart.

We were able to get about four hundred workers who became the nucleus of our association. The secret was that these people were already organized and that it was just a matter of getting them all together. You can't organize people unless there is a need. Poor people have a need. If organizers are unsuccessful, it is because they have not learned the lessons of organizing well. Organizers must blame only themselves if people don't respond. I have often heard organizers saying things like, "Well, they don't really appreciate the things that we are trying to do." "Their level of intelligence is so low that they can't comprehend what we're doing for them." Or, "They just haven't any interest in themselves." What they fail to say is "We're just not getting the message across to them." People have a very nice subtle way of telling us that they don't like our program.

There is no substitute for hard work, 23 or 24 hours a day. And there is no substitute for patience and acceptance.

We called our first convention together in Fresno, in September 1962. About 350 people were there. At that time the union was called the National Farm Workers Association. There we adopted a very ambitious program. We wanted to gradually move from a community setting in which brotherhood was created through individual help and attention to personal problems to the solidarity needed for a union that would be ready to strike successfully.

Membership Services

We also developed what is now called the Farm Workers Service Center. This Center is not like a welfare agency.

At first we pooled our resources to get legal help in individual cases. Say for instance that a man was rooked by a salesman with a high interest contract. We put all our pennies together and hired a lawyer. If the contract was for, let's say, $100, the company back in Chicago or Detroit would say, "Gee, you know attorneys would cost at least $100 anyway." So they would drop the case. If one of the workers got a traffic ticket and came to us and said, "Look, I really didn't deserve this ticket," and if we were convinced that he was right, we would spend perhaps $100 on a $5.00 ticket—in some cases even more.

Any time that we felt that an injustice was involved in a problem, we would work on that problem in two ways: First, we would let everyone know about it, especially the membership. Second, we would make sure the person involved had a commitment to follow through.

Soon we set up a credit union and co-op programs to help get such things as insurance and automobile parts. I learned bookkeeping from a government pamphlet. The most important possession for the farm worker is an automobile. A lot of money was being poured into repairing their old cars. So we developed what we call the car service center.

Our car co-op is a little different from the standard accepted co-op program operating in this country today. Instead of making the savings refund at the end of the year, we give a refund right across the counter when the worker purchases the item. In the car co-op we have always concentrated on little items, parts that are needed for a car—not luxury items such as fancy hub caps, but items such as generators, starters and the like.

Now we also have a gasoline co-op, and we are able to sell gasoline three or four cents a gallon cheaper than any station in town. We also organized a newspaper so that we could keep people informed about the things that were going on within the Association.

A Community Union

As word spread, more people heard about what we were trying to do and joined us, thus increasing our resources.

When the other unions were organizing workers, they seemed to approach the problem by using only the issues workers had with their employers. They were not doing anything on the community part of the problem. We wanted to do both things. We wanted to have a community union. We didn't have the name for it at that time, but we knew that we wanted to deal with community problems by getting the people together and showing them that there is some power in numbers.

After winning some victories we began to pull things together, started some programs, and gradually moved into a union setting where we would be really ready to strike and confront employers.

In the four and a half years before the strike we had a lot of time to do this. Only once did the press find out what we were doing. Only once did it get through. Otherwise, for four and a half years no one knew what we were doing except for our most immediate friends.

We had many tests and some early victories. Even before I left CSO we demonstrated. Braceros were getting jobs before resident workers even though the law stated clearly that residents should get first preference. I would take groups of unemployed workers and have them fill out an employer's work card. We did this day after day, keeping records of the results. We then had a protest march and a card burning ceremony to symbolize our protest and to show the worker's contempt for such hiring practices.

Later, when we discovered that Kern and Tulare counties were actually making money on the filthy, slummy migrant camps, we were able to encourage the migrants who lived there to demand that they be closed down and new ones erected. I felt we were getting close to being ready to strike. Our situation was different from that where the other strikers failed.

In many of the early strikes, the organizers who actually were conducting the strikes blamed the people for their failures. In almost all cases, the people blamed the unions and the organizers for the failure. The unions came in with a paid staff and quite a bit of money, but after having spent a considerable amount of money, they all gave up the idea of organizing. There was in all attempts one most noticeable parallel. The unions were attempting to do two jobs in one: They were attempting to organize the workers and simultaneously to strike.

Most of the unions were going into the fields to organize workers after the workers had revolted. The workers were out on strike (on one of those suicide strikes) and the unions couldn't put things together to hold with any permanence.

In the end the people felt that the unions had sold them out, and the union leaders felt that the people really didn't want a union. With this past history we had a number of failures to contend with and we wanted to change that.

When we came in, we decided that the job was too big to do all at one time. If we were going to organize a union, it would have to be done quietly, incorporating the idea that is now known as a community union.

First, of all, we wanted to convince ourselves that the workers really wanted a union this time. They had to show us that they wanted a union. They did this by their paying for the initial organizing drive.

By building a strong base we felt that someday we would be ready to strike, conduct a boycott, and exert other legal, economic means needed to get our union recognized.

The Strike Begins

In September of 1965, a few days after the Agricultural Workers Organizing Committee (an AFL-CIO union led by two Filipino organizers) struck two of the largest growers in the area, we voted to strike the rest of the industry where we had membership. We called our meeting on September 16, Mexico's Independence Day. We brought in 2700 workers for the night of the vote. This represented 60 to 65 percent of the total work force in the area. There wasn't one "NO" vote. Our members said they too wanted independence—from poverty, brutal working conditions, discrimination. I asked our members not to strike until four days later which would give us enough time to make contact with all the growers, asking them to meet with us to negotiate the issues without a strike. Our demands were identical to those of the AWOC. We sent "return receipt requested" letters to all the growers. We called all the growers. We sent them wires and asked the State Conciliation Service to call them to see if we could get together. They did not answer our letters. They even refused to accept our wires.

We knew that in the many attempts to organize workers, violence had played a large part in the suppression of the unions and we knew that from the moment we struck justice would be about 20 percent for us and 80 percent for the opposition. I asked the workers to vote that this strike be a nonviolent one. Many of them didn't really know what this meant. But many did know that there was another group in the country that had been making progress for human rights with a commitment to nonviolence, the civil rights movement. It was decided that night that we would be nonviolent and we have kept to this pledge throughout our struggle, but not without difficulty.

On September 20, 1965, at 5:30 a.m., our strike started. During the first ten days almost all the workers left the fields. Nothing was done in the fields. Most of the outside strikebreakers stayed away—not because they believed in the strike, but because they feared violence.

The moment they found out that we weren't going to do anything to them, they went to work. Many of those who went into the fields, when asked about it said, "we're with you 100 percent, but we just want to work to get enough money to leave the area. But we are with you." In the first three days wages went up from $1.15 to $1.25 because of the shortage.

We began to send strikers to stand by the fields with picket signs. "Huelga," we shouted. We tried to convince the strikebreakers that they were wrong, that they should be with us. If one man walks off the field during a work day, then an official strike is certified. It is important to get someone to walk off.

The picket line is the best place to train organizers. One day on the picket line and a man is never again the same. The picket line is where a man makes his commitment. The longer on the picket line the stronger the commitment. A lot of workers think they make their commitment by walking off the job when nobody sees them. But you get a guy to walk off the field when his boss is watching and, in front of the other guys, throw down his tools and march right to the picket line, that is the guy who makes our strike. The picket line is a beautiful thing because it makes a man more human.

Some of my best organizers and more faithful members hated the union before they joined. But when they see the light, they never desert us because they have been on both sides. The converted ones are our best members. Nonviolence has made it possible to survive, although there have been injustices and injuries. Union members always get arrested. Growers never do.

The strike brought us many surprises. We thought we were striking the growers. We thought the church groups, the city council, and the school people would at least remain neutral, if they would not come to help us. Within 24 hours the Delano City council had held a special meeting and passed a resolution condemning our "communist ties." Both the high school and the elementary school boards passed similar resolutions. The Chamber of Commerce passed a resolution that was similar except that it was more wordy. The Ministerial Association for the very first time in the history of Delano consented to meet with the three local priests, and they too passed a resolution condemning the strike. This really shook us up. We were looking to them as the arbitrators and conciliators. There was, then, only ourselves on the west side of town, trying to meet all forces.

"Huelga"

For the first nine days of the strike the sheriff's office and the police department in Delano played it cool. The very first day of the strike the Kern County Sheriff assigned a squad of deputies to Delano. The sergeant in charge, whose name was Dodd, told us he was here to look after and protect the farm workers on strike. I thought it was a welcome sign and I thanked him.

Nine days later, I was called to an emergency meeting with Sergeant Dodd at the Special Sheriff's Station in Delano. I was told that there was a lot of feeling in the community about the strike. Those poor workers who had crossed the picket lines had become so incensed and disturbed by our attempts to recruit them that there was bound to be violence. He asked us to refrain from speaking to them or even shouting "Huelga." He told me that if we complied, this would further our relationship, thus helping both groups. We had an emergency meeting of the strikers that evening, and I put the problem to them. They put up quite a lot of argument, but I asked them to please do it for this time to prove that we were fair and wanted to keep our friends.

We voted to refrain from shouting "Huelga" at the strikebreakers.

Three days later I was called to another emergency meeting with the sheriff. This time he was complaining because we were still using the word "Huelga." We were not shouting it; we were just saying it in a normal tone of voice so that the strikebreakers would hear us. When I asked why was there such opposition to the word, he replied, "Well, because all the people know that there is a strike. There's no need to tell them. After all, you are in the United States and you should be speaking English."

He also said that there were a lot of complaints from the powerful people in the county that the only reason we were using the word "Huelga" was that we were trying to attract the attention of the Communist Party in Latin America. When I protested he said, "Well, the word sounds downright nasty."

I brought the membership back to another meeting and I told them what had happened. I said, "We cannot use the word "Huelga." Could we use a different word?" They all got up and told me where to go.

The next morning 44 of the strikers and nonstrikers picketed one of the larger growers in the area. Included in this group were my wife, 9 ministers, 11 other wives, and 23 strikers. They lined up about 50 feet from one another and started shouting "Huelga" at the workers at the top of their voice.

Sure enough, as the sheriff had promised, all of them were arrested. I went down to Berkeley to the University to beg money from the students to bail the pickets out of jail. I got there just before lunchtime, and I spoke from the steps of Sproul Hall. I asked the students to give me their lunch money; and they gave me $6600, which was enough to bail the pickets out and cover the cost of legal aid to fight the case.

About a year later all 44 cases were dismissed.

Peregrination: Pilgrimage, Penitence, Revolution

We gave Delano a new word. While the word was very dirty in the beginning, now it has become a very accepted word. "Huelga" is used by the high school kids as a means of saying, "Hello. How are you?" It is our symbol.

A symbol is an important thing. That is why we chose an Aztec eagle. It gives pride. My brother squared off the wings so that it is easier for members to draw. When people see it they know it means "boycott" and we know it means dignity.

A year after the march from Selma, we decided to have our own penitential march ending on the Capitol steps in Sacramento. The American press can make little things into big things and big things into little things. A lot depends on how well they understand them. We tried desperately to put it into the right perspective so that they would understand. Father Keith Kenney from Sacramento wrote a beautiful explanation about the march, but it was not understood.

The first reason for the march was that we felt that personally we had to do penance for those things that we had done wrong during the six or seven months of striking prior to the march. We wanted to discipline ourselves to keep our commitment of nonviolence. When soldiers are drafted into the army the first thing they do is march. They march back and forth all day long. This is discipline training. They don't say that only 99 percent of the people march. They say everybody marches.

We wanted to come back after marching for 26 days and part of the nights with new dedication. On the march we went through much suffering. This helped us find ourselves, understand ourselves, and discipline ourselves for a strike that we knew was going to take a long, long time. The theme of the march was "pilgrimage, penitence, and revolution." People understood a little about pilgrimage, very little about penitence, and hardly anything about revolution. We were talking about changing things to make a better life. We came back with new dedication and more commitment. We had religious services two or three times a day during the march; and, while we were marching side by side along the road, we were reexamining ourselves. Some of our members, some of our organizers, and some of our friends did not like the religious nature of our march. They felt La Causa should not be a religious affair. But self dedication is a spiritual experience.

I am not a doctrinaire religiously. I want to break down the barriers. In my fast, I encouraged much different religious activity. I wore a mezuzah around my neck. Jesus must have worn one. Certainly he did not wear a cross.

The march was very successful. Many of the farm workers to whom we went understood the strike a lot better. After we left them they were really a part of the movement. By the time we arrived in Sacramento on Easter Sunday, one grower was ready to sign. Others were ready to give us support.

It takes a lot of punishment to be able to do anything to change the social order. It is such a difficult thing to do, especially when the matter of money is involved as it is in our case. It was only after we went on strike that we began to accept money from others. Walter Reuther pledged $5000 a month for the duration of the strike as support from the UAW. The AFL-CIO offered $10,000 per month. Other money began to come later.

The Boycott

We have won our major contracts mainly through economic pressure on the growers. As farm workers, we are specifically excluded from the protection of the National Labor Relations Act. Under the present situation we can't go to the employer and say, "We have 30 percent, or 50 percent or 100 percent of the workers signed up and we want you to recognize our union." We can't even go to the Board and ask for an election. Even if we had a thousand percent signed up we would have no rights. So our only hope has been the pressure of a consumer boycott.

When we started our first boycott, we were told by some experienced and very friendly unions that it wouldn't work. But it has, because we have received the support of thousands and thousands of rank-and-file labor, students, civil rights people and church groups. We have developed a nationwide network of support by sending out strikers to cities throughout the United States and Canada. We had pickets in 237 communities at one time during the Schenley boycott. This is what got us our first contract at the time that we got it. If we had not launched the boycott, our strike could never have been successful.

There are lots of people who are ready to say that this generation of farm laborers has to be written off, and that legislation, education, and so forth have to be aimed at the children. Well, I for one am not ready to be written off. This generation of children will get the food and the education it needs when the parents have enough money to take care of them.

UFWOC—A New Union

In September of 1966 our Association merged with AWOC to form the United Farm Workers Organizing Committee. At that point the AFL-CIO chartered our union and gave us the jurisdiction of organizing farm workers. This merger brought together both unions.

I'd say that it took about six months before we really brought the two unions together. For although we were together on paper, there were problems to be dealt with. First of all, AWOC was almost 100 percent Filipino: our union was 90 percent Mexican-American and about 10 percent Negro. Growers had traditionally played ethnic groups off against each other. That way they could keep wages low.

At the beginning of the strike everyone was giving us from two to three weeks, saying that we would lose like the other strikes had been lost. If you had asked me about it then, I would probably have said that failure was very possible.

But in our case something different happened—something that the other unions had never had happen in their attempts to organize workers. We received public support in our attempts to organize like no other union had experienced.

The church people, organized labor, students from SNCC and CORE, and other persons who were interested, came to our rescue, and they were able to see us through to our first victories. From then on the possibility of success was assured.

On Organizing and Being an Organizer

I am an organizer, not a union leader. A good organizer has to work hard and long. There are no shortcuts. You just keep talking to people, working with them, sharing, exchanging, and they come along. People can be organized for anything, even the worst of causes.

The reactionaries are always the better organizers. The "right" has a lot of discipline that the "left" lacks. The "left" always dilutes itself. Instead of fighting a common enemy, the "left" splinters, and the splinters go after one another. Meanwhile the "right" goes after its objective, pounding away.

From my experience I would say that bringing about community organization is a lot harder than labor organizing. In a labor union, at a certain point you can say, "Well, it's organized." But in community organization I could never see an end, a time I could say it was organized.

When I say community organization I mean the grass-roots type. It's not the type in which you take existing organizations and put them together in a coordinating agency. When I went into an area as a community organizer, I tried to stay away from the leaders of all existing agencies. I found my best leaders by going deep into the grass roots. Unfortunately, it has been my experience that some grass-roots leaders don't remain grass-roots very long. The more successful they get, the less effective they seem to become.

Another reason it is more difficult to organize community groups is that they often tend to be erratic. The organization of these groups doesn't go along smoothly; instead, there are peaks and valleys. Say you have been working in a community, and after a whole year of hard work it is organized. You go away for a few weeks and when you come back, your organization has crumbled away. You cannot organize unless there is a need for it. And until you have well developed and recognized leaders, there is no secure structure.

A movement with some lasting organization is a lot less dramatic than a movement with a lot of demonstrations and a lot of marching and so forth. The more dramatic organization does catch attention quicker. Over the long haul, however, it's a lot more difficult to keep together because you're not building solid. One of the disappointments of community organization is that it takes an awful lot of time to build. It takes a lot of time because people are not developed overnight. A lasting organization is one in which people will continue to build, develop and move when you are not there.

Everything in life is contagious. If you work hard enough, the other guy is going to work. Not so much because you convinced him, but because he's downright ashamed of his not working. At first he usually doesn't know how to work in an organization. So if you work 16 hours a day, he's going to work 5 hours a day. If you work 24 hours a day, he's going to work 8 hours a day. As an organizer you are going to have to work more hours than anybody else and like it. If you can't work without complaining, then you'd better get out. What it takes you a week to build, you can destroy in one outburst.

If you're not frightened that you might fail, you'll never do the job. If you're frightened, you'll work like crazy.

Being of service is not enough. You must become a servant to the people. When you do, you can demand their commitment in return.

Chavez Was Right!

George Nee

There are no shortcuts. It doesn't matter if you're building up an athletic team, a community organization, or a labor union. Not many people are willing to put in the four or five years of ground work they need before they're able to do the things they're really aiming for. In organizing, there are few quick victories, and even when they come they're likely to lead to defeats unless the organization is well grounded. I don't think many people have a concept of time, a concept of history.

Chavez and the Farm Workers in Delano did. They knew there was a long struggle with much sacrifice ahead. They never expected victories in the short term, never even aimed for them. One thing I have learned from the farm workers is to pace myself, and to have faith that we will win, even if the successes don't come for a long time. The Farm Workers' concept is rooted in the history that it's going to be a long struggle. I'll tell you a little about myself and what I've learned—from my own experience and from my association with the Farm Workers.

Back in 1968, when I was still in school in Boston, I met some farm workers on a picket line. I was impressed and I decided I could learn more from them than at school. Within six months I started working full-time with the Farm Workers, mostly in New England. In 1971, I left and started the Rhode Island Workers' Association. We were an unemployment rights organization. What we learned from the farm workers was that you could not just focus on issues without also taking care of people's individual problems. We didn't just work on the larger issues through action and demonstration. We did it by building in a service component. We did unemployment appeals, food stamp appeals, we developed the organization out of one-to-one contacts. And we got money and technical help from outsiders who felt that we were an important element in righting injustices.

I stayed with it for years. By 1975, though, it was pretty clear that we hadn't really found a way to establish a permanent force for social and economic justice. First of all, there was too much turnover, it was very unstable. One-to-one services don't build permanence unless each of these "ones" takes personal responsibility for other people. The funding was always a real circus and I just didn't feel that we were making any progress—or that I was progressing as an individual. I kind of reached a crossroads. So when Chavez's son-in-law, an old friend, called me and asked if I'd come out to California to work with the Farm Workers, it sounded great. It was a good chance to make a change and learn something.

I had been in touch with Chavez over the years. He was aware of the work we were doing in the Rhode Island Workers Association and was always very supportive. Chavez feels an obligation to repay the help that the Farm Workers union has received from all of the various church and labor organizations and community organizations throughout the years. The one way he feels that he can repay that debt is to help train organizers.

I spent forty or fifty days with Chavez, walking the highways. Chavez had committed himself to a 1,000 mile pilgrimage. During the day we marched and at night we spoke at rallies. The law had just been changed. Provisions under the National Labor Relations Act of 1935 and the Landrum-Griffin Act of 1959 had finally been extended to farm workers. It had taken 12 years of patient education, extensive grass roots action, and effective lobbying. This march was designed to educate farm workers all along the valley to their rights to organize, and how to conduct elections.

Working with Chavez and talking with his organizers and union members helped me clarify my own concerns. I discovered that here, 3000 miles away from

Rhode Island and in another state with a different population, some of the same problems and some of the same principles of organizing applied. I began to see that the point that I had got to, after five years of doing community organizing, was pretty much the same point that Chavez's organizing group had reached when it was at the crossroads of becoming the Farm Workers union. I felt that our group in Rhode Island had to transform itself also. It was interesting to talk with Chavez about what happened when the Farm Workers changed. His staff had the same fears, the same reluctance to try something new. I think there are some universal problems that exist and are not related solely to farm workers in California.

I realized that we had to change the Association from a nice guy organization where we gave help to anyone who walked in the door and where most of the financial support came from well wishers on the outside, to a totally self supporting organization. When I returned to Rhode Island and tested out some of these ideas, I ran into a lot of reluctance. Even some of our most steady supporters betrayed some pretty condescending attitudes towards the poor. Like on the issue of paying dues. They said poor people can't afford it or won't do it. Well, that's a lot of shit. Poor people can drink, they can smoke, they can waste a lot of money on other things, too. And they can pay dues, if they believe in something.

At that point our attitude became kind of cold. I had a couple of people who came into the office who thought of me as their private social worker. When they had a problem, they'd come and they'd want me to help them. I was pretty good at getting people straightened out or winning appeals. When I said "I won't work for you any more unless you pay dues," they said that I'd sold out and didn't care about the poor. You must be willing to take that kind of crap from people. You must have a certain faith that what you are doing is correct, and let the chips fall where they may after that.

I even had problems with the staff. They liked being helpers, doing good. But doing good all by itself doesn't build a power base and it doesn't necessarily build up people's capacities to do good on their own behalf.

So in 1976 I left my position as director of the Association and started a union called the Rhode Island Workers Union. I'd made a decision that we should start a union for people who no one else was organizing or even wanted to organize. I started with no members, with no money, and with my present wife (we weren't married at that time) supporting me for the first two years because we didn't have enough money to pay me. We were able to use some of the money we'd gotten from churches to pay for rent, the food, and paper supplies. Where we differed from the Association was in our insistence that members had to support the union with money as well as time, and in the issues we set for our agenda. After five years of working in the area, we began to see the kinds of common problems that people had on the job—like unjust firings, lack of health insurance, and poor wages.

There is a lot of slop being thrown out about poverty being glamourized and romanticized. It is basically a lack of money. If you give people money who have no money they will fix their house and have some money to take care of their kids—put clothes on them and feed them. All they need is money. They do not need a lot of charity. They need some goddamn decent wages. We decided to go after the three largest groups of unorganized workers: the jewelry industry that had 30,000 low income workers, underpaid workers in the health care industry, and office workers. We decided to do it on our own, without any affiliation with national unions. Like the farm workers, we realized that we had to build up our own strength first, then we could talk to others.

We have a lot of contacts in the community and we still do the service work that we were doing during the Rhode Island Association days. We learned that instead of just saying "We will help you with your appeal" we could say "Listen! The real answer to your problem is to organize to get a contract on the job. Then you can't be fired. Then you can get some health insurance benefits." This is a serious problem in Rhode Island because a lot of workers don't have health care benefits provided by their employer.

Our union has been involved in more organizing drives in this state than any other union even though we have only just over a thousand members. In six years we've been involved in 25 elections, and our record of wins is a little over 50 percent. Our biggest frustration is people quitting. If you start off with an organizing committee of 10, you usually have 5 people by election time. People will quit when the heat gets on because the bosses make it very tough.

It took us 6 years to get the first contract. I was fully prepared if I got the first contract in less than 10 years to consider that a success in an industry that has never been organized. We've learned a lot out of our elections and even our lost strikes. Just last month, we organized a place where we lost an election in 1978. It took us four years of going to the courts before we could finally bargain. We just received our first contract for 85 workers in a jewelry factory. The thing I had to keep remembering during those years was that once the auto worker was also unorganized. If they succeeded, we could too. I learned from Chavez that there are no unsuccessful strikes. "Strikes aren't lost," Chavez taught me, "They are abandoned." You don't lose when you don't get what you aimed for. You chalk it up to experience and start rethinking your strategy. You have to think. You have to get the right information. You have to keep people's spirits up and keep them focused on the end goals. It takes persistence. Like I said. There are no short-cuts.

It's one thing to say the word "persistence" and another thing to live it for four years. The hardest thing in organizing is to develop a realistic time perspective. You are always asking yourself if you are in the middle of a success or the middle of a failure. Because if you look back on all the struggles for social and economic justice, whether it's a fight over minimum wage or child labor, or women's right to vote and all the decent social and labor legislation that's been passed, someone just didn't come up one day and say let's do this. Those people must have asked themselves after four or five years, "Is this thing ever going to work? Or are we in the middle of a real losing campaign?'' It requires constant research, analysis and thought.

In the beginning, I thought it would be easy to make the transition from an association to a union. I will tell you now, the problems are ten times as hard and the stakes are ten times as high. People who have nothing and never did aren't likely to stay with it unless it becomes a movement kind of thing with them. They have to not only believe they can win, which means they've got to have had some life experiences with success, and they have to believe in the justness of their cause. They have to be able to get mad. Maybe that's why we sometimes had more success with foreign-born workers than with the native-born. We had a strike where there were 100 Hispanics and 100 ''anglos.'' The Hispanic workers struck and stood out to the person. The American workers gave in and broke the strike. For those who stayed with it, it was as much a strike against discriminatory treatment as it was a labor strike. For people who are here illegally and in many cases living hand to mouth to support themselves, three or four weeks out of work is risky and it feels like an eternity. But we got terrific support from the community. When it comes right down to it, a lot of folks are against discrimination. And it helps a lot when you discover that other people believe in your cause too.

In looking back, I am amazed at some of the things we have been involved in. We now have a self sufficient labor organization of 1,100 dues paying members. Like the Farm Workers, we're now in the AFL-CIO. We represent 20 percent of the nursing home industry in the state of Rhode Island. We've made significant changes for those workers and introduced concepts into the industry of better staffing. Our members are on the average paid $1.00 an hour above the minimum wage in a traditionally minimum wage industry. They have family health care coverage for the first time. I feel proud that we have some significant improvements. A friend of mine who is an accountant for a major jewelry company has told me as a result of our two organizing drives and our one strike, that many of the major personnel directors of major jewelry companies have sat down and are starting to improve wages, benefits and working conditions in an attempt to head-off unionization. We really didn't lose the strike!

Still our biggest problem is people quitting; not just the union, but the job too. The average employees we are after may have been employed 7 to 10 times before. They feel that if they quit work they hurt the boss. It is a twisted logic. They don't realize that they own their own labor when they say things like: ''I showed them, I didn't give any notice and I quit.'' They don't realize that the bosses encourage turnover because when people have been around, they get to know a place and feel entitled to more. If you leave because you didn't get the raise you asked for, it just plays into the boss' hands.

Organizing a work force means educating people. That's why we are now meeting them on the unemployment line. You have to organize workers, not the workplace! If you keep that in mind, whatever you do and whatever the short-term gains or losses, you haven't wasted your time.

The labor movement is beginning to look into this concept a little more. In fact, I am beginning to work with the AFL-CIO in Rhode Island to establish a community service immigration center to do voter education, social service work, political education and labor history among the immigrants. It is important to focus on the immigrants, especially the Hispanic, the Indochinese, and the Portuguese because the labor movement can be the place that these people can go to and get some assistance. Then, when it comes time to organize, support strikes, not be scabs, be good union members, they will have positive experience with the labor movement even before they became a member. That is essentially what Chavez understood. People with a positive sense of organization, they are the ones who will be the back bone of the union.

Dealing with Illegal Surveillance and Provocations

Sam Abbott

I'd like to talk about something that doesn't get discussed very often but that can be a real problem for some community organizations—especially groups that look as if they might be successful. I mean the problem of illegal disruption by police agencies. We were faced with this problem in a group that I've been part of, and our experience might be helpful to other people. In our case I'm glad to say it looks as if it's going to have an upbeat ending.

I was involved, starting in 1963, with a group in the Washington, D.C., area called the Emergency Committee on the Transportation Crisis. We fought the construction of freeways and posed public transportation as an alternative. We had an incredible coalition built up. The freeway plan would have displaced 25,000 people, most of them poor but not all of them. Our group organized mainly among poor people, mostly black, but there was tremendous support that cut across race lines and income lines. The affluent white Georgetown Citizens Association was shoulder to shoulder with us on this issue.

We were effective, too. We were the pioneers in pushing for legislation which got through Congress in the late sixties, allowing the transfer of highway money over to public transportation. The Metro system in Washington would never have gotten underway if it hadn't been for that law and our fight against the freeways. The battles were extremely protracted, constant. It was like social guerrilla warfare.

The skirmishes could be won or lost. There were many times when it became necessary to inculcate everybody with the idea that continuation of the struggles, more intensification, was necessary and that is exactly what happened.

We had a single-minded slogan of "Not another inch of freeway." And we won. For the first time in the anti-freeway struggle in the U.S. the result was a wholesale victory over the local officials, the state officials, and even the Federal Government. Those who say "You can't fight City Hall" were wrong that time. We beat City Hall and we beat Congress and the White House too.

I'm not saying all this to toot our horn, but to show the context of the police tactics that were used against us. We posed a real threat to some vested interests, and that's a situation where you can expect that dirty tricks are almost certainly going to be used against you. Let me give you some examples of what happened, because these tactics are in some ways typical.

On the first Earth Day, April 22, 1970, there was by coincidence—a happy coincidence for us—a big National Highway Users Conference at the Hilton Hotel in Washington. This was a lobby that was headed up by the big oil companies and paving companies. They were always testifying at public hearings that one in every six jobs in this country depend on the automobile, that progress can't be stopped, and so forth. We had a noon-hour picket line outside the hotel, with about 350–400 people.

A lot of TV and radio people covered it. After most of them had gone, though, one unidentified camera crew stayed. Two young "hippie"-type males in old Army-style jacket costumes were pulling blacks out of the picket line and putting them in front of the camera. I had given a statement to that particular camera and I remembered that some of the questions were not too relevant. When I saw they were pulling out just blacks from the picket line and having them make statements to the camera, I got suspicious. I went over and identified myself and demanded they do the same. I was verbally abused by the two of them. They called me a dictator and a Communist, a restrainer of free speech, and so on. I looked down and they had brand new, Navy-issue shoes which didn't seem to fit in with the rest of their clothes. So again I demanded their identification, this time so loudly that 50–100 people gathered around us, including police. Suddenly the two guys split in different directions and the police escorted the camera crew away.

The incident stuck in my mind. Several years later the Senate committee investigating intelligence activity reported that the CIA and other outfits had used fake camera crews as a tactic. They listed five cities where this was done, and Washington was one of them.

We also met up with undercover agents in our work. The Metro Police of Washington had a sworn police officer, a young black Vietnam veteran who had served in the Military Police. He was assigned to work in the Emergency Committee on Transportation Crisis ECTC to find out what was going on. He did a year's full-time free work for us and he had no visible means of employment. He drove our chairperson around the country to speak to groups that had called upon us for help in their freeway fights. He ate supper at my house. I became friendly with him. It was only after he left us that I found out—accidentally in fact—that he was a police officer. I happened to be in court in Washington and there he was in a uniform. He came over to me and spoke to me in a friendly manner asking about my grandchildren. He'd become disenchanted with undercover work and he'd asked for a transfer to a uniformed job. Later, when we sued the police for their illegal tactics, he testified that he'd never been able to find any evidence of lawbreaking by the Emergency Committee—or by the Black United Front, which he'd infiltrated at the same time.

So far I know what I'm saying must sound really harmless. But it wasn't always harmless by any means. One incident was really scary. We had built up a strong Student Support Committee, with as many as 1,000 to 2,000 people attending the rallies. Incidents would break out, such as stone throwing and that would be the signal for the arrests and tear gas. At one rally, we'd been warned of possible trouble with the police, so when I spoke I asked the audience not to go down to the construction site. I said we had reliable information that everybody would really get clobbered once they got to the site. This was the first time I had ever done that after participating in planning an event. I was called every name in the book from a coward to a bullshit artist by two young men, but about 200 people followed these two young men down to the site, and they were really massacred. It was so bad that there was a court case, and the victims won awards against the police for the excessive violence used against them.

I got a good description of the two guys who led that crowd. They had old Army uniforms on, and parachute scarves in which they had microphones and broadcasting equipment on their backs in a pack. A car about two blocks away was coordinating them. They were sworn police officers. This was verified by an officer who became disenchanted with the Police Department and resigned from it.

I was also involved in the peace movement against the Vietnam war. As the peace rallies began to grow, we noticed the absence of blacks in attendance. Since we'd been so successful in building a coalition against the freeways, I arranged a meeting to see how we could involve the local black population in these peace demonstrations. Some members of the Black United Front were present as well as members of several local peace mobilization committees. At that meeting, a proposed tax of $1 a head on demonstrators was demanded. The money would be used for printing presses, and to promote the campaign to develop the struggle for home rule and statehood for the District of Columbia. This was to finance a movement where blacks, who were maybe four-fifths of the population would have an equivalent say in the city. I supported that demand. Later, though, the demand got completely changed: No peace rallies would be allowed in D.C. unless a $1.00 head tax for each demonstrator would be paid to the Black United Front! How did that happen? It poisoned relations badly.

Sometime later an FBI agent named Robert Wall became disenchanted and quit. He wrote an article which appeared in the New York Review of Books and the Washington Post, and it said it was the FBI that initiated the demand that the $1 a head should be collected from peace groups. One of the goals of the FBI's COIN-TEL program was to prevent any unity between blacks and whites. The obnoxious and dirty result of the $1 a head demand was evident later when forged leaflets were mailed to prominent blacks. It was a drawing of an ape eating a banana and a heading saying "Let them eat bananas." It denounced the blacks for the $1 a head tax proposal. The leaflet was put out by the FBI. By using the Freedom of Information Act, we were later able to get a file copy of the leaflet shown in court, with a proud notation of its authorship and a warning that under no circumstances should the authorship of the leaflet become publicly known. All the COINTEL acts of this type were accompanied by the order that they should be kept secret.

Over the years I've learned that when you're working in an organization and you know there are provocateurs or agents, you have to avoid paranoia. If the idea becomes widespread that you are infiltrated, everybody looks askance at their neighbor. You can't do that. The leadership should be aware of it, but you have to be very careful that you don't divert the group's efforts or destroy people's trust in one another. That's the first salient point. Number two is that you cannot allow yourself to be put into a defensive position. I found it very sad when the Black Panthers, who started by working on issues, very quickly found themselves involved in one law suit after another. The police wanted it that way. You avoid going on the defensive by keeping your nose to the grindstone as far as the issue is concerned. Never allow yourself to be diverted into putting the majority of your efforts into defense.

Even though we handled the surveillance and provocation pretty well, we are still angry about it. After Watergate, when a lot of information about illegal police tactics began to come out, especially at the federal level, we decided to go to court ourselves. Because we'd had such broad support, and in fact had won the freeway fight, we figured we'd be an ideal group to bring a lawsuit. It wouldn't be at all easy to discredit us before a jury. So we brought a case with the help of some really good lawyers. One of them, David Rein, died two years ago but we continued the case with the help of young lawyers from the National Lawyers Guild. We've had to raise a lot of money for secretarial help, transcripts, and so forth, but we've never had to pay a nickel for the lawyers—they've worked for free. At the same time as we filed our case in 1975, 1976 we formed a group called the D.C. Committee for the Bill of Rights with the aim of getting the D.C. City Council to outlaw all noncriminal surveillance by the police. It hasn't passed yet, but we're still trying. The court case, on the other hand, was a big success. It was like pulling teeth to get the public documents we were legally entitled to, but eventually we came up with enough to prove our case thoroughly. When the jury decision came out just before Christmas 1981, in fact, the plaintiffs, both individuals and groups, got awards ranging from $80,000 to $94,000. I wouldn't be at all surprised to see the amounts get reduced a lot after all the appeals now underway this late summer of 1983 are done, but for us the important thing is that we want to teach them a lesson. And in that respect we've already won.

Defending the Wilmington 10

Anne Braden

Wilmington, North Carolina, is a port city. It's on the coast of North Carolina. It has quite a history of struggle there. In the late 1960s in Wilmington as in many communities around North Carolina, there was a tremendous battle over school desegregation. There were court orders that had been issued in a number of cities in North Carolina. What happened in Wilmington as well as other places was that the school authorities had desegregated the schools. In the process they closed up a lot of black schools. The same thing happened all over the South. In the desegregation process they had technically complied with the court order and desegregated the schools but had done nothing to try to combat the racism in the school system. You can't really have successful desegregation unless you've got some sort of program to overcome all of the racist history and deal with the racism of white teachers who aren't used to teaching black kids. A whole body of things can be done to make desegregation work, and they've been done in some places—but not in enough. When you don't do that, you desegregate the kids but you throw the black kids into an impossible situation because they're going into schools where they feel like they're in enemy territory. And they are. It's just an impossible situation for them and the white kids too. It's just very unhealthy.

What happened in North Carolina in that period in the late sixties is that black students began to organize to try to deal with this situation. That's what they were doing in Wilmington. They organized themselves in two or three high schools to try to get treated like human beings. They had very simple demands. They wanted some black history taught in the schools; they wanted more black teachers. They weren't demanding anything outrageous at all. But they were doing it in an organized way. The school administration just wouldn't talk with them at all. They kept suspending them and that kind of thing. So they began to escalate their struggle and have demonstrations, perfectly peaceful demonstrations, marching to the school board and so forth and so on.

At the same time, that part of North Carolina was a hotbed of organization by extreme racist groups—the Ku Klux Klan, which had had a decline in the '60s in most places, was strong in that area. This wasn't an area where there had been a strong civil rights movement. There were other organizations that considered the

Klan too mild. There was a thing called the Rights of White People, and they were having rallies. People said publicly that they were going to shoot black people down like rabbits in the streets. And in fact, by 1971 there were whites riding through the black community just shooting at random. It was a terror situation, and it was all building up into a sort of a crescendo.

In the winter of '70–71, the student organization there asked Reverend Ben Chavis to come and help them organize. Ben Chavis was a young black man from Oxford, North Carolina, in the process of becoming a minister. He already had a history in the movement in North Carolina. He'd gotten into things when he was thirteen or fourteen years old, when the sit-ins were going on. Ben had been a leader in Charlotte. He had gone to work on the staff of the Commission for Racial Justice of the United Church of Christ. They had a state office in North Carolina and they sent Chavis to Wilmington. That was about January of 1971. He began leading marches. Meantime these Klan-type groups were stepping up their attacks on the black community. The police were sitting doing nothing all this time. And the situation was getting tenser and tenser.

By the time Ben Chavis went to Wilmington early in '71, the black freedom movement had grown all over the state and was making itself felt in communities everywhere. Ben Chavis was key to it because he was traveling all through the state. You need somebody sort of tying things together. He was a very dedicated and charismatic person. He inspired people. He had also worked for SCLC and did some union organizing. The unions were beginning to get organized in North Carolina and the Vietnam Peace Movement was growing too. In other words, the state was in ferment. The people who run North Carolina were really uptight. That was true all over the South, but probably intensely in North Carolina because it had been a very tightly controlled state.

A lot of us believed there was a very carefully designed plan to chop off the leadership of this movement. Because if you chop off the leadership, you can cripple a movement. You don't destroy it forever, but you can cripple it. Chavis, in fact, was a particular target. Even before he went to Wilmington, he was under two or three hundred thousand dollars bond on trumped-up charges in other cities.

The kids were meeting in a Congregational Church in the black community. It happened to have a white minister named Eugene Templeton, who supported them. Everything came to a head one weekend when the attacks by the racist groups were constantly happening. The students and Ben Chavis were trying to get the police to declare a curfew or something to keep these murderers out of the black community, and the police wouldn't do it. They finally barricaded themselves in the church and started to shoot back. It was a pitched battle that weekend. One of the armed whites was shot and killed when he started toward the church with his gun drawn, and a young black was killed by the police. Chavis was on the phone constantly calling the police and saying ''You have to declare a curfew'' and so forth. The police finally did declare a curfew when the white was killed.

Considering what happened it's almost funny what the county prosecutor came up with that weekend. Some fires had broken out around the church Saturday night, and one of the places that was burned was a place called Mike's Grocery. Nobody thought much about it because there was so much else happening. But about a year later they indicted Chavis, eight black students, and one white VISTA worker who had supported them for conspiring to firebomb Mike's Grocery. It was bizarre. Nobody had thought too much about Mike's Grocery before that. There were a lot of things on fire. The only way the charge made sense was that it was a way to get Ben Chavis out of the movement work. But the state had its witnesses and even though their testimony was completely discredited later, they got a guilty verdict against all ten defendants.

When there's so much repression and so many poeple get put in jail on phony charges, it's really hard to fight them all at once. You've got to have local organizations everywhere who do that and some of that went on. But you sometimes have to focus on a few cases to bring out what's happening everywhere. The idea is that if you win one, it's going to help other people. This case in Wilmington was so atrocious that it cried out for particular attention.

One organization that began right away publicizing these things was the Southern Conference Educational Fund—SCEF—which I was with at that time. We had our monthly publication, we also had a network of people all through the country who were concerned about things like this and a good machinery for getting information out. We had been covering all this stuff happening in North Carolina for two or three years. We had this conviction that if you can let the people know the facts of the gross injustice, you can build a movement against it and often stop it. The main thing is to get information out that people just don't know. The big press is not going to cover things like this. The North Carolina newspapers covered the Wilmington 10 indictments, but they just presented these people as being guilty. They didn't tell what really happened.

We found over and over in SCEF that we had to have our own publication first off, where we could tell what really happened. We had a news service that sent stuff to other publications. While the *New York Times* was not going to print our news releases, the small press would, the black press would, the student press would, and the church press would. We'd built up over a period of years a reputation for accuracy. People knew if we said it, it was correct. We would send things to these smaller papers that would be printed. We kept pointing out this was a general pattern, repression and not just a frame-up of the Wilmington 10. That began to build a fire. You do it long enough and one day you pick up the *New York Times* and they'll have a story about it because the more people begin to hear about it and talk about it and eventually it becomes news. So we were doing that around these cases. Unfortunately the role of SCEF in these cases was short-lived because SCEF broke up through a very unfortunate set of circumstances about 1973. The organization I'm with now, the Southern Organizing Committee grew up later to try and do the kind of thing SCEF did, but we didn't have all the machinery that SCEF had. We played a supporting role.

The organizations that really built the campaign around the Wilmington 10 were the National Alliance Against Racist and Political Repression and the United Church of Christ Commission for Racial Justice. The Alliance was a new organization, formed in 1973. It grew out of the successful campaign to free Angela Davis in California.

Ben Chavis got involved in the Alliance in the early stages. The Wilmington 10 had been convicted in the Fall of 1972. Ben got 34 years, and they all got long sentences, but Ben got out on bail a few months later. The United Church, because he worked for them, had put up his bond. This was a fluke that couldn't be duplicated for everybody. The United Church did have money. Later he persuaded them to put up bond not just for him but for the others. It amounted to something like $400,000. Almost nobody has that kind of money. This was a big step for the Church and to their credit. It was important that Ben was out on bond because he could go around and tell his own story. There's nothing as effective as that. The Church also raised money to pay good lawyers. Attorney James Ferguson of Charlotte was the main defense lawyer.

Meantime the Alliance began to do the kind of thing that SCEF had been doing earlier of getting out the facts about this case and building a movement around it, both in North Carolina and outside. One thing that happens when people get under attack like this and they've got cases in court, the first reaction, unless someone organizes, is fear. People stay away. They feel they might get caught too. It is very important to get the initiative and show people that they don't have to be afraid, show people that they've got to stick together, and whoever is under attack, well that's where I'd better be.

In 1974, the Alliance decided to have a big march in North Carolina. There hadn't really been any big marches in the south since Martin Luther King was murdered. People had tried to have them but it didn't click, because there was so much repression. The late 60's and early 70's were a period of intense repression. There was a major counter-attack against the civil rights movement and black organizers were being jailed everywhere on charges that later proved to be frame-ups. The Alliance decided to mobilize a national march on July 4, 1974.

Some said "Why spend all that time on one March?" You do it to focus attention on these cases. Ten thousand came to Raleigh to that March on July 4th. It was a big march for that period, bigger than anything since King died. But the importance of a march like that is not primarily the 10,000 people who came and marched in Raleigh, though that did impress the state of North Carolina. More important, there were all the people around the country—several hundred thousand, maybe more than that—who were touched by the organizing for that march. There were posters all over the place with a map of North Carolina. The laboratory of repression, we called it. Literature was printed. The name began to get on the map.

A lot of people in Chicago or Birmingham or wherever who did not go to Raleigh went to rallies to raise money to send people to North Carolina. In other words, by organizing for the march we were organizing to let people know about this case.

This was also true in North Carolina. The Alliance had sent people to North Carolina including Angela for some weeks ahead of that march. They were traveling all over the state and had meetings and so forth. Even people who didn't come and march were touched by this. It was a very successful march.

On the heels of that they began circulating petitions. Nobody thinks a petition by itself will do any good, but that's another way of getting the word out to people. In the course of the next few years there were literally hundreds of thousands of people signing petitions for the Wilmington 10. In May of 1975 we had another march in Washington, D.C. It wasn't as big but it was important. We got the city council to declare the day of the march Wilmington 10 Day. That's how well-known the case was getting to be.

Then we got the people in the Alliance talking to people in Congress who were sympathetic. That has an effect because they get listened to. People like John Conyers and Parren Mitchell and other people in the Congressional Black Caucus plus some white Congresspeople like Don Edwards of California began putting things into the *Congressional Record* about this case. That gets some publicity. It's little drops of water beating on a rock. In the meantime you have all these people who have been on these marches to Raleigh and Washington who are back home talking to people about this case. They go to their city councils and get them to adopt a resolution. All those little things, each one of which wouldn't do much good, add up to a campaign. It's important that someone is coordinating it—sitting in an office somewhere keeping track of what people are doing in Podunk, what people are doing in Chicago, and getting material back out to people.

By that time the case of the Wilmington 10 was wending its way through the courts. Finally it got to the Supreme Court and the justices refused to hear it. So the 10 went to prison in February 1976. But that didn't stop the defense campaign; if anything it brought us more publicity and more support.

One thing the Alliance did was to contact groups in other parts of the world, so that petitions began to come in from all over the world calling the Wilmington 10 political prisoners—which of course is exactly what they were. It became a real international issue. The day we had another march in Raleigh in '76 there were demonstrations in other countries too.

Finally all of this agitation through the channels of information that people like us can create—by word of mouth, by organization, by going to the churches and unions and so forth—started to break through into what I call the big press. James Baldwin, the author, wrote an open letter to Jimmy Carter about the case, and it got widely printed.

As a consequence, in early '77, the State's case literally fell apart. All the witnesses who had testified against the 10 recanted—said they'd lied. The press in

North Carolina, some of whom were decent reporters on papers, even though ownership might not be so good—got very interested in exposing all this. The reporters went back and interviewed the jurors. One juror said, ''The case has really collapsed, hasn't it?'' Anyway, it had. And all this was highly publicized.

Then the TV show, ''60 Minutes,'' did a whole thing on the case. Of course the power of television is ridiculous. I remember going to places and speaking to people about this case and somebody saying ''Well that's true because I saw it.'' Somebody had said ''Well are you sure that's true?'' ''Of course that's true'', she said. ''I saw it on 60 Minutes.'' It was like suddenly that made it real—to be on ''60 Minutes.'' But of course CBS didn't just go discover the Wilmington 10 all by itself. They went there because of all this activity that had built up.

By that time it was a national issue that took off on its own. Well, we had to keep pushing it, but pretty much it rolled on its own momentum after that. Finally there was pressure from people who didn't even know what the facts were. All they'd heard was that these black people and one white including a minister were in prison because they were fighting for human rights in North Carolina.

We didn't win a dramatic victory, with everyone walking out of the prison at once, but we got them out one at a time. By the time a federal appeals court overturned the convictions, they were all out on parole. What happened was that Governor Hunt refused to give them a pardon, but he cut their sentences to make them eligible for earlier parole. Ben Chavis was the last one to be paroled, and that was December 1979. For our part, we decided not to let the case drop. The Wilmington 10 had taken the position all along that they wanted complete vindication in the courts. They were innocent and they wanted that recognized. And finally in October 1980, after a lot of organizing and agitation there was a hearing in the Fourth Circuit Court of Appeals and it reversed the conviction. It took nearly ten years, but we won. The state of North Carolina meant to put those people away forever, and they were stopped from doing it because of people organizing. That is the main lesson.[1]

---

[1]The Wilmington 10 case was only one of many situations in which black organizers in North Carolina were jailed on spurious charges in this period. At one point, at least 40 movement activists in several cities were in prison facing long sentences. Another famous case was that of the Charlotte 3—Jim Grant, T. J. Reddy, and Charles Parker—activists jailed for allegedly burning down a riding stable. Grant and Chavis had worked closely together, organizing throughout the state. The struggle to free the Wilmington 10 became the best known nationally and internationally, but the activity around this case was joined with campaigns to free the Charlotte 3 and other victims of repression. Eventually, all of them went free.

Alinsky Starts a FIGHT[1]

Robert Perlman

THE SCENE BEFORE "FIGHT" WAS LAUNCHED

Rochester, New York State's third largest city, has a population of approximately 350,000. It is principally a manufacturing center, with 45 percent of its labor force employed in some 800 plants, Eastman Kodak being the dominant firm and Xerox a rising newcomer. The city had a Democratic administration, Republicans regaining control in 1970. It was estimated that there were 35,000 blacks in the city in 1964; there are close to 50,000 today. This represents a tremendous growth since the early 1950s.

Unemployment[2] of both blacks and whites was exceptionally low in Rochester, about one percent at the time Alinsky arrived at the scene, and the industrial leaders are "enlightened," far more so than, for example, in Syracuse. Rochester has a highly skilled labor market. The public schools had been doing some things to meet the need of blacks: In 1965, 1000 black children were placed in schools outside the ghetto. It may be of interest that the late 1960s witnessed a rise in lower-middle-class racism, putting a stop to integration. The housing occupied by blacks, however, was and still is generally substandard. The city's blacks, regardless of social and economic status, are concentrated in two ghettos. The Third Ward contains most of the better-off blacks. The Seventh Ward, which had been the receiving area for blacks displaced elsewhere by urban renewal, contains the bulk of low-income people who live in an area with prostitution, numbers, rackets, and the like. Transportation in Rochester is a mess, but this is not peculiar to the black community.

In the face of strong civic pride about what the city has done for its people, there were what some whites and blacks considered "serious riots" in the black community in the summer of 1964. Others considered these as the beginning of "black rebellion." One opinion held that the riots were a revolt against the Rochester police, following a history of incidents of police brutality. Protest committees had accomplished nothing. Then three whites and three blacks staged a sit-in at City Hall and received support from some of the University faculty. The clergy wanted action through a Police Advisory Board that had been set up by the Democratic administration. Black leaders wanted two or three men on the police force fired.

The NAACP and the city's Human Relations Board were considered to be ineffective in the situation. The press, radio, and TV—controlled by the ultraconservative Gannett chain—opposed the interests of the black community. Shortly

---

[1]Edited version of a case written by Robert Perlman of Brandeis University.

[2]Unemployment of black men may currently be up 5 percent and that of black females 10 to 12 percent.

before what the press subsequently defined as "riots," Malcolm X had a meeting attended by 800 blacks. Some observers feel that his presentation may have sparked the "riot." Other observers disagree. During the disturbances that followed, four men from Martin Luther King's organization (Southern Christian Leadership Conference, or SCLC) were invited to organize in Rochester. They came. After surveying the scene, however, they indicated that SCLC was currently committed to its endeavors in the South. Because of the press of these involvements they did not feel equipped for organizing efforts in a Northern city.

The Urban Ministry of the Rochester Council of Churches then turned to Saul Alinsky's Industrial Areas Foundation (IAF). The Council is a corporation of denominational churches, supported by local contributions collected through its member churches and affiliated with the National Council of Churches. The Urban Ministry is a somewhat autonomous group within the Council; its function is to develop strategies for inner-city church programs and to administer such programs. The Urban Ministry has its own board of directors and its own executive. It gets its funds from national and local judicatory bodies of the various denominations and is therefore, to some degree, free of control by the local churches. The Urban Ministry's executive director—with full support from the Executive Director of the Council of Churches and from the lay chairman of the Urban Ministry board—sparked the first move toward Alinsky by bringing together a small, informal group of white and black laymen and clergymen and arranging for them to go to Chicago for an initial contact with Alinsky. The group invited him to come to Rochester to discuss an organizing program.

PREPARING THE WAY FOR ALINSKY

In January of 1965 a meeting was arranged in a black church in Rochester, but Alinsky's plane was grounded in Chicago and he did not appear. In his absence there was a brief discussion revolving around such questions as whether the black community needed a "white Moses" or a black leader. Some felt that the black community was divided and needed a miracle. Perhaps Alinsky could provide it. Others argued that the black community should not depend on a white man but should organize from within. Later in January, Alinsky came to a similar meeting and answered questions, described the organizing work of the IAF in other cities, explained the role the IAF would play if it came to Rochester, and clarified the possibilities and requirements of an organizing drive. He was very clear on the financial arrangements. These would have to be secure, not subject to political promises, and capable of supporting the first two years of organizing efforts.

Meanwhile, public knowledge that Alinsky might come to Rochester had begun to agitate and polarize the whole community. The Protestant ministers were busy explaining and defending Alinsky and neutralizing the growing opposition. Petitions asking Alinsky to come were circulated in the black community. Individual civic leaders (a member of the board of the Council of Social Agencies, a Jewish businessman, a prominent Republican, and others) let it be known, mostly in private conversations, that they favored Alinsky's coming to Rochester. Ranged against them was the press, the business community's top leadership, the President of the University of Rochester, the executive of the Council of Social Agencies, and some members of the Divinity School faculty. During this period, the Urban Ministry obtained commitments, from its national and local sources, of funds in the amount of $100,000 for a two-year organizing drive, half of it in cash for the first year and pledges for the second year. This fact was widely publicized in Rochester.

In mid-February, a Citizens' Committee for Alinsky created by the Urban Ministry held an open meeting in the ghetto. Black and white ministers fielded questions from the floor. Again there was discussion of goals and tactics, of the need for unity among blacks, of their responsibility for organizing, and the like. In this meeting the Ministerial Alliance, an organization of black clergymen, took the stance that they were inviting Alinsky to Rochester.

A few days later, there was a second meeting attended by an all-white audience in another section of town. Members of the Urban Ministry saw to it that the proposed arrangement with Alinsky was explored from all angles. Would there be violence again? How does IAF proceed? What would be the effect on social welfare agencies? Shortly after this a meeting was held in a black church to bolster the campaign for signatures on petitions to bring Alinsky to Rochester and to give evidence of growing support for him in the black community. The Ministerial Alliance took responsibility for this one.

Throughout these weeks Saul Alinsky had not given a direct answer to the black and white leaders who were urging him to come.

ALINSKY AGREES TO COME

The next significant event was a meeting in Syracuse between Saul Alinsky and 18 people from Rochester, with more blacks represented in the delegation than had been the case in previous meetings. Alinsky again explained his approach, what could be expected of him, and what he expected of those who wanted to organize. He stressed the fact that there must be no rioting in the summer of 1965. If riots occurred, he said, it would be the end of the organization. Alinsky told the group he was willing to come to Rochester, but that some steps had to be taken to define issues and rally more support before a public announcement could be made.

A MILITANT CORE AND A LARGER ORGANIZATION

In March, a crucial meeting of blacks who had been involved from the beginning was held by a small group in which they tested among themselves what they were prepared to do and risk if Alinsky came. They decided to assume leadership and planned a public meeting to consolidate the decision to have Alinsky get started. Two hundred people took part in this meeting. At the end of March, Alinsky held a second meeting in Syracuse with the Rochester leaders. He introduced Ed Chambers as the organizer he was assigning to Rochester. A press and TV interview was arranged to follow this meeting. This constituted the public annoucement that Alinsky was going to organize in Rochester's black community.

Chambers assumed the organizational responsibility at this point and recommended some structure—an organizing committee, a steering committee, and preparations for a "convention of delegates" of local organizations to be held within six weeks. On April 20, 400 people, half of them blacks, met as "the body" of FIGHT and heard representatives of organizations give evidence of their support. Four committees were set up:

1. Constitution
2. Policy and Issues
3. Convention Arrangements
4. Urban Renewal

The Steering Committee was legitimized by "the body" and was authorized to take action against slum landlords. This issue was selected by the Steering Committee and Chambers because it would draw universal support and was a symbolically meaningful target.

The IAF organizer at this juncture made a decision to concentrate organizational effort in the Third Ward, where the church-oriented people who looked at themselves as "respectable" lived because it was stable, and he felt that the important thing at that time was to get the organization started. Alinsky and Alinsky organizers have subsequently been criticized for this approach and for their frequent reliance on already organized black middle-class groups. The IAF organizer did not, however, give up his determination to maintain and in the long run increase the participation of the antichurch, more militant group from the Seventh Ward. Chambers then hired some organizers, all blacks, from the neighborhoods in which the organization was beginning. Soon thereafter, FIGHT staged a picketing demonstration against a landlord.

During this period the Steering Committee was meeting every week or two. In mid-May a public meeting took place at which new organizations affiliated with FIGHT. A Nominating Committee was established to prepare for the "convention" that was to be held on June 11. About 700 people participated as delegates in that convention. Some 130 organizations were represented. While about 70 percent of these organizations existed before the convention, the others were paper organizations. Hundreds of white people attended the convention as observers. The constitution was presented and some sections were discussed and amended from the floor before it was adopted. A slate of officers was elected. All the preparatory work had been handled by a convention committee under the general direction of the Steering Committee. FIGHT was established!

REEXAMINATION OF ALINSKY'S STRATEGY

Alinsky's operation resembles the process of organizing a local labor union. As the union moves into a plant or a community that is unorganized, the organizers make contact with some people who have indicated their interest if not their commitment to organizing. The union then tests whether there are sufficiently good prospects for expanding this nucleus to warrant an investment of a union's resources in an organizing drive. The union may also be concerned about exposing a small group of militant people to defeat. During this feeling-out process, the union explains that the goal is to set up a permanent organization. The union also makes clear that the basic responsibility for organizing rests with the workers and particularly with the nucleus of emerging leaders. The union brings to bear its previous experience and offers, in effect, a kind of technical assistance to the organizing drive.

The analogy breaks down in one important respect. The union must ultimately be able to produce a majority of workers as card-carrying members of the union. In the Alinsky type of operation it is not at all necessary to enroll a majority of the target group. In fact, in Alinsky's *Reveille for Radicals,* he points out that building an organization with 5 percent of a target population will constitute success. In this respect it may be more appropriate to compare Alinsky's operation with the organization of a local chapter of an environmental action group. These considerations lead directly to the first of a series of propositions about his organizing methods that will be advanced and illustrated here.

Step 1. There needs to be a nucleus of support and the availability of financial resources outside the disadvantaged community in order to initiate an organizing process.

The process begins when an actor or group of actors makes the decision to undertake organization of a target population. In the early and mid 1960s this target population was usually a black community or a low-income neighborhood without regard to race. While individual members or leaders of such groups often initiated the goal of organization, they rarely if ever possessed the financial resources needed to carry it out. The growth of social movements in the mid-1960s and the experience of population groups with the antipoverty programs considerably changed this picture.

The leadership of the Urban Ministry in the Rochester Council of Churches first took the initiative in bringing together a group to seek out Alinsky. It was also this group that raised $100,000 for the organizing drive. It was necessary, however, to help the community shift the responsibility from the white Protestant leadership to the leadership of the black community. Alinsky made it clear at his first meeting with the Rochester group that he must have an invitation "from the people" as well as financial support from the churches. He explained that if a church group wants to make money available and is able to get the support of the people, then the Industrial Areas Foundation must have the money in advance in order to protect its organizers' income when the going got rough and pressure was applied to call off the organizing. Once the sponsors advanced the money, however, they would have nothing to say about what happened after that; the people would make decisions.

While the initiating group was not without some anxiety over this, some of the people who favored Alinsky clearly saw him as an alternative to more nationalistic and "dangerous" leadership emerging within the black community. From the outset, Alinsky faced the test of avoiding "the riots" that the white community feared in the summer of 1965. This made it necessary for him to move more rapidly than usual.

Step 2. Alinsky sets certain tests as conditions for his coming and in responding to these conditions, the local leadership begins the process of organization before Alinsky commits himself to enter the situation.

Over a period of months Alinsky structured the situation so that while he did not give a definite answer about his coming to Rochester, more and more people were asking him to come. He held two meetings in nearby Syracuse, where he had been a consultant to Syracuse University, rather than in Rochester itself. At the first meeting he held in Rochester, Alinsky was asked whether he would come, since he had whetted the people's appetite. He replied that he was not sure, that he had many other bids for his services in other cities. At the next public meeting, which was held without Alinsky, the question was asked, if the black community is unorganized and divided, how can it respond to Alinsky? When Alinsky next met with the group in Syracuse his first question was, "What is the mood of the churches, is it militant?" He was told that the churches were not leading and that some of them feared reprisals. At the end of this meeting Alinsky made the statement, "We will come when you are organized."

This process of testing reached its climax at the meeting in March, when a small leadership group consisting only of blacks met to discuss their position. They were still uncertain at this time and were asking themselves whether they were willing and able to act. At this meeting the leaders finally committed themselves to bringing Alinsky in and then asked how they could prepare for this and how they could mobilize support to convince Alinsky that there was a sufficiently strong base to warrant his coming in.

Step 3. Alinsky helps the local leadership meet his set of conditions.

He used a variety of devices to educate his leadership: he recounted past successes in order to convince the local leaders that it could be done; he sought to increase militancy by polarizing the situation, by identifying the enemy, and by developing a situation in terms of "good guys" and "bad guys"; he helped the leadership to anticipate some of their problems, such as the role of informers and sell-outs; he provided leadership in setting goals and helped them to anticipate the kind of tactics they would need to employ; and he schooled them over and over again in the mutual rights, responsibilities, and expectations of his role as the professional organizer and their role as the local leadership.

This approach may be illustrated in some detail by quoting from Alinsky's early meetings with the Rochester group. At the first meeting in January, Alinsky began in his characteristic way, not by making his own presentation but by asking for questions. One of the first questions was, "Is integrated housing a goal?" Alinsky answered, "The whites don't want to live with Negroes." He went on to say that he would not be telling the blacks what to do; that after they had put together their organization they would have only black organizers, he would not be present much and would sit in the back and only speak up if asked to. Alinsky said, "I am not after anything for myself, but white skin can be useful in getting an audience downtown."

Alinsky was asked how leaders are recruited. He answered that you start by looking for angry people who are willing to learn and if they are intelligent, you take them. He added that the IAF does not reject existing leadership and went on to recite the history of the Back-of-the-Yards movement. This presented a problem that Alinsky had to deal with again—he explained the growing tendency of workers in that part of Chicago to become part of the establishment and said that he might have to go in and start a new organization there. A question was raised about his attitude toward social workers and Alinsky warned that settlement houses would try to buy people off by giving them certain services. He emphasized that he tried to organize people so that they could acquire dignity and a sense of identity that can only be achieved by fighting the enemy. "Power is organization," Alinsky said, "and the sources of power are either money or numbers." Since blacks lack money, they must organize power through the use of numbers. "Power is neutral," he continued. "Whether or not it is desirable depends on the values involved and the immediate situation."

When asked about sit-ins, pickets, and similar demonstrations, he answered, "We do nothing so unimaginative." He cited the instance in Chicago of mobilizing three thousand blacks who went to one of the department stores as a means of getting jobs there for other blacks. They carefully looked over all the merchandise and made small purchases to be delivered C.O.D. (in order to tie up the department store's trucks). Purchases were all for $5 worth of merchandise, the minimum that could be purchased C.O.D. All orders were refused on delivery. The presence of so many blacks turned away many white customers. Alinsky then used "Uncle Toms" to get the message to the department store that they were willing to negotiate. Within a matter of hours and at the insistence of the department store, 113 jobs were made available for blacks. Alinsky was asked whether he could bring a factory to Rochester as a source of employment for blacks, and he answered that the IAF had done this in several places in Chicago. He was asked about salaries for his organizers and said that they usually started at about $4700 and if the individual did a good job he could work his way up to about $6500. In a press conference following this meeting. Alinsky was asked about violence and replied that violence occurs when people are discontented and have no understanding of their potential power. He said that organization overcomes that sense of desperation and removes the need for violence.

It is important to note that this process of interpretation was carried on by other individuals in Alinsky's absence. At one such meeting it was explained that Alinsky would organize politically and that he would use the techniques and tactics of the union movement. In the course of this discussion more and more stress was placed on the development of pride, self-help, self-responsibility, and the like. One speaker said that blacks need to organize in order to unify themselves in the way that Italians and Jews have done in Rochester. Some interest was expressed during this meeting in generating public opposition in the white community as a means of lending legitimacy in the black community to Alinsky's presence as an organizer.

The process of preparing people for the struggle ahead continued when Alinsky met with a leadership group in Syracuse. He warned the group that the antipoverty program would try to control black churches by moving in as tenants, paying rent and providing funds for their programs and then insisting on certain controls. He also warned against "professional Negroes," by which he meant the gradualists. He expressed his concern about people being bought off and kept out of the organization. Alinsky told the group that his staff would guide and offer their experience, but "the job of liberation is yours." He said he would pick the local director who in turn would recruit and train black organizers.

Immediately after Alinsky told this meeting that he was willing to come to Rochester but that this was not the time for a public announcement, he added, "Let the whites worry, let's first find the issues and get people to declare themselves." He urged them to put together a list of people for the organizing drive. All of this had its impact on the small leadership meeting that was described above. At that meeting there was a discussion of the major issues, which were defined by various individuals as jobs and education, urban renewal, and the need for real and lasting representation downtown. The strategy that was suggested was to line up black leadership and organizations, and the man in the street would follow.

Alinsky used the events of the moment to define for the leadership his role and his tactics. At his March meeting in Syracuse he said that he had received an invitation to meet with the City Manager of Rochester. He first assured the group that they would decide by vote whether or not he would accept this invitation. He then made three points: "(1) They want to know me as a person. If I say 'No' to their invitation, they will think they are dealing with a madman; (2) I assure you they will be more nervous after my meeting with them. I'll show strength and toughness; (3) We should realize that we will have to negotiate sooner or later, we can't be suicidal. I also want them to know I keep my word but that we are strong. I will stress treating Negroes with equality." In the discussion that followed, someone wondered whether Alinsky's meeting with the City official would jeopardize trust on the part of blacks. The group made a decision to approve the meeting because they felt that Alinsky was going as their representative and not as someone picked by "downtown."

While Alinsky was concentrating on preparing the black leadership for what lay ahead, the white Protestant ministers were equally hard at work in the white community preparing both friends and enemies. At the meeting in February attended only by white people, the white leadership recounted the history and experience of the Industrial Areas Foundation, pointed out that violence was not a part of this plan, and emphasized that Alinsky had worked with churches in various parts of the country. It was emphasized that Alinsky had no program for Rochester but that he would make the black community work together and gain power through such devices as a rent strike, efforts to improve code enforcements, and the like. No answer was given at this meeting to the question as to whether Alinsky would be working with white people to educate them. There was a discussion of the reasons for the riots in Rochester, and these were given as the flooding of southern blacks into the city and the antagonism of blacks to merchants and to the police.

One of the ministers reviewed the TWO experience in Chicago and said that social workers do some organizing but prove to be helpless when their demands are rejected. The Alinsky-type organizer was compared to St. Paul as a passionate man and at the same time a strategist. With regard to relationships to existing organizations, it was pointed out that in Chicago settlement houses, the American Legion and others have cooperated with Alinsky organizations. As to whether there would be conflict with social agencies, the answer was that this choice would be up to the social agencies.

Throughout this meeting it was reiterated that Alinsky's operation is not a program but a process. In dealing with the question as to whether Hitler-type leadership could arise in this process, one of the speakers made it clear that the white community could not control the process and was not in a position to organize the black community.

The stage in the organizing process that this material illustrates might be restated as follows. *Alinsky helped the local leadership to meet the conditions he had set and thereby accelerated the process of organization. Simultaneously he offered them technical assistance, such as instruction in how to set up a press conference, and confronted them with the choice of whether in fact they wanted to play the role that he defined for them.*

Step 4. As soon as Alinsky commits himself to organizing, the development of a militant and disciplined core of people becomes the overriding objective. Issues and programs are converted into tactics to achieve that objective.

Alinsky suggested using a "program ballot" in which people were asked to state their goals at the beginning of an organizing campaign. However, this is essentially a tactical device that Alinsky used to build and protect the developing organization. Alinsky's rationale for this device is that it makes people in the community aware of the organization's existence, it gives some of them a feeling of participation, it helps to identify potential recruits for the organization, and it is a defense against the charges of lack of democracy in the organization. In other words, Alinsky used this program ballot not to formulate goals but to build the organization.

The data on the first few months of organization, which bears on this point, will be summarized here. When Alinsky moved into action, one of his first statements to the group was, "Don't be specific on issues." This can be interpreted as a recommendation to keep the stance of the organization flexible in order to seize opportunities as they present themselves. He also stressed the use of humor, ridicule, and surprise to throw "the enemy" off balance, while unifying "your side."

At the same meeting Chambers reacted when, in the discussion, it was made known that the local Community Chest was giving $40,000 to start an Urban League in Rochester. He said, "If the Urban League is getting $40,000 to educate Negroes, let's ask for $40,000 to educate poor whites about Negroes." This brought an immediate and favorable response from the group. Chambers then got down to the real business quickly. He asked if there was a need for the nucleus of an organizing committee and which community groups should be signed up as part of the selling job that would take place during the next six weeks before the nominating convention. Chambers always threw out ideas as questions.

When the steering committee met, there was some discussion and listing of issues. These included the needs of migrants, youth problems, enforcement of housing codes, school segregation, police activities, vocational counseling, and urban renewal. The committee then discussed the coming convention and agreed that every organization would be invited to send five delegates. It was in this discussion that the rules for group discipline began to be made explicit. Chambers urged that none of the officers or committee chairmen leak information prematurely and that they not take their disagreements outside the executive group. Throughout these meetings in the spring there was considerable concern with questions of solidarity, not breaking ranks, being seduced by the establishment, backbiting among blacks, and identifying and removing Uncle Toms from their midst. The sense of black solidarity was further reinforced at these meetings by making it clear when welcoming whites that this was a black organization.

It is evident from the record that as an organizer, Chambers made a clear-cut decision in his own mind concerning strategies. He would present his strategies and argue them before the leadership group. Subsequently, over a period of time, he would seek out those people who supported his strategies, and in turn support their rise in the organization if they corresponded to his image of leadership.

Chambers also recognized that there was strong factional feeling between the Third Ward where the "respectable" people lived, and the Seventh Ward. He made a conscious decision to begin working through the more stable, church-affiliated neighborhood where the ministers told him they could count on mobilizing 2000 of the 10,000 to 14,000 black adults.

Wanting to see some balance maintained between the two groups, Chambers saw himself as a catalyst. He encouraged them to bring their conflict out into the open and battle it through. Apparently Chambers hoped to build the organization with support from both wards. Consequently, he embarked on a strategy of involving the ministers of black churches and encouraging them to assume roles as militant, visible, and committed leaders. In one tactic, for example, he set quotas for black ministers to bring a certain number of people to the picket line that was demonstrating against a slum landlord. He cautiously walked a middle ground between factions and hired two organizers from the anti-church area and one from the church-oriented neighborhood. Alinsky and Chambers chose as the president of the organization, Reverend Franklin D. R. Florence, a minister known as a militant and a black nationalist. Chambers was careful not to move without the support and approval of his new president and, in fact, held off from action for many weeks while Florence had to be out of town.

Chambers defined his role as one of constantly trying to push people into doing things they wouldn't otherwise do. He moved through the community and kept widening his contacts. He set goals and tests, such as by telling the leadership that if they could not produce 60 pickets for a demonstration, it should be called off. He suggested program ideas such as negotiating with landlords who were holding back on maintenance and also complaining about their tenants, and suggested arranging to reduce the rent for "a house mother" who would then keep order in the house. He saw this as a prelude to starting tenants' clubs later on. It seems clear that Chambers screened and selected the issues for action. He resisted efforts to involve the organization in service programs. When it was suggested at one meeting that FIGHT participate in the literacy program by providing teachers, he pointed out that this was not a central concern of the organization.

Alinsky is concerned with "people's organizations" and strengthening their influence on service organizations. Working at the level of the local community, he seeks to change the attitudes and behavior, with respect to power, of both kinds of organization. The essence of the Alinsky process is to exploit action situations so that a "people's organization" will perceive itself as more powerful. Forming a disciplined organization, it may test its power, inevitably finding itself increasingly effective in asserting its interests against those in authority who have hitherto disregarded the group because they perceived it as powerless. The salient point here is that the Alinsky-style operation is designed to redistribute power in the decision-making arena and to place more of it in the hands of the previously powerless. It is quite different from efforts that are directed toward some specific policy change, such as improving the quality of education for disadvantaged children or enhancing the job skills of school dropouts. Concrete program objectives are the means for Alinsky, not the ends.

TWO YEARS LATER

There are, of course, a series of epilogues to FIGHT's early history. No organization stays the same for long, and a militant organization based on a shaky alliance cannot expect to maintain allegiance of all its supporters forever. Some of the organizations founded by Alinsky foundered after some time. Some, like Back of the Yards, became conservative and reactionary. Most changed their character considerably. Alinsky counters his critics by explaining that this is the nature of the dynamics of all organizations and all collaborative efforts. His job is to help a community organize, not to tell it what it should do with itself after it is organized. If helping the "have-nots take it away from the haves" results in giving more than its rightful share to the group he is helping, then maybe "I'll have to help another group of have-nots take it away from them," he says.

Two years after Alinsky and Chambers began organizing, where was FIGHT? In keeping with the times, the "I" in the organization's acronymic name was being largely ignored (the letters stand for Freedom, Integration, God, Honor, Today). Whites had been firmly pushed out of the organization, but were now all organized into the Friends of FIGHT. FIGHT as an organization was now a conglomerate of more than 100 organizations, including settlement houses (those social workers Alinsky had argued against), pool halls, gangs, and Black Panther clubs. According to its chairman, it was led by "dissident young blacks ready for a change."

The Council of Churches was trying to raise $35,000 for a third year. Several denominations were refusing to contribute. Others pledged money, but only after bitter internal struggles, and with victories of small minorities. Still, most gave, and the money was eventually raised.

Friends of FIGHT were in disagreement. Some deplored attacks made by some of FIGHT's leaders on several Jewish community leaders. Stokely Carmichael, then chairman of SNCC, came to town to address a FIGHT rally, promising that in a forthcoming battle with Eastman Kodak over 600 jobs for hard-to-employ, unskilled blacks, he would organize a national boycott against Kodak. When it came, the boycott was a dismal flop, proving that FIGHT could not rely on help outside Rochester, and that there was a certain aloneness in a local organization that is not part of an organized national movement (another criticism leveled at Alinsky). "When we are through," Carmichael had claimed, "FIGHT will say 'Jump,' and Kodak will ask 'How high?'"

The Kodak issue provided good press for some time. A vice president of the company whose wife was a member of Friends of FIGHT had signed a rather confusing agreement with Florence to allow FIGHT to recruit the 600 black to be employed. "Kodak's killing FIGHT with kindness," wrote a local news columnist. A few days later, higher-ups within Kodak repudiated the agreement. "If I were Alinsky, I would have bribed Eilers (president of Kodak) to repudiate the agreement," said Ben Phelosof, acting president of Friends of FIGHT.

FIGHT at the time was engaged in a number of fights, perhaps too many. The Gannett chain stepped up its attacks. Prominent white supporters were repudiating the organization, or at least wavering. The Urban League, organized by middle-class blacks to counter the Alinsky organization, was picking up some support and somehow weathering the accusations of "Tomism." New, more militant organizations were expanding within the Seventh Ward, where Chambers had not organized early enough. But FIGHT continued to maintain its rather characteristic Alinsky style for some time. It should be noted that while this case illustrates Alinsky-style organizing, vintage 1960's, he has recently moved progressively out of the black community and into organizing lower- and middle-income whites around other sets of issues.

The Boston Model—
A Success Story?

Lee Staples

For a time the organizing was very successful. We had a fairly strong group of organizers in Boston, led by staff director Bill Pastreich. The organizing model that we used came to be known as the Boston model and I want to describe it in some detail. Basically, it was built around organizing to obtain special needs benefits from the Welfare Department. These were benefits that could be given out at the discretion of the social worker, two prime examples being grants for furniture and school clothing grants. In Massachusetts, we looked at the limited precedent that had been established by social workers giving special needs payments to certain individuals. We tried to break that open on a much wider basis, essentially using that discretionary part as a "handle." In other words, we could leverage special needs grants for *all* recipients based on this discretionary power. We broke this open on a statewide basis in 1968.

The state of Massachusetts had taken over the county system of welfare in late '67 or '68. Everything was unified in 1968 under a statewide system. This meant that if we could establish precedents in one office, we would be able to replicate them in offices across the state.

The first breakthrough was won in the Roxbury Crossing office. Bill Pastreich organized a large group of recipients from the Mission Hill Project to go into the Roxbury Crossing welfare office and demand special needs grants for furniture. They were initially refused, but they sat in for a long period of time and finally won. I don't think the Welfare Department realized it, but at that point what they had done was to give Welfare Rights a precedent. It was the organizing handle that we were looking for, and we ran with it across the whole state. That's how each of the fifty-five chapters was built: each one around a special needs benefit campaign.

The following is a detailed description of how a special needs organizing campaign was conducted. The organizing drive was essentially done on a six-week timetable. Generally one paid organizer (full-time) and a couple of volunteers from local churches were needed. The first step was to do basic groundwork in the area we wanted to organize by visiting various social service agencies, poverty programs, churches, and so on, talking to sympathetic workers and clergy involved in the neighborhood. We tried to enlist their aid in several ways. Most importantly we attempted to get contacts of good people to see who would potentially become involved in an organizing project. Secondly, we tried to get a number of these early contacts involved as volunteers to help in the organizing drive. Thirdly, we asked them to let us use their offices and their resources, a telephone or a mimeo machine, whatever. After we gained a reputation, we always tried to get a local office we could work out of. Later, this early phase of the model changed in that we were often approached by a group of welfare recipients asking us to come into their neighborhood to help get an organization started.

After doing the initial groundwork, we would immediately go about the work of building an organizing committee. Essentially we were looking for ten to fifteen recipients who were anxious to get an organizing drive off the ground and had some leadership potential and had a fair number of contacts in the neighborhood. Ideally they were people who were known and respected in the neighborhood, who had the time, energy, and commitment to involve themselves heavily in an organizing drive. The organizing committee would hold a meeting and begin to plan the drive. We would set a date, time, and place for our first meeting about five weeks in advance. The meeting would usually be in the morning. That's when people were available and offices were open. Meetings were held in a local church or a similar place. Before picking a date, we would choose an issue to organize around. They were virtually always for special needs campaigns for furniture or clothing. The bulk of the most successful organizing was for furniture. Next we would design a leaflet or flyer and a letter from the organizing committee to other recipients. The letter would say something to this effect:

> We are all recipients living in the neighborhood here who feel the need to get an organization started. We are not getting our rights met by the Welfare Department (or we're being mistreated by the Welfare Department); social workers aren't telling us what we're entitled to. Because of this we've asked the Massachusetts Welfare Rights Organization to help us get an organization started in the neighborhood, so we can fight for what is rightly ours.

The letter would also talk about the four ultimate goals of the National Welfare Rights Organization: adequate income, justice, dignity, and democracy. Then specifically it would refer to the special needs campaign, asking if the people knew that they were entitled to furniture or clothing for their children, and that in order to receive these benefits they would have to organize. It stated that a meeting was going to be held on X day and in X place and that someone would be around knocking on their door to give them more information and more specifics about the meeting. We also tried to get a commitment from people on the organizing committee to go with an organizer doing the door knocking or the home visits to find people later. We lined up those commitments at the meeting.

Recipients were a special constituency, it wasn't particularly efficient to go randomly from door to door. We needed a list of who was on welfare. The best method was to get a sympathetic social worker who would steal the list for us. That happened in a number of cases with social workers who were totally disenchanted with the welfare system and its lack of response to the needs of people. In other cases we were able to slip into the office and make Xerox copies of the lists. In public housing projects we were able to go door to door because of the density. Probably the most creative thing we did to get a list of recipients was to use tables in supermarkets on check cashing day. At the table we'd always have a priest or nun and some people from the organizing committee. We'd all be wearing Welfare Rights buttons and the tables would be decorated with big signs saying "Did you know you're entitled to furniture from the Welfare Department?" or "Do you need school clothing for your kids?" or another poster saying "We're getting organized to get what we need."

As the lines moved pretty slowly, it was a great chance to talk with people and interact with them. We'd explain that an organizing drive was taking place and that there was going to be a meeting. We'd pass out a leaflet designed in consultation with the organizing committee, telling about the meeting. The most important thing was to get people to sign up their name, address, and phone number indicating they were interested.

We'd tell them we would be around to their house to give them more information, to help determine what they were entitled to.

We had a sample form that we would take to figure out a budget with people and decide what they were going to ask for. That was extremely successful and often we would come away with hundreds of names.

Timing was very important. We would want to have the initial organizing committee meeting take place one or two days before the first or the fifteenth—check cashing days—so that we would immediately go into the supermarket with our tables. Once we'd done the tabling we then moved into the meat of the organizing drive. We'd make home visits to people on the lists and talk with people about the benefits that they were entitled to and the fact the organization was getting started. We always would try to go with a recipient from the organizing committee, so usually there would be a team—an organizer and someone from the committee. The members of the committee were able to get us into the door because they knew a lot of the people in the neighborhood. They were able to tip the balance.

The first step in a home visit would be getting into the house. You can't really convince anyone to participate in a meeting if you're standing outside their door. You need to get into the house and sit down. We would immediately explain our goals and appeal to the person's self-interest around a pretty basic material benefit.

We would ask questions in a fairly agitational manner: "Do you have all the furniture that you need?" or "Would you like more school clothing?" People always said, "Of course!" Then we'd say "Did you know you were entitled to it by law?" They'd say "No!" By this time they'd be fairly angry. We'd then hand them a form which had "SAMPLE" stamped on it. Across the top of the form would be a quote from Welfare regulations saying that the recipient is entitled to a special needs grant for furniture or whatever. We'd say "Look, here it is. This is what you should be receiving. Take a look at it." We would have the person check off the different items. Each item of furniture or clothing was listed there with the price next to it, and people would check off what they needed. Then we'd tally it up at the end. A typical furniture benefit for the average person would be about $2,000. That may seem like a lot of money but in so many cases everything in the house was falling apart, everything was broken down; and so people would say they needed everything on the list. We'd tally it all up, of course. The person would say, "Great, give me a form and I'll take it to my social worker" and the organizer would say "Oh no. This is just a sample form. Your social worker doesn't have to give you this special benefits grant. We're going to have to fight for it. They can give it to you but they're only going to listen if we're organized and go in a group. Next Tuesday (or whenever the date was) we're going to go as a group and bring our forms together. They'll listen to us!"

We'd then also talk about some of the bigger issues, the most important being the whole notion of dignity. People felt they were constantly mistreated in the Welfare Office. Recipients had to wait for hours to see their social worker. Often they were insulted or treated in a demeaning way. The whole notion of dignity and the fact that as an organized group they would be treated with respect was as compelling as the special needs benefits.

We would also talk about the local neighborhood group being hooked into the National Welfare Rights Organization. We'd explain about the national movement and its goals of adequate income, dignity, justice, democracy. We'd stress the fact that recipients all across our country were organizing.

I think an important thing to remember about Welfare Rights, is that it was at least a mini-movement, as opposed to just an organization. Movement is hard to define. Movements contain organizations. Organizations are necessary but not sufficient for a movement. In movements you see a lot of spontaneous activity, like the civil rights movement in the '60s. That's one key thing. All across the country, welfare rights groups were springing up on their own without paid organizers, without using the Boston Model. People were organizing and raising hell in the welfare offices—basically having read something in the paper or through word of mouth, having heard what was happening. What I'm describing in Boston was probably the most systematic organizing that was done in the country. It was in the context of the Massachusetts Welfare Rights Organization, which had professional organizers and various serious-minded people who did things like this in a structured way.

Basically, we'd make a pitch to their immediate self-interest in receiving material benefits under the special needs provisions, and secondly we'd raise some of the bigger questions of dignity, justice, and the notion of welfare as a right, not a privilege. By the end of the visit, it was not uncommon that the person was really worked up and very angry. The angry people would usually turn out for the meeting. Before we left, we would always get the name, address, and phone number on the sign-up sheet.

Some people were reluctant to give us phone numbers, because so often people on welfare have unlisted numbers. We made it a strong point that the number was just for organization records and that we wouldn't give it out to anyone else. This was our way of communicating. We didn't have the money to send a lot of letters and the mail took too much time. We'd use the telephone.

Primarily we'd door knock between 10 A.M. and 4 P.M. It took about three weeks to cover the entire list. We had it pretty well figured out how many door-knocking hours would be required to cover the population. The meeting date was related to this, because momentum was important to the drive. If you dragged your timetable out too long, you would lose the excitement, the movement, and the momentum that were necessary for a big meeting. But if you didn't allow enough time, you wouldn't be able to hit all the doors and talk with all the people.

As we got closer to the meeting, we would try and publicize it in every way—posters, church announcements, flyers; a second mailing would go out to our list, designed to arrive the day before the meeting. Sometimes we could get the Welfare Department to send out notices with the checks saying that people had the right to organize. We often had a letter from a local priest or minister that would be enclosed with the final reminder. The letter would say that it was good that people were organizing, that people should stand up for their rights. I can remember even using a portable sound system in the housing projects, operating it off the car battery, announcing that the meeting would start in an hour or so.

All those kinds of reminders, leaflets, and mailings are not primary means of recruiting people; they are all secondary reinforcements. That's very important. So many organizers try to organize through the mail, over the telephone, or through leaflets, except in rare cases where issues are extremely hot and immediate, those methods won't work. It really takes the personal contact that comes with door knocking to recruit people. Finally, we would make the reminder phone calls right before the meeting and that probably accounted for an additional 10 or 15 percent. But again, they were reminder phone calls as opposed to initial phone calls.

The meeting itself would be held on a weekday morning. We generally got somewhere between 40 and 60 percent of the people whom we talked with to attend, which is an extremely high percentage, but of course we are talking about immediate cash benefits. You might ask why the attendance wasn't even higher. Some people were afraid. Some people still didn't want to be publically identified as being on welfare. Other people were having so many crises and hassles in their lives that they just weren't able to get there. All in all, a very high percentage of people we talked to participated.

One thing we had mentioned on the home visits was that people needed to join the Welfare Rights Organization. It cost a dollar a year for dues. In some cases there would be local dues too, at the discretion of the local chapter. We didn't collect that much money during the door knocking. We generally told people to bring their money to the first meeting. The first meeting very often would come right after a check day, so people would have the money to join. When people came through the door, we would always have a couple of aggressive people from the organizing committee signing them up as members. In most cases only members got the special needs forms.

People would often come in very late. If the meeting was due to start at 10:00, they might still be coming in around 10:40. People would fill out the forms. The organizing committee and the staff would sift through the crowd and help with questions on the form. Finally the meeting would be called to order. Generally, it would start with a prayer by a local clergy person, usally a pretty lively prayer that would talk about how it was good that people were organizing and fighting for their welfare rights. The clergy would explain that welfare *was* a right, mentioning some of the problems and horror stories around the local office. It was usually a pretty agitational, inspirational kind of rap that was designed to get people fired up. Oftentimes we'd do a little chanting or singing after the prayer.

Then people from the organizing committee would be introduced. Following these introductions, we'd have elections of temporary officers. The elections were usually for a three-month period, which was an excellent idea. It would give the leadership a chance to try out the job and give the members of the organization a chance to test their new leadership. In many cases, at the end of three months there would be a whole new leadership. The temporary elections sometimes helped prevent the organization from getting locked in with bad leadership for a whole year. The officers elected would be a chairperson, co-chairperson, treasurer, corresponding secretary and recording secretary.

Following this would be the formation of a grievance committee. Generally anywhere from 10 to 15 people would join—virtually all of the second line leadership. The grievance committee was charged with helping people who had immediate individual problems. A member from this committee would go and serve as an advocate for a person in any dispute with the social worker. Once the group got off the ground, we would have a grievance day once a week, like Thursdays. Anybody who had individual problems, as opposed to problems that we could organize around, would come in on Thursday and we'd go down to the welfare office as a group. The individual with the problem would pair off with a person from the grievance committee.

Following the formation of the grievance committee, there would be a short inspirational rap about the next steps we would take to receive the special needs benefits. We were going to walk (or march) to the Welfare Department and demand to see the director. And we'd do it—right then. We'd introduce the officers and inform the director that we now had an organization. We'd turn in our forms and give the Department one to two weeks to process our requests, then inform them that we'd be back as a group to pick up our checks. We didn't want them mailed out. A very high percentage of people who came to the meeting would march down to the office. One thing that helped was the fact that we wouldn't turn in the forms for anyone who wasn't with the group. You had to turn in your own form and see your social worker personally. The leadership would not collect forms from people who said they couldn't make it down to the Department. There was great emphasis on solidarity.

Sometimes we would be met by the police and a confrontation would develop immediately and in some cases, arrests happened. But the forms were turned in. We had lawyers with us and if there was an arrest, we'd appeal and we'd generally win. In other cases, we would simply hand in the forms after making a strong speech on how we were organized and how things were going to be different around the office. We'd inform the director that we were coming back in a week or two weeks to pick up our checks. They would oftentimes complain and say they couldn't possibly process all the forms by that time. We'd tell them that we were coming back, regardless, on that day and they had better have the checks ready or else. And in the vast majority of times they would in fact have the checks there. Occasionally they wouldn't be ready and then we'd get involved in sitting in and waiting and negotiating for a quick follow-up appointment. That basically is the outline of what the organizing drive looked like.

That would be followed by other issues and other confrontations in the office and grievances. Virtually all the initial organizing was done around a special needs campaign and generally within the framework of a six-week drive.

One mistake that was made in welfare rights, was overreliance on the single tactic of organizing around special needs benefits. When Massachusetts and New York and other states took away these special needs benefits and instituted automatic flat grants, that meant all recipients regularly received checks. They never would have received benefits automatically if we hadn't fought in the late '60s and that was a victory. But welfare rights lost its handle for organizing. It was unable to adapt its organizing methodology to the new situation. Combined with other factors, I won't get into here, that's what led to the demise of welfare rights.

We could look at any number of weaknesses in the Welfare Rights Organization. It was single issue, single constituency and relied too much on a single tactic.

Also, it probably wasn't the most democratic organization in the world, and didn't do much serious internal fund raising. It pretty much relied on staff slots through grants from large liberal foundations or the government.

On the other hand, much of the organizing that was done in welfare rights was, in fact, the precursor of the organizing that is being done today in organizations like ACORN or Fair Share. If you were to look at organizing drives in either of these organizations, the way they were built and are currently being built, you'd see a very, very strong parallel to the old Boston Model that I just described. And the organization did move huge numbers of very low-income people to take direct action and win both tangible benefits and a greater measure of personal dignity. Many of those people are still active today and many of the staff members have gone on to do other important organizing all across the country.

After Alinsky

Stan Holt

Alinsky abandoned the old neighborhood model in about 1970—totally abandoned it. He opened his training center in Chicago in '70 and didn't even field-place people in his old organization. It was a total break. At the end he was moving more toward citywide and more middle-income work. In the old Alinsky method the neighborhood controls the total agenda of what the issues are going to be. It's autonomous. Also you're building it within the structures of the neighborhood—its churches, its social organizations, its civic organizations and small business. And they totally control it.

When you're building a statewide organization like Fair Share, that neighborhood or even city unit is part of something larger. Rather than an organization of organizations, which is the neighborhood Alinsky style, where you belong because you're a member of the Calvary Baptist Church or St. Ann's parish, when you deal with a statewide organization people don't see each other often—they're spread out all over the state. You need a single membership organization, which Fair Share has, where people pay ten dollars a year to belong. That automatically says "I'm a Fair Share member. I'm part of that and all across the state people like me belong." It's a cement that draws people together.

In a state organization you have an agenda which transcends the neighborhood or the city so that you're bringing in issues rather than just evolving the issues out of the neighborhood. We're centralized. Because we're dealing with such diverse groups all over the state, we need the central membership and the central budget. Otherwise we would be balkanized. There are people who are trying to build statewide organizations from neighborhood organizations, then linking them up. I haven't seen it happen. I don't think you can do it because the people have their autonomy and their parochialism. They may join occasionally on a statewide issue but their first loyalty, the primary loyalty, is back home.

In a statewide organization your research is much better because you can *do* better research. You can afford it. We have more researchers here. In the neighborhood organization we did all our own research as organizers. Here we're dealing with bigger, more sophisticated issues, longer-term issues and you need the research. Fact sheets, research papers—they come down to the local unit discussing their interest in that particular issue.

We don't build as deeply in a neighborhood. We tend to draw people out of the neighborhood because of the statewide issues. It's different from a neighborhood organization, where people know they're never going any further than the neighborhood. We combine consumer advocacy with a neighborhood base. There are a number of professional consumer advocacy groups around. They tend to be small, good at research, but poor in mobilizing. The genius of our organization is that we can do the research, but we also have the neighborhood bases that are committed to the local issues. We can deliver people on the statewide issues also.

Very few organizations take grass-roots fundraising seriously. We have. In our thirty chapters, our six regions, we're committed to raising about $180,000 by the people raising their own money. When they raise their own money they can go on as long as they want. They aren't dependent upon anybody—either staff or grantors—to direct them.

Fair Share started off as essentially a staff organization. They had a lot of control. Gradually over the last two years, more and more of the power of the organization shifted to elected leadership. And now that they are raising more money, it's shifted even faster. The power in the organizations follows where the money comes from. However, there's no neighborhood that has the power to hire and fire staff.

Fair Share is an institution. We're no longer a movement—no longer a new thing. We're a three-quarter-of-a-million-dollar institution with thirty organizers. This is power, right? A thirty-thousand-dollar organization is never going to have much power. It's fine maybe in a neighborhood—to achieve what you want with the neighborhood—but when you start talking state, you know you've got to have an institution to deal with the utility companies, the banks, the state legislature, the government. That's been the change in organizing over the last five years, from the neighborhood organizations to the realization that you need these large institutions now. You can't go against a castle with a bow and arrow.

Fair Share has had a lot of success with issues like inflation that the old neighborhood model couldn't have given us. We've had victories over rising insurance rates, redlining, and rising utility rates. A neighborhood can't impact state regulatory agencies. Fair Share turned out about 900 people from across the state a couple of different times to pressure the insurance commissioner to rescind the new auto rates. They were going to competitive rating, which would have jumped the rates 20 percent, and we were able to get them turned back to regulated rates.

Let me give a detailed example of how we would organize such a fight. A year ago last summer we found out through our research and through calls from people, that they couldn't get heating oil. Normally people would begin stocking up on oil in the summer when it's cheaper so that when it comes fall and winter, they have full tanks. With oil prices going from 23 cents a gallon to 50 or even 75 cents, the predictions were that there was going to be very expensive heating oil. When these calls began coming, we began checking with oil dealers and found out that they were not able to get supplies because the large oil companies were drawing down, holding back fuel oil coming into New England because the longer they waited the higher price they could get. And we also found out the Shell Oil Company was getting out of the Massachusetts market completely, taking away about 7 to 10 percent of the oil supplies. We heard this from dealers who were complaining that they couldn't get oil and therefore couldn't get it to the people. The small fuel oil retailers were being hit hard.

We organized a meeting with the Shell representative for New England, a Mr. Buemer, and customers in all our neighborhoods throughout the state. We met with him and got the story that there was nothing he could do. The decision had been made in Houston, and he couldn't help it. We would just have to find other suppliers, that's all. Then we had a follow-up meeting with Mr. Buemer with about 400/500 people in Cambridge. We had done the homework to find out which oil dealers were cut off by Shell—the total number of gallons they used to order. When Mr. Buemer came to that meeting and said again that it was out of his hands, we said, "Get Houston up here."

We followed that with some actions—visits to his house, talking to his family, visits to the regional office in Wellesley in order to disrupt it. We found out that a vice-president of Shell was coming through at Logan Airport on his way to New Hampshire to go fishing or hunting or something like that. We met him at the airport with about 50 people and demanded that he come to a meeting the following week. He was so surprised that he committed himself to come. We had a meeting over in East Boston. We had about 50 people in a room with him and about 200 people in the hall. And then he negotiated restoring the supplies to New England. We won that.

We were positioned at that point to go after a number of different oil companies because they were all drawing back. Texaco made the mistake of saying that they would give 25 gallons of free oil to anybody with an emergency. Then we made a mistake at that point. We began to shift off the oil companies and on to a general energy program. We had a couple of meetings with Texaco about how this plan was going to be implemented. We got them at one point to say that they would give 25, 50, 100 gallons, whatever's needed. They opened the door for us and we never went through—which I think we could have. We could have gotten them to commit themselves to 100 and then we could have seriously gotten people taking advantage of it. But we shifted to a general energy program. It's a difference of philosophy. I think some people like myself tend to be more pragmatic with the goal of building organizations, taking opportunities that are at hand and utilizing them. Whereas other people in the organization have more an idea that they want to undertake issues that lead to reform. I say take the means at hand, which is the immediate issue. Use that to build the organization, and in the long run you can do a hell of a lot of reform. Some people jumped quickly to reform with long-range objectives that I didn't think were winnable.

There's one thing I would add—the potential of organizing Catholic parishes in an urban setting. It's being worked on in a number of cities and I think Fair Share can work on them more. There is a renewal going on within parishes. It often revolves around issues such as sex, violence, and abortion and many of those things that Reagan appealed to in the blue-collar Catholic family. It seems to me that community organizers need to grasp the family issues and neighborhood issues, link them up with the parish and move those people into progressive solutions. We're doing that some. We're doing it in Fall River and We're doing it in Lowell, where the organizers have an affinity for that. And I do some consulting for National Catholic Charities that takes me into Youngstown, Minneapolis, Covington, Kentucky, and a few other places. We're attempting to do it within Catholic Charities without the organizers. It seems to me the organizers need to realize that there are resources that can be drawn upon and channelled directly, and really turn out numbers of people. That's I think really one of the cutting edges of the eighties.

3

Organizing at the Neighborhood Level

Five examples of organizing at the neighborhood level are presented here. Each one illustrates different problems organizers face. These are, of course, only a small fraction of organizing issues at the neighborhood level. This entire book is in one sense about organizing at the neighborhood level. In all the examples given here the organizers are very experienced and articulate.

Peter Rider shows that even though ACORN follows a well-defined plan in beginning neighborhood chapters it was very difficult to get started. Part of the problem was that the organizers did not have an explicit plan adapted to the needs of that neighborhood. An action that should have taken weeks took one and one-half years because the organizers did not push hard enough at critical times. Usually ACORN-style organizing emphasizes pushing for quick victories when getting started. Community people stuck with the issue even though a resolution was so long in coming. Why do you think they did? There were two other roadblocks to organizing. People were intimidated by threats of violence, and that fear had to be dealt with. Furthermore, city agencies that could have helped them refused because a neighborhood organized by ACORN would have undermined the mayor's political machine.

Joe Drexler shows how he helped organize on national and local issues simultaneously in a neighborhood setting. He describes a carefully thought-out strategy for linking the peace issue and Reaganomics in a multiracial neighborhood in Cambridge. Although he was an outsider and a good organizer, a substantial part of the efforts' success is attributed to a community leader who was a state representative and city council member as well as on the executive board of the Peace Council. She was able to open many doors for Drexler that then enabled him to do the legwork. This involved using existing community groups to stage a "Speakout to Survive." The object was not to create a new group but to use a networking strategy to enable the very highly developed existing community groups to relate to the peace issue. There was great care taken that all elements of the community be represented and that all committees reflect the multiracial composition of the neighborhood. Two unforseen circumstances prevented a large turnout at the speakout. There was a pro basketball playoff they could never have planned for and an enclosed courtyard kept the sound of the bands from traveling and attracting people.

Larry Gross documents how the Coalition for Economic Survival of which he is the coordinator links community groups fighting for economic justice. Opposing racism is a major focus of the organization. This is done by showing community groups of different racial and ethnic compositions how much stronger they are when they support each other's causes and by having workshops and conferences specifically to educate people in the ways racism weakens working-class people of all colors. In documenting the fight to prevent displacement of residents in the Pico Union section of Los Angeles, Gross illustrates specific techniques as well as the elements he considers the ingredients of victory. The specific techniques include picketing, boycotts, rallies, leafleting, and lots of publicity. The boycotts and pickets were used in neighborhoods throughout Los Angeles to support people in Pico Union. The three elements of success included the concrete victory of having nobody displaced, the demonstration that people have the power to alter their relationship with the corporate structure, and the remaining grass-roots organization eager to take on other issues.

Ibrahim Mumin is director of an agency that is supposed to deal with housing issues but finds that the drug traffic is so bad that this is the issue that must be taken care of if progress on any other issue is to be made. He and his staff work on many levels in the community. Among them is the support of a progressive black police chief who is doing his best to help with the drug issue. It is more usual to find the police part of the problem.

Mr. Mumin lives in the neighborhood and feels the drug problem as a direct personal affront. He shows enormous courage in giving court testimony that would put pressure on judges to give stiffer sentences to drug dealers. He knows that it will be a very long, tough fight but measures progress by the fact that neighborhood people are now convinced that they have a right to live in a safe, drug-free community.

Steve Burghardt is a white social work professor who felt his skills could be of use in helping extremely poor black and Hispanic residents develop used housing stock and set up "people's corporations." He felt that his middle-class skills in dealing with bureaucracy complemented community residents' skill in doing construction work. He is very sensitive to class and race differences and their effects in an organizing situation. He uses his social-work skills not only as a community organizer but as a case worker in attempting to join personal considerations in a political context. At one point there was a viable organization with black, white, and Hispanic leadership as well as participation. Then President Jimmy Carter came through the neighborhood and said something should be done to fix it up. The apparent prospect of enormous sums of money pouring into that neighborhood caused the organizing effort to collapse. People saw no need for a community organization if the federal government was going to take care of them. Burghardt concludes that the real problem was that these people couldn't be organized because they were too poor and necessarily had to be concerned more with survival issues. The level of their oppression made it impossible for them to organize on a long-term basis. This is an issue that is very controversial among community organizers.

The Best Laid Plans . . .

Joe Drexler

The Boston area probably has more local peace organizations than any other part of the country. One that I'm involved in, the Boston Peace Council, differs from most of the others in that we try to focus our work mainly on working-class communities, especially in neighborhoods where there is a mixture of races. Most peace groups in the area are middle class and white.

This particular project, organizing in the Riverside-Cambridgeport section of Cambridge, came at the suggestion of a black woman who was the key to the whole project. Saundra Graham is a state representative and also a city council member, and this neighborhood is her home base. It's mainly working-class and has a high percentage of blacks. Saundra's idea was that the Peace Council—which she co-chairs—should try to link the peace issue to Reaganomics and the horrible effects it has been having on working-class communities. She said, and a number of us jumped at the idea, that we could use Riverside-Cambridgeport as a model of how to organize in other working-class communities around Boston. We also thought that we could hopefully broaden the membership of the Peace Council, which is really pretty young; it's only been around for a couple of years.

I was new to the Boston area myself—I'd come there in September of 1981— and this project had considerable appeal to me. It was that winter that Saundra put forward her idea. The two of us talked about it in January and agreed that we would have some type of neighborhood forum. It was very vague at first. We wanted a forum that would involve community people in not only coming to it but in planning it as well. We drew up an outline explaining what we hoped to do, that we hoped to make a distinct contribution to the Boston area peace movement by carrying out an event with a multi-racial working-class constituency.

It's important to note that the success we ended up having turned on the fact that we were able to utilize the existing leadership of the neighborhood. Saundra Graham is recognized as the primary community leader because she has been involved in so many struggles over the years related to the neighborhood. In fact she was instrumental in forming many of the groups that existed there. This meant that when we began looking for neighborhood support a lot of doors were open that might not have been otherwise—or that we would have had to spend a lot of time in getting opened. This was especially important for me, since I did a lot of the work and I was an outsider. It was great to be able to say I was working with her.

Our initial group also included another neighborhood leader by the name of Rena Leib, someone from a group called the Cambridge Peace Education Project, and Andrea Devine, who was also from the Boston Peace Council. Saundra and I and the three of them met to draw up a list of neighborhood people to try to draw in. We especially wanted people who in some way had their own constituencies and were tied into various neighborhood networks.

This is a neighborhood that's been organized around a number of issues, especially issues of housing, health centers, and institutional encroachment by the two giant universities; it is located between Harvard and MIT. Being forced to try to fend off Harvard and MIT has helped to bring about a lot of organizing and a lot of indigenous institutions. For our peace project, we wanted to try to feed into those institutions. We didn't want to start out with the idea that we would be creating a whole new organization. We had a specific project and we wanted to get all those groups to participate.

Initially we had this vague idea of a neighborhood forum in which people from the neighborhood could come together and speak out against the arms race, speak out against the budget cuts, and we would try to draw some connections between the issues of peace and Reaganomics. We wanted an open mike where everybody could speak their mind about what was happening to them. There were so many different things coming down on the people in that neighborhood that Saundra felt they had to have a way to express their concerns.

We drew up a list of people we hoped to draw in, and I wrote a letter which we made copies of. We all carried those letters around to people on our list and talked to them about what we were trying to do. In most cases we got a favorable response and, in general, no negative reactions—at worst, people said they didn't have time, which many of them obviously didn't, given the other things they were all involved in. Still, the letter itself was a mistake, and I learned something from it. It was too long, it had too many big words. It was simply out of context given the working class nature of the community and I think it turned some people off. I wouldn't write a letter like that again, but it didn't damage us in a way we couldn't recover from.

We also made a mistake in how we tried to reach some key institutions. Our first goal was to get people to come to a planning meeting at one of the three elementary schools in the neighborhood. We really wanted to get the churches involved at that stage. But we relied on one of our contacts to do that for us, and she let it slide. You can never assume that because someone says they will reach certain people, that it will be done. We lost a lot of impetus by just assuming it would get done. But we did reach a number of other groups, such as the Women's Commission which the city had set up to deal with women's issues. At the first planning meeting we turned out twenty-two people from the neighborhood, representing fourteen different organizations. Most of them were indigenous neighborhood groups. We even had the Democratic ward chairman, who'd been Saundra's old political nemesis. He had recognized the importance of doing something like this.

We had worked very hard to make the planning meeting multiracial, and it was. We didn't have just one or two people of color, but we had a composition that was representative of the neighborhood. That was crucial for us.

The first meeting was really a round-table discussion. The ward chairman was from Greece and he talked about how he'd gone back there and seen how only the rich were being educated. He pointed out that we were coming to a day in this country where only the rich would be educated here too. He was very concerned about that. One of the young people there talked about all the cuts in recreation—how the basketball courts might be closed or wouldn't be supervised, and what impact that might have on the neighborhood. People talked about health clinics being closed. They talked about the draft. They talked about the upcoming fight to overturn Proposition 2½, the statewide referendum that had forced drastic cuts in local public spending. There were all kinds of issues that came up. We agreed on the need for a neighborhood meeting to give everybody in the neighborhood a chance to come together and speak out. Since it would be dealing with real survival issues like AFDC, food stamps, and so forth, we decided on the title "Speak Out to Survive."

After that we had several other planning meetings. Every one was very well attended. We lost very few people, and everybody chipped in on the work. We did the small things that I think are often overlooked. We had very extensive and detailed minutes that we sent out to people just a few days after the meeting to give them a summary of what went on and remind them what they had volunteered to do. Every time we had a planning meeting we sent out a mailing, and in addition to that we did a follow-up call. We were in contact with all these folks throughout, to make sure we didn't lose anybody. It was also an opportunity to talk with all of them to get any special concerns addressed. We divided up the work into various committees. We had a food committee, an outreach committee, a program committee, a logistics committee and any other committee that was needed. Everybody on a committee was given a particular task. Everything was rooted in the neighborhood and we were even able to get some free food from local merchants.

We knew entertainment would be really important in bringing people out. We got a reggae band from the neighborhood, a well-known local singer, and a Greek band. The local Arts Council donated the use of a sound system, and one of the elementary schools agreed to host. They have an outdoor courtyard that we used. Overall, we spent very little money; most of the things that normally cost money were donated to us.

Unfortunately, we couldn't plan for everything. Nobody thought to look at the pro basketball playoff schedule, but Sunday afternoon, May 16, which was the time we had picked for the speak-out, turned out to be a day the Boston Celtics were involved in a big game. Really, there was no way we could have known that when we first set the date, but there's no doubt that it kept a lot of people away. On another matter, we just didn't do our homework. We thought that once the bands got warmed up the sound would carry everywhere and draw people in. We wanted to touch people who'd never been touched by this sort of event. However, the courtyard was enclosed and the sound didn't get out like we thought it would.

We did do a good job on publicity. We used all our initial contact groups as well as the churches and made sure they would all do their part in publicizing the forum. We had spots on the radio and some newspaper coverage. We had nine thousand leaflets printed at no cost to us, thanks to the Women's Commission, and we did a saturation leafletting of the neighborhood, dropping off a flyer at every doorstep. We also used the three elementary schools as a way to leaflet—every kid in each of the schools was given a leaflet and asked to carry it home to their parents. The importance of involving the schools from the start was borne out by this experience. The morning of the event we went around the neighborhood with a speaker system mounted on a car. Saundra Graham and others worked the loudspeaker, to get people while the event was going on. We had free balloons for the kids.

Between two and three hundred people attended the speak-out. That doesn't sound like a lot, but none of us was really disappointed, especially not the neighborhood people. Everybody seemed to think it was a big success, and if it weren't for the Celtics game and the problem with the music not carrying very far we could easily have doubled or maybe even tripled the attendance.

The speakers at the event were neighborhood people, each of them addressing a particular area of concern. The peace issue was brought in at every point. All the speakers drew a connection between their particular issue and the enormous size of the military budget. Basically, everyone put forward the idea that you can't solve any of these single issues without addressing the need for·peace and the need for stopping all that wasteful military spending. In addition, there was a shared perspective that in the long run you can't have peace without justice. After the speeches we had a slide presentation called "Whose Budget Is It, Anyway?" about the military budget.

Maybe the most encouraging thing is that the speak-out gave us the will to keep going, As a result of the forum and some other activities, we were able to fill two and a half busses from Riverside-Cambridgeport for the big June 12 demonstration in New York against the arms race and for funding human needs. Just as in the speak-out, these were mostly people who'd never worked politically for peace before. I think that was our major success. A few nights before the June 12 demonstration, we gathered to make a banner for the "Riverside-Cambridgeport Speak-Out Committee." The local high school also made banners for us, and we marched en masse as the neighbors of Riverside-Cambridgeport under our own banners at the demonstration.

Although the long-range impact of the speak-out reamins to be seen, we have already seen some short-range effects. The so-called "speak-out model" has been used successfully since the Riverside-Cambridge event in two other neighborhoods in the Boston area. I think we are well on our way toward a more representative and dynamic peace movement.

Starting A Neighborhood Chapter

Peter Rider

ACORN neighborhood chapters are built on two fundamental concepts: permanent indigenous organization and result-oriented campaigns. A rule of thumb is to initially concentrate on an organizing plan that focuses on a visible neighborhood problem and solves it quickly. The victory puts some concrete results behind the organizing plan, giving leaders a sense of their power when organized and attracting new members.

An example of a campaign that was ultimately successful, but which did not follow these rules, may help explain what I mean. One of the first organizing efforts ACORN made in Boston was one where we got a lot of support but didn't keep the pressure on. It was in Roxbury, a lower-income section that's mainly black, partly Hispanic. It's about 50 percent tenants, 50 percent homeowners—marginal homeowners who may have a lot of trouble keeping up their houses and paying their property taxes but who have a pride and investment in the neighborhood.

The fundamental approach that we use to organize in that neighborhood is the same one ACORN uses in all neighborhoods. We canvass the entire neighborhood door to door, talking to people about the problems in the neighborhood. We talk with residents about the need for an organization like ACORN in their neighborhood. We work from what they say to us and put together an organizing committee. As part of getting a chapter started, a plan is constructed to deal with some of the issues that are prominent in the neighborhood. That lets us demonstrate to people their own power.

One of the first issues that came up in that group was a problem with two abandoned buildings. They'd been an eyesore in the neighborhood for quite a long time. One was a cleaners and the other a garage. Several other organizations had tried to take on the issue before and really had gotten nowhere. So this was an issue that kept coming up when we went around asking about neighborhood problems. It was one that people wanted to work on. First a few neighborhood ACORN members worked with the organizer and did some initial research on who owned the buildings and then they proceeded to deal with the city. This is the point when I think the City of Boston was just beginning to realize that ACORN was in the city. For the first time we met institutional and political resistance to what we were doing. There was a resistance not so much to the issue itself as to the idea that this organization of neighborhood people was trying to do something about it.

Recently Boston under mayor Kevin White has been politically modelled on the patronage system that Mayor Daley made famous. That system also relies on the ability to punish and reward. You reward with a job or you reward with getting a building taken down or a street sign being put up or whatever. It's all done so as to build the mayor's political machine. The city saw that if ACORN were to build an organization that could do that same thing—maybe do more—that would be a threat to their power in the neighborhood. It's an interesting obstacle because I think it requires a sophisticated political analysis of the structure of government in the city, and it's an analysis a lot of people don't have when they start organizing.

We had the head of the city's building inspection department come to a neighborhood meeting. That's a typical kind of thing. We'd gone to his office with a petition asking him to come to a neighborhood meeting, and when he agreed, we built the meeting up. About eighty people came, which I think is a remarkable turnout for an issue like that. Usually an abandoned building is not an active issue. It just sits there as a constant but generally low level problem. Given the turnout, we thought we knew what would happen. Typically, you'd expect this person from the city to take a look at all the people, promise to take care of the problem within two or three weeks, and then actually do it. Because that kind of community interest can translate into votes, they will usually respond to it. But all we got was abuse. He attacked the organizer, attacked the legitimacy of the group. He did promise to come and inspect the building within three weeks, but we should have known he was lying.

Basically we had people waiting for three weeks for him to show up, and he didn't come. At that point the campaign really started to lag in a way that I think we failed to deal with successfully. He would no longer come out to neighborhood meetings. We couldn't make him responsive by getting him there at a meeting. Typically you might think, "Well, if a bureaucrat won't come to me, we'll go to his house." Well, this guy lived in a part of the city where we couldn't go—an all-white section where our black membership wouldn't feel safe going to his house. So that kind of tactic was out.

Luckily for the organization, we had a few other issues that people were carried along by. But there was still that commitment on the part of some of our strongest leaders—a feeling this is our first issue and we had to take care of it. We had a series of smaller actions ranging anywhere from five to fifteen people down at the office of city officials and when we met a roadblock there we started to explore other avenues. We went to the district attorney's office, we went to the housing inspection office, we did a number of the typical citizen lobbying kind of things: petitions, phone calls, small protests. But it hurt us that we couldn't hit in the evening, which is something that usually springs a campaign. Our largest actions will always be in the evening. I'd say probably 40 percent of our membership are holding down jobs and most of the others are involved in some kind of childcare activities during the day. So our usual tactic would be to invite this politician or whoever to a meeting, and if he doesn't show we'd do an action at his house with somewhere between thirty and sixty people. That sort of shakes him up enough to do what we want. In this case we got boxed in because we couldn't go to this bureaucrat's house.

The campaign continued, and the remarkable thing is that the people kept with it for so long. This kind of thing went on for about six months and at the six-month point we finally got one of the buildings torn down, the laundry. But the garage was a real mess. Now it was open again, with what seemed to be an outlaw band of people doing car repairs and dealing with stolen cars. So at this point we had a victory, which made people want to keep going, and on the other hand the ballgame started to get a little bit rough because there was criminal activity involved. The police were pretty consistently refusing to interfere. They'd say they'd go by and couldn't find anybody there. Meanwhile these people are doing things like pouring gasoline into the street and a lot of drunks are hanging around urinating on the walls. It became more and more of an issue, and ACORN couldn't walk away because we were so strongly identified with it. Normally you might say, "We don't seem to be able to solve this problem, so let's move on to something else." But we couldn't do that here.

All this time, we'd never really been able to figure out who actually owned the garage building. It had kept changing hands and the only name we really had was a real estate operator from Brookline who was somehow involved. So we decided to go after him. About fifteen people went in to tell him that we were going to pull an action in his office on a public business day unless he agreed to come to a neighborhood meeting. So he showed up, and we had probably fifty people there, which again was a surprise since the campaign had gone on so long. Well, this guy showed up but he came with two bodyguards both carrying guns. They stood in the back of the meeting room kind of moving their shoulders and hips about so you could see their guns going in and out behind their coats.

ACORN members started the meeting with a typical introduction, with people describing the problems they had with the garage and then we moved to the demands: ACORN wanted him to stop the illegal garage and secure or tear down the building. He sat there and he listened to about half the introduction then he said that he couldn't do anything about it. He again denied ownership, denied his interest in the building, and got up and walked out of the room. At that point some of the members wanted to try to keep him there, but because of the bodyguards people thought they had to let this guy go.

Now we started having to deal with fear. It's something that crops up a lot and often an organizer won't recognize it. Like somebody might say you can use their apartment for a committee meeting and then two days later they say no. You can't figure it out until you understand that people don't like strangers coming into their apartment because there are so many break-ins in the neighborhood. They don't know if somebody at the meeting might check out their TV set and then the next week it's gone. Well, in this situation, after the run-in with the real estate operator and the bodyguards, people started to come up with all kinds of reasons why maybe we shouldn't try to do anything more about the garage. Finally after three hours of talking with different leaders it became clear that they were just plain afraid of the guy. He had people with guns for some purpose and he had a real interest in keeping this rinky-dink operation going at the garage.

By that time we'd been working on this campaign for nine months. That's an awfully long time for an issue like this but we also felt we had a lot invested in it. So we tried a different tack. We decided to try the police and the district attorney again. For reasons that we don't understand, other than persistence, we were able to get the DA to issue a complaint. We pushed them and they went to court and got a subpoena. To this day, which is another nine months later, they are still saying that they are actually going to go over to the garage and arrest the people who are working there. In other words, it's been a year and a half now and we still haven't gotten any of what we wanted. We got the laundry torn down, and that was good, but on the garage—nothing.

So this wasn't the most exciting or militant campaign we've ever done, and it surely wasn't one of the most successful, but there are some lessons in it. It does teach something about organizing, especially about getting a group going. It somewhat calls into question the common assumption that you have to have an early victory to keep a group together. People in the neighborhood were concerned about this issue, and I think it's good that we didn't just say, ''We can't get it done, so let's go on to something else.'' But a second thing that it showed us was how messy and negative this sort of thing can get when you're not on top of it, pushing it every minute, making it a priority. Too many times we went one step and failed to take it to the next step right away. So the building commissioner tells a meeting with seventy people that he'll inspect within three weeks, and the three weeks goes by and we take another month to get down to his office. The campaign developed a pace that was unsatisfactory because we needed more action and more results. We fell into a more leisurely pattern that people in the neighborhood were used to—kind of, "No rush about it."

I think one of the things we should have done was make a clear plan from the beginning for the steps we would follow. We also should have had more of an appreciation for how confusing the whole thing was going to be. There's no reason it should have taken us nine months to find out the story with the Brookline landlord. We should have found out in the first few weeks that, one, he was a public figure; two, he had an office in a very public place; and three, based on people calling and dropping by his office he was willing to come to a neighborhood meeting. We spent a lot of time playing around with the question of who was really the owner, following this or that trail and saying, "Well should we deal with the real estate person or shouldn't we?" When we finally decided to go after him, we got stymied. There's a real need to press ahead on a campaign once it's started—get all your research done and see the beginning, middle, and end of it and not let it trail on.

I think the third problem had to do with city politics. Early on, it seemed to us that the city was messing with us not because they cared about the building but because they didn't want people to get organized in the neighborhood. But at first we kept that belief to ourselves. Now it may be that one reason the campaign was sustained so long, was that this revelation would come to people in the group at different times. They'd get angry when they realized it, and it would kind of pump new life into the campaign. But I'd say it was a lesson probably learned by five or six leaders, not by the whole group.

The final thing was the whole question of intimidation and how you deal with it. Certainly violence is a part of daily life in a crime-ridden neighborhood like this one. Typically people will carry some kind of defensive weapon with them if they are out walking around. The ACORN organizer was just so foreign to that experience that he couldn't talk to people about it. He didn't know whether it was responsible to encourage people to do an action on the real estate guy's office when he had obviously threatened people with violence. The organizer first started to encourage people to do that and then ran into a roadblock—one excuse or another until we finally threw the issue on the table and identified it.

The campaign had maybe the full complement of pitfalls that you run into when you're starting to get a neighborhood chapter together. A lot of organizers will say, "If I have to work on one more stop sign I think I'll go crazy," but those are the kind of issues you work on first.

Communities Must Support Each Other

Larry Gross

I'm the coordinator of the Coalition for Economic Survival. The Coalition has been around for ten years. We're a grassroots, multi-racial, multi-ethnic community organization of about 5,000 members and a number of affiliated organizations— community groups, labor unions, senior citizens groups. We have five full-time staff and a projected budget of $100,000. We have chapters in a number of communities. We also have a democratically elected Board of Directors, which is made up of activists and community leaders. Our chapters have representatives on our central board and so do our affiliate organizations.

What we basically have been is a vehicle for people—mainly low and moderate income people in the Los Angeles area—to participate in the fight for economic and social justice.

Over the last ten years we've had a fairly successful track record. We've been responsible for defeating a number of utility rate increases, and changing the rate structure of the municipally owned Department of Water and Power in L.A. We've stopped some bus fare increases, we've lowered milk prices, and we've helped item pricing in supermarkets. Recently we've been involved in housing issues and we're at the forefront of the fight to bring rent control to the city and county of L.A. We've also been working on trying to force government to build low and moderate income housing.

We believe that people have the right to basic economic needs—the right to a decent job at a decent wage; the right to affordable decent housing and food and utility rates, fair taxation, etc. We're trying to build a grass-roots challenge to big-business control over our economy and our government. We feel big business is more concerned about maximizing its profits than providing basic needs for the people. We also feel that government has been unresponsive to those needs. Our elected officials are put into office by big business, and that's who they respond to—not to ordinary people.

Another big concern of CES is that we see a need to actively oppose racism in this society. It's one of the biggest obstacles facing groups and organizations fighting to bring about change. In all our organizing approaches and in everything we do, we try to educate people as to how racism works in this society. We actively try to make sure that CES is a truly multi-racial organization: our board, our staff, and the communities we work in. Unless you bring neighborhoods together, people together, your movement's going to fail. When we organize chapters, we try to build bridges between black, Hispanic, and white neighborhoods. On the basis of this unity we feel that we have a better chance of achieving our goals.

A good example of our helping neighborhoods help each other is what happened in Pico Union, which is a mainly Latino area right next to downtown. I have to explain the setting first. It's really a run-down neighborhood. It's like a port of entry for people coming into this country from Mexico and Latin America. All together it's about 85 percent Latino. A lot of undocumented people live there— people who are forced into living in substandard conditions and can only get poor jobs. They are living in fear of deportation and are not able to function in society because of the lack of English.

It's also a neighborhood that's being threatened with gentrification and displacement due to urban renewal. Federal funds have been coming in to displace people and tear down buildings, so that big businesses can expand. We believe it's part of a master plan to expand the city of Los Angeles. Over the years the downtown area has been developing. The process dates back to the displacement of people in the Bunker Hill area where low-cost housing was supposed to be built. Instead we have the Music Center and Arco Towers and the Security Pacific Bank on that site. Chavez Ravine, which now houses Dodger Stadium, was supposed to be a low-cost integrated housing project, but this was undermined by big business downtown. So Pico Union is basically part of a master plan, because there's a whole corridor of low-income minority areas that border downtown L.A., and if downtown is going to expand it has to expand in that direction. And the people who live there will have to go. We believe it's a conspiracy.

We got involved in this neighborhood because we were asked to come in. A number of residents in Pico Union were being faced with displacement. The Pep Boys auto parts store was getting something like one and a half million dollars in federal funds that we felt should have been going to build low-cost housing. Instead, it was being used to help them expand—build a parking lot, build an office building, and expand their retail outlet. As a result, thirty-two families and eleven small businesses were going to be thrown out. We got a phone call. They had seen us in the newspaper or on TV around some other issue and they wanted to link up with us. So we went there and we helped them form a chapter of CES. They took on the name People United to Save Our Community. We basically helped them to learn organizing skills, gave them resources of our organization, and helped develop leadership in that community. The people who were affected had never been involved before in any type of community organization. They consisted of families with lots of kids, small business people, a restaurant owner, a printer, a bar owner, and so on. Most of them had lived there for twenty years, and now one day they wake up and the city is saying, "Hey, we want to take over your property and give it to a multi-million-dollar corporation and we're gonna do that with your tax dollars."

We went through the whole process of showing people how to organize. We had a number of meetings and helped strategize with them together. That's a long story, but what I want to stress here is the way we helped them reach out to potential allies around the city.

We also started a boycott of Pep Boys. It was right in the community. We felt that, if we can't impact on the city directly, maybe we can get help from the Pep Boys. Their concern was making money, right? If you can hit them where it hurts they may get mad and put some pressure on the city. So we started a boycott of Pep Boys. We got people from all over the city to come down and we had an incredible kickoff event. We had hundreds of people out there, and lots of press. And then for six/seven months—every Saturday—people went out there and picketed Pep Boys. In addition, our other chapters helped in their communities. Pep Boys is throughout the area.

This is an example of how we try to link white neighborhoods, black neighborhoods and Chicano/Latino neighborhoods together. We had people, for instance, in our Venice Chapter, picketing the Pep Boys outlet in Venice. Some other community groups helped us in other areas. We try to work with as many types of groups as possible on every issue that we work with. We believe no one group can do it alone—that basically you have to go coalition, as we say. The picket lines, taken together, had a big effect. We did hit their sales and Pep Boys stores started putting pressure on the city.

In addition to that, we did a lot of visible things like rallies, leafleting in the community, getting a lot of press. We also had a candlelight vigil in front of Mayor Bradley's house on Thanksgiving Eve. We had about 200 people out there saying these people want Thanksgiving too, and we had lots of press.

All of this resulted in a substantial victory for the people because we forced the city to make concessions. The city agreed to pick up a seven-unit apartment house and move it to a lot in the neighborhood. In that way we saved low-income housing from being destroyed. In addition, the owner of those apartments was given the ability to buy a $20,000 house—a three-bedroom, two-bathroom house that the city brought in from Monterey Hills and did all the landscaping and rehab on it in the neighborhood. The city picked up $18,000 in legal expenses. In addition to that for those remaining tenants still in the area, about ten families, the city has agreed to build thirty-two units of low income housing. No one else can be evicted until that housing is built up front. This was an important victory because one of the things behind gentrification is the attempt to dissolve a political base. Minority communities, low-income communities—as they develop political muscle they become a threat. If you can't make the threat go away through gerrymandering, you do it through displacement. So if a community group can keep the people *in* those neighborhoods then that's an important victory.

A lot of times if people win they'll just sit back and enjoy their house or whatever—but not these people in Pico Union. These people have become leaders in the community. They've been in the struggle. They know what it entails. And they're now going out and helping other people organize.

By the criteria we set for ourselves this was very successful organizing. There are basically three things that we look for. First, we want to bring concrete victories into people's lives and some relief to the economic situation they're facing. In this case they won better housing. Second, we want to show people that they have the power to alter their relationship to the corporate structure. We did that. And third, we want to build organization. We want to come out of any campaign leaving behind a substantial ongoing grass-roots organization in the community, able to take on other issues. We think that happened in Pico Union too.

We think that bringing other neighborhoods into the fight in Pico Union was really important. We always emphasize solidarity between communities. For example, you might think that West Hollywood, which consists mostly of white senior citizens, is about as different from Pico Union as you can get. And maybe it is. But they were involved in an effort to win county-wide rent control. And while we worked with them we were trying to show them that low-cost housing is also important—that the fight for low-cost housing in Pico Union was the same fight that they had in West Hollywood.

At any meetings in West Hollywood during that period, we got people from Pico Union to come. We put them on the agenda and they talked about their fight and they asked for support. They asked for either letter writing or phone calls or to come down to the picket line. When we had the picket lines at Pep Boys we had people from many of our chapters coming out. They held signs that said "Fairfax Chapter" or "West Hollywood Chapter" or whatever. It showed the unity. The people in Pico Union felt that "Wow! We're getting support. We're part of this county-wide organization, we're not alone." That was very important for people to see. At the same time, when we had hearings around rent control at the Board of Supervisors or rallies in West Hollywood, people from Pico Union would come in support.

It's a big challenge to build that unity. It's one of the most important fights that progressive organizations face today. A lot of organizations with our general approach feel that if you just bring people of color together with whites, and they work with each other, a lot of racist ideas will just melt away. That's true to some extent but not totally. Our particular slant is different because we actively try to educate about what racism is and where it fits in society. We do it through newsletters, meetings, speaking engagements, and conferences. For instance, our Venice chapter put on a conference against racism in Venice. Venice is an area where there's a lot of racial tension. Within Oakwood, an area in Venice which is basically black and Latino, there's tension between the two groups. And then there's tension between them and the white neighborhood there. About 300 people came out and participated in the conference, including a lot of white people. A lot of people were able to talk about things and it helped a lot. It wasn't just CES that put on the conference—other organizations worked on it too.

We gamble a lot of times but we feel that it's important to take that gamble—to bring people together.

I've got a good example. The question of health care to the undocumented workers was a big issue. There was a lot of racism around that—people saying, well, they're illegal, they shouldn't have health care. Meanwhile you figure they're paying taxes. Also you know there's a health problem here, and everyone's affected if people aren't getting medical help. This is the richest country in the world and everyone should have the right to basic health care, regardless of who they are. We were down at the Board of Supervisors on rent control with mainly white senior citizens at the same time they had the question of health care for the undocumented on the agenda. They basically had us pitted against each other: which issue would come up first? They shoved the rent control question off for the afternoon and then dealt with the health care question in the morning. A reporter from the *Los Angeles Times* grabbed one senior (I don't know whether she was with our group or not) and got a quote which appeared in an article the next day: "What's more important— health care for illegals or rent control for us." It was an obvious attempt to pit us against each other.

They were bringing back the two issues again on the same agenda two weeks later. We had discussions in our chapter on the issue of why it's important to both support health care to the undocumented and show unity between the two groups— that we shouldn't be pitted against each other. The group accepted it, understood it, and when we went down the next time to the Board of Supervisors we wore little tags that we'd made up. They said "Rent Control Now" and right under it they said "We also Support Health Care to the Undocumented." Everybody wore them. The other group—the health care group—really appreciated it. It helps us develop a better relationship with the groups working on that issue too.

President Jimmy Carter Came to Visit

Steve Burghardt

I'm a long-term community organizer and political activist who teaches community organizing at Hunter School of Social Work. My most frustrating experience as an organizer may have been the work that several of us did a few years ago in Morrisania, in the South Bronx. It's the poorest part of the South Bronx, which tells you that it's very poor.

We had friends in the area who were working with Legal Services. They saw a possibility of doing neighborhood revitalization work, and they encouraged me and several others to get involved in it. We shared a commitment to working-class and minority populations and communities.

When we went in, we went with the recognition that this was going to be incredibly difficult. This is an area with more burned-out buildings than good ones. The people have been chronically unemployed most of their lives. The ones who do have jobs are mostly in the service sector at low pay. It is mostly a lumpen population, and the people have real problems housing and educating their families.

Most of us went in knowing that it's hard to organize in a neighborhood like that. As most of us were white we also recognized that we were going to have to deal with our own racism and our own fears of working in the neighborhood. The people there are mainly black with a few Hispanics. If we were going to develop a solid multi-racial grouping we knew we couldn't be condescending on the one hand or romanticizing on the other. That is, we couldn't view the people as terrific just because they're oppressed.

And in fact the initial problems we had were because of our fears and our vestiges of racism. When people would challenge us—"What the hell are you here for?"—we responded badly. We'd say things like, "We're here to try and help you," or "We don't know what we can do," or "We really care." Caring isn't what people in that neighborhood need. They need work. It took a couple of us about one session to realize that. What we had to do was admit what we were: middle-class white people who had skills to give and had things we could actually do.

What the neighborhood needed was to know that people in the neighborhood had real talent, real ability, but it had been denied or been underused. We could help them to try to use it. We regrouped quickly. The way we faced at least part of our racism was to say, "Okay, we have certain things that we are going to do. We'll work hard at it. We're not going to deny who we are because that would be unfair to you. But eventually in order for this to succeed we'll all have to do this work."

The way we wanted to use everyone's skills, ours and theirs, was in the rehabilitation of some of the housing stock. People's Development Corporation was up there and we wanted to model ourselves after them to an extent. They've done some very exciting work. We would go with people to the bureaucracy, help them fill out the forms, try to get them to get a sense of what power is. They had a sense of what powerlessness was, but not power. Our idea was to show them that by working on different institutions you could get them to do something.

We also tried to convey skills related to how to function in meetings, how to communicate with people. These people have never genuinely communicated with each other, and therefore didn't know how to work together. They had to learn the normal kinds of very basic organizing skills that one needs in order to maintain a simple community group. In fact it was rougher than that—they had to learn things like what was needed in order to go for a job, how to be on time for interviews, that sort of thing.

In planning our work on the housing rehabilitation, we decided to start with one building, not with many buildings. We worked out the tasks that were needed. Then we found out the indigenous skills that were available in the neighborhood. Often people would deny, or just not recognize, that they had skills that would be helpful. You overcome that not by saying, "Yeah, you can do it," but by a whole series of interactions with them. You yourself work hard and show your skill and don't deny it. You say, "Yes, I know how to work with the bureaucracy and make them do things. I learned how to do that, now maybe you can help me." At a later stage we say, "Now look, you've got to help me. Otherwise we're not going to get this building fixed up because I don't know diddleysquat about rehabilitation. My skill at handling the bureaucracy and your skill at being able to look at this building and know how to fix it have got to come together."

In this stage we began to move from a group that talked about what people wanted to accomplish and what was possible to specifying how we wanted the organization to actually function. People were given organizational roles. Now, that sounds as if it should be easy, but it wasn't. The street culture rewards people for all sorts of things but not for being able to follow through on long-term commitments. The street culture can't allow for that because in fact it's dangerous. If you're planning what you're going to do in the future you may miss out on the fact that you have something coming down on your head right now. Planning for a day ahead or a week ahead is okay, but you can't plan for a month ahead. Poor people use the word "survival" a lot. White liberals and radicals pick up the term without ever really understanding what it means. When you have two kids and have to figure out how to give them food and your food stamps run out, it's literally survival. What are you going to do? It's not like you can go to your mother or your aunt or your friends to lend you money, and yet the need is still there. Are you going to plan a month ahead given a reality like that? So consistency and planning for the future are things you really have to work to build into an organization like ours.

Formal leadership was a problem. We could have set it up with all poor blacks and Hispanics as leaders, but in fact the white organizers would still have been doing some of the skilled things that the others weren't trained for yet. The way it's often been done in the past is to deny this reality and make believe that the neighborhood people are the leaders. In fact it's not true and everyone lives with the tension of knowing that it's not true. Instead of really trying to work together, people use each other. The whites can say, "See, I've developed this great organization that I have nothing to do with. Look at all these leaders I've developed." And blacks can say, "See, I'm running an organization that is my organization." And underneath it everybody knows that is not true. The resentment and hostility that is in fact there—that must be there—is kept inside and denied. Eventually it all comes out in huge fights and the organization falls apart.

It was not easy but we began to say, "Look, we can set up this fake dummy corporation as if it's all you, but that's bullshit," which everyone agreed with. "We don't want to do that because it's dishonest for the work that I do and it's dishonest for the work that you do." And people could relate to that. This was a suggestion, by the way, that did not originate with whites but it originated with the black leaders that they weren't going to be part of some front group. It was terrific. It was the right way to go and we saw that. We set it up so it had white and black and a little Hispanic leadership but it was proportionate to the membership itself.

At this point since people were taking responsibility with organizational roles and there was a lot of work on what that meant—we also had to have some payoff. We had to do something that had some success. That meant getting the city to lease us the building and/or to get a small grant to help us pay for the maintenance of the place. We needed a little symbol of success through paper and stationery. These things were very important to people up there. They had to see something that was real. The name they selected was the Freedom Spot. They had another place they called the Spot that was a hangout and they wanted the Freedom Spot because it meant going beyond that. We were able to get a small grant, about $2,500 and we were able to begin.

We began the process with people going to the bureaucracy and showing them what we had as an organization. People wanted to do it but it was incredibly hard to get people to go to these meetings, to show up on time, to present themselves as best they could with officials. We had to be able to distinguish between the environmental stresses that come up with poor people so they can't show up and those that are based on vestiges of the attitude "I can't do it." One of the realities of poor people is that if someone gets sick they go to the hospital and that's their day. If your kid has a fever you have to go to the Bronx Lebanon Hospital, which is a pit to look at and be in, and you're there all day. Those things would happen and we would have to know if it was that kind of thing that caused people to not show up. We had some real confrontations on this that were very important for all of us. You must make demands on people. You must say, "Look, you've got to do it. I'll do it with you, but this is bullshit. I'm not doing it alone any more." It is very scary to do it because people are poorer than us. They don't have as much as we do, and we feel, "Who am I to walk in and say they have to do this shit?" We can go home to our comfortable apartment and our cushy job and stuff. But this fact is both true and irrelevant to the immediate situation at hand. The fact that I am middle class and have a comfortable apartment will in no way change whether they get housing. If I move out of the house and go somewhere else and live poorly or become richer it will do nothing for whether their housing is rehabilitated.

We were able to make some progress. We had about 12 people who were working more or less at varying levels of activity. The group had maintained itself. We had a small grant and had moved from a group to an organization. We were moving ahead toward the establishment of concrete objectives that could be reached through the rehabilitation work. Politically we had moved ahead in the development of a method that was really beginning to make us mutually share our work because of our understanding not only of politics but of our personal lives. In general there was a sense of movement. It's a wonderful thing when blacks and whites and Hispanics really work together. Not that color is lost or that racial differences are lost, but there's a sense of genuine sharing. At that stage, we felt safe in an area that police were afraid to come into. It was terrific.

At this point it was getting toward summer. President Jimmy Carter decided to take a walk through this area to show his concern for the poor. He took a walk that went literally a block and a half away from where our little Freedom Spot was. Our group hadn't even seen a state representative, had not seen an assembly member, and here the President of the United States of America comes walking by their door. This had such an overwhelming impact that all of the old assumptions about how change takes place cropped up—how when wonderful leaders come along they will do everything for you. All those old feelings that still lie within all of us at different times came rushing back. There was a tremendous elation on the part of the people from the neighborhood that *he* had been there, that the head of HUD had come walking through as well and they'd talked about hundreds of millions of dollars of investment to turn the South Bronx around.

All this talk was really strictly rhetoric but it had a tremendous power on people who'd been so oppressed. I could understand it. Here they were piddling around with a small grant and the chance that if they busted their ass we could fix up a house that they could use. Then they could use the skills so they might be able to get other jobs. Now they saw a chance for a hell of a lot more and a lot more easily. Our whole effort really fell apart. While we were able to continue to work together for about four more months, there was so much emphasis on talking about what could we do to get Carter's money, what could we do to hook up with the political machine in order to get things done. People didn't want to deal with the reality. They wanted quick bucks and we could do all the political raps we wanted and it didn't matter what we said. So it fell apart.

Retrospectively as I assessed what happened I concluded that you can't underestimate the power of the official leadership, of the power the media has in making people feel as if change was easy and accessible merely by some leader's presence. An organizer has to deal politically with this from the very beginning in educating about self-determination. But in reality I believe that we *did* do that. We did do political education. We weren't heavy-handed about it—you can't go in and start talking about socialism or the nature of class oppression and so on, that's stupid. But I do think that we did a decent amount of educating through the metaphors of the actual work that was going on at that time. We used concrete situations. We talked about power. We talked about the nature of change and so forth. When "socialism" came up, it made sense.

What if I had it to do over again? Quite simply and sadly, but it is a reality that I think an organizer has to face, I would have worked with a different population. It is not possible to work only with lumpens or very, very poor people and expect long-term success. This is not to say they are not good people. It is not to say they don't have the innate ability and all the rest, but the level of oppression does determine the ability to mobilize on a long-term basis. It is possible to mobilize on a short-term basis on any variety of things ranging from small rent strikes to Jimmy Carter coming or not coming. But the stresses in their lives are too great and have been too great for too long to allow them to stay focused on anything but the immediate present. This is not a condemnation. An organizer has to look at context and context includes the people and what they're able to do over the long haul, not just what he or she wishes were possible and what he wants to have happen. There are lots of parts of the South Bronx with a far more stabilized working-class population of Hispanics and blacks, where people are doing terrific work to bring about better conditions for their lives. Realistically I say choose a population that has stabilizing environmental factors so that people are free to be able to work on long-term problems. Terrific methodology, experienced organizers, and very dedicated and good people cannot substitute entirely for the realities of a completely debilitating environment.

We Have a Right to Safe Streets Too!

Ibrahim Mumin

I started off as an officer in the youth council in the NAACP in Columbus, Georgia in high school. I was arrested when I was fifteen in a demonstration against segregation in public facilities in Columbus, Georgia. When I came to Howard University here in Washington I got involved in the student movement and in 1969 I was arrested at Howard at a student takeover of the whole campus. Shortly after that I kind of got disillusioned with the September-to-June movement and so I got involved in the broader community because I thought the students had a tendency to just deal with student issues. I got involved with the Black United Front and with some community-wide issues like housing, bus fare increases, and things like that. In 1973 I joined the then Nation of Islam, which is now the American Muslim Mission, and I've been working actively in it. In 1978 I joined the Shaw PAC[1] as a community organizer. When the director and deputy director quit about a year and a half after that, the board asked me if I would organize the staff until they could find a permanent director. After I'd been doing it for a month, they said, "We don't need to look any further." So I've been the director since then.

I'm interested in my staff being professional and being courteous. This is not a hippy outfit. I'm an activist, I'm a fighter, but I think that people who call should be handled courteously and promptly, messages should be recorded. I believe that people should come to work on time and work during that period and they should be honest. I expect honest and straightforward answers when I ask them because that's what I give. So in some ways I guess I'm old-fashioned. I think that morality is

[1]The Shaw Project Committee, called Shaw PAC, is funded by the federal Department of Housing and Urban Development through the D. C. Department of Housing and Community Development as a community development organization in the Shaw neighborhood of Washington, D.C. It has a full-time staff of four, plus two interns.

important to our being successful as an organization. I don't try to hit on the women on the staff and I don't encourage or entertain that kind of thing from other people. I have a wife and family and I'm happy with that and I think that's important in terms of running an organization. I've been a part of many organizations that were broken up because of moral things that came up, like trying to go to bed with everybody on the staff or asking all the clients for dates. I think really if you can focus on the mission of the organization and try to do things that can help the community that really pushes you on a long way. There was a quote by Paul Robeson that I read once, and I find it very apropos. He said that once you get to a place in your life where you can't be intimidated and you can't be bought then you really are ready to become an effective organizer. That's kind of the bottom line because an organization like the Shaw PAC may have a lot of weight in terms of influencing which developer may get a parcel of land. Many people will pay for that kind of influence, and there are people who've indicated to me that if the Shaw PAC will vote a certain way that they'll arrange for me to have a lot of things. So common sense tells you it's very important to have some strong moral principles in this kind of work.

Most of what we do at Shaw PAC has to do with housing and economic development. That's what we were set up primarily to do. But in the spring of 1981 we decided that we had to get involved in dealing with the problem of drugs in our neighborhood. Some of the streets like Seventh and T and Seventh and S, Fourteenth and U and Fourteenth and V were flooded with people selling illicit drugs. It was literally an epidemic in our community, with maybe 150 or 200 people on the corner at one time. You couldn't even walk down the sidewalk. It bothered me just as a man living in the neighborhood, having to put up with that.

We didn't see how we could avoid the issue. Having adverse things like that going on in the neighborhood was bound to affect our work. It was a disincentive to any sort of housing or economic development project. No developer was going to put up an office building under those conditions, nobody was going to put a decent housing project in a place where dope was being sold right outside the front door. Until we could address the drug issue everything we were working for was going to be put on hold.

Since then we've been doing everything we can to get neighborhood people involved in the issue. We see the people who are carrying on with narcotics—and prostitution too—as victims. It's not just a question of getting criminals off the street and locking them up. If a person is an addict, locking him up isn't going to change that. We know from our sources that there are as many narcotics in jail as there are out on the streets, and once an addict comes out of jail he's going to steal in order to support his habit. We're working on things to prevent the addiction and crime in the first place.

We're working with people in the high schools and junior highs, doing a lot of workshops and seminars for older people too. A lot of older people just don't know about drugs. At first they have a hard time accepting the fact that we're in this kind of epidemic and that it's throughout the whole country. People should be aware of what PCP or other drugs look like, so they know what their children are getting hold of. A lot of older people didn't have that kind of exposure when they were younger.

When we decided to work on the drug issue one of the first decisions we made was to work with the police. Here we don't have the tremendous brutality problems that people in a lot of jurisdictions have. The problem here has been mainly one of unresponsiveness. The current commander of the Third District, Deputy Chief Rodwell Catoe, is very sharp, and we've been working with him. We invited him to come to a Shaw PAC board meeting and he came down and talked with the board members. He talked about some of the things he wanted to see in the Third District and he reminded us that there are a lot of problems. He said our district had the highest concentration of drugs of any police district in the city, and he said a lot of citizen involvement would be needed.

At present, in fact, we've been involved in supporting Chief Catoe against the people who'd like to get rid of him. He's an Afro-American and he has a lot of Caucasians under him who resent his style of leadership and his emphasis on community involvement. He's got all these rednecks under him who do everything they can to undermine his position. Without our support, he'd have been transferred out of the district a long time ago.

Lately we've gotten embroiled in the Third District Advisory Council, which is supposed to be a way for citizens to have an input into police policies. It's been run by middle-class whites who run it as a kind of country club. They had a membership committee which had to vote you in, and there's a $5 fee, which operates like a poll tax to keep poor people out. The chairman, who lives in maybe a $300,000 house over in Logan Circle, would really like to get rid of Chief Catoe. She and her friends used the police in the past as kind of their private army, and they don't want to see someone with the kind of community consciousness that he has. So we're working to gain leadership in that organization, and see if it can really be used as a community voice. If civil servants serve us, which the chief does, then we've got to protect them. Usually what you have is the opposite—you're lobbying to get rid of somebody who's been ineffective or unresponsive—but in this case we've got somebody who's good and we're fighting to keep him.

One tactic we've used has been something that's called allocution. That's a very obscure part of the D.C. code, but it means that citizens of a neighborhood are allowed to speak up at the sentencing of any repeat offenders in drug or prostitution cases, and ask the judge to give stiffer sentences. The drug dealers and their lawyers and some of the other people involved with them are sitting there in court, so it takes some courage to do it. But basically my faith in God really wipes out that kind of fear so I can deal with it. So this is a tactic we've used. We've done it working with the U.S. Attorney's office, though they haven't been as helpful as we'd like them to be. Basically they want us to bring them air-tight cases, not cases where they have to do a lot of work.

We had a particular judge who interrupted me when I was doing one of these allocutions. He said instead of having drugs and prostitution spread out all over the city, it made sense to have them concentrated in one neighborhood. It made it easier for the police to deal with it. I didn't say it, but I was really tempted to say, "Yes, okay, judge, we'll have it in your neighborhood." You can imagine how much he would have liked that. Fortunately I've had that experience already when I burst out in court—that was in my earlier days. At that time I was held in contempt of court. So now I don't do that.

It's a real struggle that has to go on. It's not going to be a short-term thing. It took a long time to get like this so it's going to take a little while to change. We think within the next year we should see a real diminishing of most of the street activity in terms of having large crowds of people. What we've done recently is get them to move from one corner to the next but that's not solving the problem. But I think the biggest thing that's happened is that people decided we have a right not to have this sort of thing going on in our neighborhood, and we're not going to accept it. We think that we have the same right to have a safe street as people who live in American University Park or Glover Park or Chevy Chase or wherever. Living in a low income neighborhood doesn't mean we should be bombarded with crime and drugs.

Organizing and Racism

Of all the issues that confront organizers one of the most critical as well as the most difficult is that of dealing with racial issues. Throughout this book cases have been presented that tackle this issue. In Chapter 3, Joe Drexler discussed the necessity of having equal racial representation on all committees in a multiracial neighborhood. Larry Gross described techniques used to educate people in racially segregated communities and the strength they gained by supporting each other's causes. Steve Burghardt described the difficulties of overcoming the chasm of a white middle class organizer working with an extremely poor black community. In Chapter 7, women working with the Massachusetts Coalition of Battered Women Service Groups speak eloquently of the need to fight against racism and why ''racism is the problem of white people.''

In this chapter organizers discuss many aspects of this issue. Loretta Roach discusses mistakes of white organizers with middle class backgrounds. Peter Rider takes the position that white people can be effective organizers in black communities. Gary Delgado and Don Leaming-Elmer describe contrasting approaches to recruiting, training, and keeping minority organizers. Ashley Adams describes the ambivalent position of an organizer who feels racial issues must be dealt with but is afraid to alienate his white membership. Henry Allen describes techniques used to bring white and black parents together to fight for better quality education in the

Boston public schools. Anne Braden describes building coalitions among existing groups under crisis conditions involving critical racial issues in Louisville, Kentucky.

Loretta Roach, a very experienced black community activist and organizer, tells it "like it is." She explains why poor people, whether black, white, or Puerto Rican, will not work in organizations dominated by white, middle-class intellectuals who come into their communities to organize. She has watched these organizers make the same classic mistakes countless times. Either they push forward into leadership positions inexperienced community people, setting them up for failure, or, conversely, they prevent the strong, competent leaders from assuming leadership roles because they, as organizers, would lose power and control. She feels that class and racial differences create so many difficulties and tensions that for black and white to come together to build a community or an organization is almost impossible. What do you think?

Peter Rider takes a clear position that white organizers can be effective in black neighborhoods. One of the dangers he sees is that it gives people an opportunity to attack the organization but he feels such an attack can be handled effectively and could even strengthen the organization.

Gary Delgado, like Peter Rider, is on the staff of ACORN, Association of Community Organizations for Reform Now. He is in the process of developing a summer training program for minority organizers. In the past they have not recruited people from their lower-income black constituency because potential organizers must already possess certain middle-class skills that this constituency lacks. In addition, ACORN trains people according to an organizing model that makes a clear-cut distinction between community organizers and community leaders. For many reasons, in black and Chicano communities this distinction is artificial, and that makes it difficult for minority organizers to follow the ACORN model. What do you think of his plans for overcoming these pitfalls in training Third World organizers? He plans to have Third World trainees paid more. What do you think some repercussions for white trainees might be? What about the use of a white core staff?

Don Leaming-Elmer describes the techniques developed in Washington, D.C. that ensured an all black organizing staff. Some of the techniques were different from those used by Delgado. The people used to train the organizers were black and the entire history of the organization was that of a black project. The pay was again more than that usually paid to organizer trainees. Not to be overlooked is the fact that most of the trainees were college graduates and came into the training with middle-class skills.

Ashley Adams is a relatively inexperienced organizer who is starting a chapter of Fair Share in a Boston neighborhood that has a very racist reputation. He is confronted by people who want his help in stopping the harassment—really terrorizing—of a black woman who had just moved there. His organizing supervisor didn't want him to work on the issue because it might be divisive in that neighborhood.

They worked on it because community people insisted they work on it and did get the harassment to stop. Adams is very frank that he was relieved that the group did not push to work on issues like integration because "It would have blown Fair Share out of the water before we even got started organizing." He feels that one must work not on the most important issues but those that will involve the most people. Do you think he is right?

Henry Allen, a white community activist, describes the building of multiracial parent councils in Boston as part of the school desegregation process. The situation was extremely difficult as the active white parents were more likely to be against desegregation. He details the successful struggle to institute a multicultural curriculum in a magnet school that involved forcing the principal to comply with court orders. They not only had to build a black-white coalition but a teacher-parent coalition. He is very honest about a basic weakness of the parent councils in that they did not directly confront the issue of race. They had thought it was enough to have black and white parents discussing common school issues. Another basic weakness was the small number of black parents in leadership positions. They seemed unable or unwilling to deal directly with that issue. What do you think they should have done?

The situation described by Anne Braden took place almost 15 years ago, and is from the first edition of this book. It is reprinted here because the organizing lessons it teaches are timeless and because, unfortunately, the social conditions are such that rebellions of the kind described in this case are still a possibility. The SCEF organizers simultaneously attempt to deal with an immediate *crisis* situation, while building understanding and communication links within the white community and between whites and blacks. Not satisfied to deal only with the manifestations of community hysteria, they sought to expose the underlying hypocrisy of racist institutions. A variety of tactics typical of radical organizing efforts—leaflet distribution, mass meetings, and picketing—are demonstrated.

Anne Braden describes organizing against a resurgence of the Ku Klux Klan in Louisville, Kentucky in the late 1970s. She feels that anti-Klan organizing is important because it always leads to organizing against the more respectable forms of racism. Again a variety of tactics were used: rallies, picketing, education in the form of fact sheets and workshops, petitions, etc. Heavy emphasis was placed on building anti-Klan coalitions among already existing organizations. As in the previous case a crisis situation was used to mobilize people to fight racism.

I've Had It with White Sectarians!

Loretta Roach

I am a community activist and I have been for twenty years. Over that time I have always had contact with predominantly white groups that have been trying to organize poor people in my neighborhood. Whether the issue is education, electoral politics, housing or whatever it is, these groups have been around and I have seen the same mistakes over and over again. It gets tiring.

Mainly they are groups that are left or ultra-left in a way that's highly intellectualized. They come in with these strong political theories, and yet they are not able to organize poor people—poor blacks, poor whites, poor hispanics—into any type of cohesive organization that's going to move. They insist on making very classic mistakes.

Now the average black, the average Puerto Rican, the average poor white hasn't had four years of college education, hasn't had that kind of time to get their heads on politically. We don't intellectualize things. We don't intellectualize racism or poverty or the lack of housing or lack of health or lack of good schools. We live it. And we live it every day.

These groups are really isolated, sectarian I'd call them because they're so wrapped up in their particular program. They don't see what I think are some basic fundamentals, principles of dealing with people. One, you take people at their level. If they're willing to do a mailing for you, and lick stamps for you, leaflet door to door—whatever people offer and whatever they give you, you take that and you work with it. The mistake of a lot of these groups is that they want more, and they want it right away. They want to compensate for the lack of blacks and hispanics in their organization, so this incredible process starts occurring where they push blacks and poor people into leadership positions even if they aren't competent for them. And most of these blacks and hispanics, rather than say, "Look, I can't do this, I don't know how to do it," get swept up into the leadership. Not knowing what real leadership is, they get angry and frustrated, and they leave. Most of them just burn out and quit, and by and large stop being active. Groups like that manage to let loose and burn out more blacks, hispanics, and poor whites than they've organized.

And it's interesting what often happens at that time. There was strong black leadership capability, competent leadership capability, and the sectarian group was afraid of it. They wanted to put into leadership black people who they could work around, who they could manipulate and control. It's easy to control someone who doesn't quite know what they're doing. But I've seen genuine leadership bypassed because those people can't be controlled.

These individuals in sectarian groups are also highly egotistical and arrogant. My experience in dealing with them at this point, after twenty years, is to watch and listen but to keep them at arm's length. They lack experience, knowledge in dealing with people, all kinds of people. They see themselves in the leadership role, they do not see themselves as workers. They see themselves as leadership. That fact alone, as far as I'm concerned, is confrontational. Very often, the leadership in some of these groups will say, "Why can't we get the blacks involved? Why can't we get hispanics involved?" First of all I keep telling them they're putting the cart before the horse. They start with an idea—somewhere an idea is born that suits their politics. They hitch it on to a community concern and after they've gotten a group organized with the right politics, predominantly white, they begin to look for black and hispanic participation. They put the horse after the cart.

This one group I've worked with in the past year is highly secretive, amazingly secretive. It's like a caricature of the Communist Party during the thirties and forties. I have seen them attack people within their own ranks with this massive hostility when they don't toe the line politically. And when a black person who *isn't* in their group dares to criticize their positions in a community organization, they're totally outnumbered. This group will come down on them hard. For the average person in my neighborhood, who may go to church but doesn't belong to any political groups, it's a bewildering situation—and it's embittering, too.

In terms of academics, the academic analyses are fine but when it comes to working with people they fail miserably. And they will continue to fail. I don't know what the answer is but the question is how to get blacks and whites and hispanics and other people to work together to build some type of organization to have some political impact. I don't know what the answer is. But I know that inbred white arrogance is a real obstacle. They are born with power and they don't understand that their own upbringing is the reason why they can't build anything in the black and hispanic community. The black and poor white are at the other end of the spectrum. We've never had power. You've got to have some type of egocentric sense of yourself to do what some of these groups want to do. You've got to have a massive ego. And we get those people's egos inflicted on us. When I say we, I'm speaking about the black community. I will go so far to say that sometimes whatever those groups organize becomes secondary, the issue becomes secondary, whether it be welfare rights, whether it be over education. It's secondary as long as the leadership maintains its control.

There's a case in point. There's a Fair Share organization in my community. It has a committee with predominantly older blacks, mainly women, a sprinkling of other blacks and one or two white members. They're active and some have a good sharp political sense and in the midst of all this was a Fair Share organizer, a southern white boy, born in Mississippi or Alabama or someplace else in the South. It was interesting for me to watch the interplay when he sat in on the meetings. All of a sudden this heavy southern drawl would come out and he'd be sitting there talking to one of the older black women saying, "When are you going to fry some fried chicken? I'm going to come over and eat some fried chicken and sweet potato pie." From my perspective, he had a very condescending manner with these women. He didn't talk about racism, there was never any conversation about racism with this man.

Their primary focus at the time was housing. These women would volunteer days to go sit down at the Registry of Deeds to look up absentee landlords and tax rebate information and they did a lot of really good important stuff. And they fundraised, they had fried chicken dinners and made lots of money for Fair Share, but I decided I could no longer do it. I couldn't deal with the whole range of how he was using them. Once they asked me to be a lead speaker at one of the Dorchester meetings, and when I walked into the meeting that night they had registration tables and information tables. As you walked in there were six or seven tables and there were these elderly black women sitting there doing all the work. Yet I knew when I went inside that they had no say in what was going to happen, what was going to be said at the meetings. They had no say in setting the agenda, or the political content of the meeting. They had absolutely nothing to say. In other words they were up front as showpieces. Fair Share operates that way—I know it. But there are a lot of other sectarian groups that do the same goddamn thing—more subtly, but they do it. And you have to be pretty sophisticated to be able to pick it up, but it's there. And when you confront them with it, and I've confronted some of these organizations with this stuff, their response is to say, "Well, why don't you join?" I laughed. I think it's funny.

It well may be that the whites in this country have been the masters too long, it well may be that the blacks in this country have been the slaves too long, for them to come together to build an organization or build a community that benefits both sides. I don't know what the answer is. I don't think anybody knows what the answer is. But I'm a perennial optimist.

White Organizers in Black Neighborhoods?

Peter Rider

It is clear that whites are able to function well as organizers in black neighborhoods. Even in Boston, where there's probably more racial polarization than in just about any other city ACORN works in, having white organizers doesn't hurt us too much. It's a disadvantage in the sense that there's so much racial hatred in the city—understandably, black people have a lot of distrust of whites. But once you are going door to door and talking to people directly, what comes through is your own personality, your sincerity, and ultimately the appeal of organizing.

I'd say that you can break through the race barrier with about 90 percent of the people. Race is not an issue that stops the group from forming. Mainly this is because the way we organize. When people ask us whether we live in the neighborhood we're ready to say, "No, I don't live in this neighborhood. I'm an organizer. I'm trying to help you get together an organization that deals with the problems that you see in the neighborhood. I'm not going to tell you how to do it, but I'm here to help you." Then we move to questions like "What do you think are the problems in the neighborhood?" I think that kind of technique—as opposed to coming in and trying to play more of an actual leadership role—lends itself to minimizing the problems.

Having a white organizer does give people who want to attack the organization a handle, there's no denying that. One of our members had a friend who worked at City Hall, and she asked her friend what he thought of ACORN since she didn't know much about it. He said, "Oh, ACORN, that's a bunch of white organizers telling blacks what to do—using them for their own aims." That kind of race baiting can hurt. But our experience has been that we can live with it.

For our best leaders, in fact, the innuendoes make them much clearer on the racial issue. We're a multi-racial organization and proud of it. If somebody stands up at a meeting and says, well, this is just white organizers manipulating blacks, that's an attack on the organizers but it's also an attack on the neighborhood ACORN leadership we have up there. It's telling them that they're just puppets. And of course our leadership acts in a very predictable way. They say, "What are you saying—that I'm a fool? I'm not a fool." The defense is always there. I've never seen a situation where people who've been in the organization get turned around by that kind of race baiting at a meeting. What it tends to do instead is to make people much more sophisticated on the race issue, and make them understand that race baiting has been used to divide people and destroy organizations.

A Training Institute for Third World Organizers

Gary Delgado[1]

There are a bunch of reasons why you don't find black folks doing this kind of organizing and the first has to do with the issues. We don't do issues that are racially based. We stay out of, for instance, education issues which many people perceive to be racial. Community organizations are interracial and are afraid to alienate white membership, therefore don't deal with those issues. In my opinion, they don't even give their leadership a chance to be progressive because they never attempt to push those issues.

---

[1]From *Just Economics: The Magazine for Organizers*, Vol. 7, No. 2 (April/May, 1979), pp. 12–13. This magazine is now entitled *The Organizer* and is published by The Institute for Social Justice.

For young blacks, if you want to get into what's happening in your community, an ACORN or a Fair Share is not the place to do it. People still do not, in the Black community, believe that the primary reason for discrimination is economic, or class; they believe it is racial. People will join ACORN but when you talk about what young blacks want to organize, they want to organize something that deals specifically with racial issues as sort of the focal point for the organization.

Second, the organizations are inadvertently racist, and I do mean inadvertently. I don't mean they're anti-Black or anti-Hispanic but what they do is they treat everybody the same way. If you don't take into account the fact that there are real differences culturally you're going to have problems. For instance, for any white person who comes on staff, there are natural social relations. If a black organizer comes on a staff where there are few other black staff, the social relations have to come from that very small group or from the constituency and that messes with the whole organizer/leader dichotomy. That causes role confusion for people. They get confused about who they are, what they're doing because the hierarchy is reflective of essentially what society is; it's all white and mostly male.

Also, if you look at who we recruit, we recruit the best and the brightest. There are already a requisite number of skills people have to have in order to just become an organizer. They have to be somewhat analytical, they have to be hard-working and they have to have a certain amount of resources.

We can only seriously afford to take people who have resources and have those skills. When I was trying to recruit basically out of the constituency we organize for ULO we couldn't because their education wasn't that tight; they couldn't do it. Therefore, to put them on an organizing drive makes double work for anybody in terms of training because you have to train them but you also have to deal with the skills deficiency and that kind of tension always makes the new person feel like shit and the trainer feel like shit and that's another reason we end up losing a lot of people. There's a primary contradiction in terms of our attempting to hire people from within our constituency. Basically, organizing skills are middle class skills.

I also think the money stuff is integrally related to some of the other concerns. People often say they quit because of money but there are a number of other reasons why they really quit and the money is sort of a bottom line excuse. If you have resources, or access to resources, the money is less of a problem. If you don't and you come to work here and you're not making much money and you're working 12 hours a day, it becomes problematic. You're having other problems, training, role problems, etc. and then money becomes more of an issue.

The last thing I'd say is there's a big problem about the style of organizing. There's a model, you don't deviate from the model. There's a dichotomy between organizers and leaders and to the extent that it's a white model it's a problem because it doesn't allow Third World organizers to play to their strengths. There's a different history in the black and Chicano communities that makes the whole leader/organizer thing less clear cut. If we take people who don't have certain kinds of skills they could compensate for them if they were allowed to develop a different style of organizing but because they're not that compounds the problems we have in terms of recruiting, training and retaining.

WHAT CAN WE DO DIFFERENTLY TO DEAL WITH SOME OF THESE PROBLEMS?

I think if we seriously want Third World organizers, we're going to have to make some concessions both in the organizing and training models. First, I think that we can not continue to hire people and move them immediately. They have to have a chance to develop their stuff if not in their own community, at least in the same town.

I also think that you need to develop in people, in all organizers, a sense of history, the history of organizing and a sense that there are different kinds of organizing. I think some of the parochialism has got to go.

In the training program we're putting together this summer, I think one of the big selling points is we're going to bring a number of people together at one time to go through the same experience. We're going to bring in outsiders who are black and Hispanic to talk to them about different kinds of organizing.

WHAT ELSE WILL BE DIFFERENT ABOUT THE TRAINING?

People will only be sent out of here in teams and only when they're ready. After four months minimum here they will go back to their own communities. There will be reunions, skills up-grading sessions three or four times a year. And it will not just be an organizing drive. There will also be two sessions a week, one on the history and one on issue development. The other thing is we're paying more money than the usual ACORN trainee. I think what we're trying to do is create a little bastion of Third World staff. All training for Third World staff will now be in New Orleans and I think that's a good move.

Insuring an All Black Organizing Team

Don Leaming-Elmer[1]

When you started organizing in Washington, D.C., six months ago, you recruited a whole staff of local black organizers. I want to talk about why and how you did it.

[1]From *Just Economics: The Magazine for Organizers*, Vol. 7, No. 2 (April/May, 1979), pp. 13–14. This magazine is now entitled *The Organizer* and is published by The Institute for Social Justice.

When I got here, it was obvious that because the area we're working in is almost all black, that we were going to have to find black organizers. The sponsoring committee's assumption, of course, was that there were a lot of black organizers around the country. Then we began to talk about it and I told them about my experience of finding very few at least with this kind of organizing experience. What I figured was if we're going to have a black staff, we're going to have to train them.

So, one strategy was let's recruit young black staff from right here and then get in a couple of real good experienced organizers to help train them. But I thought, well, as long as we're starting from scratch, why not just train them and not attempt to bring in experienced organizers from the outside other than the director.

What I was afraid of was we'd have the experienced organizers come in and they'd be white. I wanted a situation where the blacks felt like if it was going to work it was going to be because of them and where I wouldn't rely on white experienced staff too much and then come out with a staff that simply gave the whites more experience and the blacks a kind of inferiority complex about organizing from the start.

Was that feeling based on some past experience?

At NCO (in Chicago), we had a heavily Latino population. We brought in sometimes as many as three or four Latino staff onto a staff of 10 or 15 in all and of course the Latinos had absolutely no experience. They started from the bottom and there were a lot of white staff around with experience and it never seemed to click.

Another experience I had in Chicago with NCO that affected the decision I made here was that when I started there in 1970 there were no women organizers whatsoever. In fact, I remember times when there would be women coming in and it was just a joke. The feeling was that they could not organize, period. What happened was Susie Simms was the first woman at NCO who really took off. She was dynamite and then gradually she attracted other women in and I discovered that once we had close to 50 percent women—I don't know what the magic number was—but when there was a sense that it was fair and there were a couple of stars among the women as well as among the men, the whole atmosphere changed.

So I decided let's just start with an all black staff so I don't throw out any unconscious vibrations about what the chance of blacks versus whites would be. I was fortunate in that one of my black staff had a little organizing experience he picked up in Chicago, not a great deal but at least he knew what organizing was and had a couple of good experiences under his belt. So there was a black organizer that was looked to as having some experience that the rest were scrambling to catch up to.

Again, there was this sense, if it was going to work, they were going to get the credit. If it didn't work, it would be on them. My feeling is that as a result this organizing staff is at least as good as the best organizing staff I had at NCO or

MAHA or anywhere in terms of ability when you look at them after the six months we've had on the street.

Where did you find the staff?

We just put an ad in the paper, in the *Star,* the *Post* and the *Afro-American.* We ran it one time and got 142 resumes. Part of the reason we got such high quality people is the job market in the District. A huge number of them had at least four years of college experience, a lot of them above that. The other piece was that I had some contacts, Daryl Sabbs at The Youth Project gave me a bunch of leads as to where I could find some black organizations around the city that could refer people on and that was really effective.

How much are you paying?

That's another thing I think is a factor. The wages have been so shitty in organizing for so long and it's still not really high here but for beginning organizers we're paying $10,000 for a trainee slot. That obviously has a lot to do with getting really good people because the people on staff now don't think in terms of I'll stay here six months or whatever. All of them have commitments to stay more than a year and I'm going to have to take very seriously trying to find some more money to give more incentive to stay but I think that's just the real world.

Is Washington unique?

It may be but my sense is that we might have been able to do more in Chicago than we ever dreamed. We just never had a good success under our belts to know how to do it and I think if I went to another city I'd probably spend a whole lot more time digging out black staff. Everybody starts with the assumption you can't find them so it's almost a self-fulfilling prophecy. I think it's harder in another city but I think for instance that some organizations might do well to even go to a city like D.C. to find staff instead of assuming you have to do it right in the town you're in.

Any other organization I was part of was an existing group that had some history already. It already had the history of a majority white organizing core. Here, one of the reasons it works is because it doesn't have that. I'm white obviously but there's more a sense that this is a black project. In an existing organization, if there was a way to take a piece of the organization, say one black neighborhood, maybe the way to start would be to attract black staff there. I think you need more than one or two to make it happen, to pull together a sense of identity. I think what I would do is attempt to attract an all black staff of four to eight people and create that identity. Later on they could work with white staff too but I'd want to create the identity first so they would go into that experience with the sense that they had skills and wouldn't be intimidated by white staff. I think my staff now could handle any white competition, period. But I didn't want that as an excuse for not producing or an excuse for me to rely on whites instead of blacks.

Going Slow Against Racism in White Neighborhoods

Ashley Adams

When it comes to bringing up issues of racial equality in white neighborhoods, I pretty much believe in going slow. But it's possible to be so cautious that you end up alienating people who are ready to move on a particular issue. Sometimes it's so clear-cut that you don't risk anything by going ahead and standing up for what's right.

When I was hired by Massachusetts Fair Share in December 1979, I was assigned to test out the possibility of organizing in a particular section of Boston. The community is, I think, 99.7 percent white, mainly Irish Catholic with some Italian and Polish and a few Jewish families. Middle-class and upper-working-class people, relatively affluent for a Boston neighborhood. My job was to look for people who were interested in working on neighborhood issues and try to develop them into leaders who could establish some form of organization in that part of the city. To start with, I had a list of about 150 people who'd given $10 to Fair Share as a membership contribution when our canvassers had gone through the neighborhood. I started going through the list, calling people and setting up appointments for home visits to meet with them and talk about various problems.

When we finally had a meeting of people who'd expressed interest, I found that one of the key issues on people's minds was a problem of racial harassment. A white woman at the meeting said she was a close friend of a black woman who'd had a shop in this neighborhood for about ten or fifteen years. She hadn't really had racial problems until about five years ago when she'd bought a house and moved her family into the neighborhood. She bought a house on a very beautiful street, a very nice house. And at that point both her home and her shop became objects of violence—not just brutal name calling but she had people chasing her, threatening her kids, spray-painting "Fuck you nigger" on the side of her house, all sorts of things. Most recently someone had driven a car or truck several times into the door and the wall of her shop, trying to break it down. The police had refused even to write up a report on the incident—they said that it was probably just some drunk.

When this came up at the meeting, my organizing supervisor interjected that we shouldn't deal with it at that point. She said, well, perhaps we might want to work on other things first, because we wouldn't want an issue that might be divisive. The woman who'd brought it up got really indignant at that, and my supervisor backed down, but she still felt the group would be making a mistake to take up that issue at first.

I can understand the theory behind what my supervisor was saying. The issues you want to work on aren't always "the most important issues that exist in the community," but those that will involve the most people. I think racial integration is vital and important, but as an organizer I'd choose to stay away from pushing integration in a racist neighborhood. In this case, though, the issue wasn't integration as such but violent harassment. It was so clear-cut that very, very few people would be opposed to fighting for this woman's right not to be harassed. Even if people thought the attacks were okay they'd never be able to come out and say it. So not only morally but strategically this was a good issue to take on.

So we had a house meeting and the target of the harassment came. She's a very quiet woman but she's been fighting this for five years. We had about thirty people at the meeting, a lot of them friends and neighbors of hers because she's got a lot of friends in the community. The people there weren't really gutsy freedom-fighting radicals—it didn't require all that much guts to say that somebody's shop shouldn't be driven into.

Now if I'd been in that community as an individual, I'd probably have been pushing the race issue. I'd have said that it wasn't just a violent attack on someone who happened to be black but part of a citywide problem and we should work for integration. But as an organizer I was hoping that nobody would be standing up and saying those things, because it would just risk offending everybody. It would've blown Fair Share out of the water before we even got started organizing. So I was nervous at the meeting. But nobody did bring up that sort of thing. I think they felt good about themselves, in a kind of righteous way, and I encouraged this. I let them feel righteous as hell about helping their black neighbor, but at the same time we weren't encouraging lots of other black people to move in, or attacking realtors for discrimination. Maybe it was kind of liberal guilt and a concern about their image that was leading people to want to work on this issue, but if so, that's okay. We're all motivated by self interest, and if I assumed that people are involved only for the purest of motives I wouldn't be a good organizer.

What we did in organizing around the issue wasn't really very militant. We had a community meeting at a church where people spoke about the importance of protecting people and wasn't this a terrible incident. The police were there and they said, well, we don't really have the manpower to do anything permanent but we'll send a patrolman by there for the next couple of months and write up these reports in the future. The state attorney general's office took some interest. We made a couple of research trips to offices downtown, state and city offices, so that we could bring it to the attention of other people. We didn't get anything that you could call a clear-cut victory, but the people involved felt good about what they'd done. Even though we didn't get hard-and-fast concessions from the police, in fact the harassment dropped off a lot. The expression of community concern really helped.

It's ironic that even though Fair Share as a statewide organization decided at a convention to work for racial justice and harmony, this episode was one of the few times that a local chapter had worked with whites around a race issue. Even our more progressive chapters hadn't taken up those questions. It was in this white, upper middle class neighborhood, considered the most racist neighborhood that Fair

Share works in, that we actually addressed the issue. It's not that we planned it that way, but this was an issue that came up and we were flexible about it.

Some generalizations don't apply to specific cases, and the generalization that you should stay away from racial issues in a white racist community didn't apply here. There were a number of people in the community who were happy to work on this issue and liked working on it because it made them feel good about themselves. We were right to respond to that and take up the issue.

Multi-Racial Parents' Councils

Henry Allen

When the federal district court in Boston ordered desegregation of the public schools in 1974, one of the things it did to try to make it work was call for the creation of multi-racial parent councils. The idea was to bring white, black, and other parents together and give them an incentive to cooperate by giving them the right to have an input into the school system. At that time there was a long tradition in Boston of excluding parents, even preventing their physical presence inside the school buildings.

So the judge said that a network of multi-racial parent councils should be created, and he ordered the School Department to cooperate. What happened at that point was many parents who'd been involved in school reform and desegregation since the 1960s got attracted to these new councils. It seemed like a chance to make a positive contribution. I myself was elected to the school-based council where my kids went to school and then also elected to the district council and later the city-wide council. In those first two years, 1974 and '75, there was a large group of activists in neighborhoods across the city who were taking leadership. It took a hell of a lot of effort. We were organizing the councils and we were exercising leadership in them at the same time.

The context was pretty discouraging. City officials were ambiguous at best and in most cases hostile to desegregation. The first year of busing brought strong opposition in the form of an anti-busing movement in some of the white neighborhoods. That first year, probably most white parents who were active around school issues were active specifically in opposition to desegregation. Boston is one of the most segregated cities in the country to begin with, and there was very little experience of black, white, Hispanic, and Asian parents working together. And now the atmosphere was in some ways more bitter than ever.

The immediate issue that created a common ground was the issue of safety. It was something that white and black parents were equally concerned with. It had to do with the safety of the buses, with being safe while waiting on street corners, with what happened to the kids when they got to school. We had to work toward a climate in the schools that could somehow be immune from the general level of hostility and near-violence that existed in the city. What we said to the parents we were trying to organize was that only by *being* organized could we all get what we wanted for our children in terms of safety. It's not that the schools were really battlegrounds—the problems were concentrated mainly in a few high schools like South Boston and Hyde Park which were in the news. But there was a potentially dangerous situation *unless* the parents organized. This was something that most people understood. If we held parent meetings based on the safety issue, people would generally come out.

Sometimes the meetings couldn't be held at the school because of where the school was located, so we'd try to have the meeting at a neutral site. We'd try to think of things like multi-cultural fairs or multi-ethnic dinners, which sometimes was the most effective organizing technique because people like to share things like food and music. The idea was to bring parents from different backgrounds and neighborhoods together—which, when you think of it, was a radical step for Boston. In a number of schools these social events were very, very effective. They did bring people together and people began to talk about serious educational issues: curriculum, teacher attitudes, administration, that sort of thing.

I don't want to make it sound easier than it was. In fact, many of these meetings never happened. I mean, you might work very hard with a few parents at a school and talk about how to put a leaflet together—what it should say and how to make it as attractive as possible and how to distribute it—and how to do follow-up phone calls, all the traditional organizing tactics, just to get a meeting held. And then comes the night of the meeting and maybe only two or three parents show up. It demoralized a lot of people badly. They felt, "What difference does it make? I'm the only one who's interested." The difference between successful and unsuccessful organizing might simply be the attitude of the active parents. The ones with more staying power might say, "Well, okay, if it doesn't work the first time, maybe it'll work the second time."

There were over 160 schools in the system in 1974, so people were trying to organize in 160 different locations. Every school really was potentially a place to organize. Many of them were all but hopeless, either because of the level of hostility or because there wasn't an active core of parents ready to do the work. Those of us who felt a stake in the viability of the parent councils did what any organizer does—we put our biggest effort into places where we had the best chance of early successes. These were schools where there were active parents, both black and white—people had been active even before the desegregation order. If the councils wouldn't work in those schools, they couldn't work anywhere. In fact, not only at those schools but at a lot of others where there was no active organizing going on, black and white parents did start meeting together.

There were other issues besides safety that people wanted to take on. The broad issue of quality education was more and more on the agenda. Let me give you an example. A number of schools were designated as magnet schools where they were supposed to have certain themes or educational programs that would make them attractive to black and white students so that parents would voluntarily decide to send them to those schools. One school that we worked with had as its theme a multi-cultural curriculum. A number of the teachers were quite interested in really developing it. They wanted to shape the curriculum materials so as to give students a good multi-cultural education. But the principal of this school was extremely antagonistic, both to a multi-cultural curriculum and to any level of parent involvement. He did everything that he could do to set up barriers. He refused to hand out flyers, refused to let people see the list of parents of children in the schools, refused to make phone calls or even to return calls. These were all very basic things that parents had a right to—and they were in the court order. But he'd been principal there for ten years, ever since the school opened, and he thought he could get away with anything.

Finally it got to a point where the parents and some teachers decided they ought to try to remove this principal. Now this is almost unheard of in the history of the Boston schools. You had alcoholics, you had incompetents, you had no-shows— you had almost any imaginable kind of principal and they were extremely hard to get rid of. Most of these people were tied-in politically through the patronage system, and they had connections with higher-up administrators or School Committee people. So that meant the activists at this school had to devise a very, very carefully plotted-out campaign to get rid of the principal. They knew that teachers are very vulnerable, and that unless they approached it very carefully they might end up with parents on one side and the teachers and the administration on the other. If they could get the parents and the teachers together, there was a much greater chance of getting rid of that principal. Over a number of months of meetings I was co-chair of the Community District Advisory Council, which was responsible for providing support to the local parent councils. So I met frequently with the active parents at that school, and I developed a lot of respect for them. I think by the end of about six months we'd done an exceptionally good job of laying the foundation for getting rid of this principal.

They held meetings with parents, between parents and teachers. They documented every instance of violation of the federal court order. Every time he refused to allow the parent council to send home a flyer, that was a violation of the court order. If we wanted we could call the district superintendent, and he'd call the principal and say, "Look, let them give out the flyer," and at that point the principal would give in. Instead of going through that every time, the parents decided to build a case for getting him removed. They recorded every instance of obstruction, from the most blatant to the most trivial. The coalition we built between parents and teachers was something that was almost unheard of in the Boston schools. Generally teachers were very aligned either just with themselves or with the administration. Here we had black and white parents aligned with black and white teachers. Rather than go through the bureaucracy, we decided to take the case directly to the School Committee. We got on the agenda of a School Committee meeting and we got a lot of parents to turn out for it. We presented the evidence, which was quite overwhelming. Even though the School Committee members had known most of this themselves, they were shocked to see it all documented and presented to them. When they tried to put off a decision, we fought them on it. There were some angry exchanges between them and the parents. They finally put it off, for a week. During that week, there was a series of meetings held between the parents and superintendent of schools. At that point she was trying to build some alliances with parents, because her job was on the line and she thought it would help her if she showed she had a lot of parent support. (It proved futile, because that wasn't what the School Committee was interested in, and her contract wasn't renewed.) We convinced her to recommend that this principal be transferred out of that job. Now at that point the parents didn't feel any stake in where the guy was transferred—they just wanted him out of that job. Well, she was going to transfer him to a school in Charlestown. The people in Charlestown found out about this and at the next School Committee meeting, with all of our parents showing up for our big victory, you also had all these parents in Charlestown saying "No way will you have this guy transferred to our school." The superintendent pushed for the transfer anyway, which on the one hand was an enormous victory for the parents, but on the other hand you had black and white parents from the Charlestown school very upset. We hadn't thought out our strategy well enough. It hadn't even occurred to us that we might be strong enough to have the guy fired. So we hadn't really dealt with what would happen to him. And in fact the transfer never actually happened, after all the months of work. But what did happen was that the whole struggle radically changed his outward behavior. He had so much pressure put on him that in fact for the next year or so—while you still had that active group of black and white parents—he kind of stepped out of the way. A multi-cultural curriculum was put in place, with significant changes in what was being taught and the materials being used. That was a victory in itself for the black and white parents. It was a very, very important example for us in terms of what we could show citywide. Here was a school where we cleared away a big obstacle to implement something very important for the parents and their children.

    When I think about our overall approach to the organizing we did around the parent councils, it seems to me that one of the weaknesses is that we didn't confront the issue of race very directly. We thought it was enough to get black and white parents to a meeting and talk about issues that affected both of them in the school. In retrospect, I would say seven years later that we chose the right direction generally, but we should have dealt more directly with the issue of race. I think we saw real problems later on with teacher layoffs, and the issue of whether they should be on the basis of strict seniority. That would have meant a drastic decline in the percentage of black teachers in the system. There was distrust between black and white parents on this issue. Part of that may have reflected our not dealing directly enough with the issue of racism.

In general, black parents haven't been as involved in the councils as white parents. Partly that has to do with the fact that in a number of schools white activist parents tend to be too dominating and that is a turnoff to black parents. But also, some of the leadership of the black parents had been siphoned off into other areas. There is a program called METCO which buses black students from Boston into white suburban schools. Many of those black parents who you would expect to provide leadership and organizational talents are not in the Boston public schools at all—they are in the suburban schools. This is a continuing problem, because the school system now has a majority of black and Hispanic students but most of the leadership in the parent councils is coming from whites. On the other hand, I would say that, both among students and among parents, there is more black-white contact than at any other time in the history of this city. There is more working together on common ground, on common issues, than ever before. It means that we made a beginning. We showed that people can work together and that sometimes they can even succeed.

SCEF[1] Responds to a Crisis

Anne Braden

THE WHITE COMMUNITY RESPONDS TO THE BLACK REBELLION

The rebellion in Louisville erupted on a Monday night, May 27, 1968. It followed a street-corner meeting in the heart of the ghetto to protest a flagrant case of police brutality. There would have been no violence if police cars had not roared into the crowd of black people who were peacefully leaving the meeting.

Our city and state governments responded to that night's uprising by an immediate and tremendous crackdown. All available police converged on the area and the Governor sent in the National Guard—2,000 of them by the next day. An immediate curfew was imposed. Before dawn more than 100 black people were arrested, mostly for curfew violation. Four were shot.

Our first thought was to get white observers at the jail to try to discourage the mistreatment of black people being arrested. At the jail, we found that the Louisville Council of Churches also had observers on hand—ministers, mostly. The Council had set up its own skeleton organization back in the winter to respond to a possible rebellion and to set up a "rumor center." They had a telephone number where people could call to see what was happening. Because things like this were

[1]Southern Conference Education Fund.

being take care of by the church group, we were able to turn our attention to other kinds of action.

Early Tuesday morning, we decided that our job was to attempt to get some kind of public expression from the white community protesting the imposition of a police state to deal with the black rebellion. It is our opinion that this is the task of the white activist at this moment in American history. We saw it as our job to help the white community to see that as long as there is oppression there will be rebellion and that if the white community attempts to crush this rebellion instead of facing the conditions that cause it, this can only be done by the imposition of a police state that will enslave everyone. In other words, aside from all the moral questions involved, it is in the self-interest of the great majority of people to stave off a police state— because the kind of society it would bring is one they would not want to live in. This was the political and philosophic base of all our actions in Louisville—and it still is.

That first morning, a few of us got on the telephone, called all the white people we could think of who might respond, and asked them to meet at City Hall at 3 p.m. to attempt to see the mayor. The demands of the delegation were to be (1) removal of the National Guard, (2) lifting of the curfew, (3) release of prisoners on their own bond (bonds had been set at $2000 for curfew violation and $20,000 for looting), (4) firing of the police officer whose misconduct had caused the protest in the black community, and (5) establishment of a program to deal with the real problems in the West End of Louisville where the rebellion was in progress. Militant black leaders were making similar demands on the city. We also distributed a leaflet in downtown Louisville calling on white people to support these demands and to meet at City Hall.

The downtown leafleting recruited only a few people for our City Hall demonstration. However, it served the purpose of letting great numbers of whites know that other whites were opposing the policies of the city government. Most of those who actually came to City Hall did so in response to the telephone campaign. There were more than 50 of them—a good turnout for Louisville on something like this and one that included some people we'd never seen at a demonstration before. White Southerners don't often demonstrate on the behalf of blacks.

Terrified city officials locked the doors of City Hall when we got there. We waited on the steps. Finally, the executive director of the Human Relations Commission came out to talk with us. We insisted on seeing the mayor, and when he insisted that the mayor was seeing no one, we insisted that he immediately take our demands to the mayor. He did—with no results, of course. But our delegation stayed an hour or more talking on the steps with the Human Relations man. Police were crawling all over the place; we asked why, and he finally asked them to leave. We had two official spokesmen—a Catholic priest and a Baptist minister—but everyone whom the spirit moved was able to talk, and we did. We made two main points: (1) the practical short-range one that the use of force, the presence of the Guard, and the like were actually making matters worse and prolonging the disorders in the West End, and that (2) if the city continued its policy of meeting rebellion by force it could only succeed by increasingly repressive measures, a garrison city, and an unthinkable and unlivable situation. We fear that the officials were moved more by the former short-range argument than by the latter, more basic one—especially since our argument was at that moment being documented (we learned later) by new West End outbreaks in the very areas where the Guard was heaviest.

Finally there was nothing more to say to the Human Relations man—so one of our delegation hastily went into town and bought cardboard and we made picket signs and set up a picket at police headquarters. When it came time for the 8 p.m. curfew, everyone left except seven people who decided to stay and be arrested—which they were. We later had some doubts about the effectiveness of this kind of protest against the curfew. There were hundreds of black people in jail by then and no one really had time to fight about these people's right to picket. However, those who went to jail had important and significant experiences in communicating with the Black prisoners—many of them understood why the white people were there too, and important lines of communication were set up.

The City Hall delegation did have an impact in the community far beyond those who saw us there—as it was written up in the paper the next morning and others knew about it by word of mouth.

That night there were more disorders throughout the West End, more blacks arrested, and four more shot.

The next morning we decided that instead of spending our time getting out a new leaflet and organizing a continuing picket line, we needed to take time to get more white people together to broaden our base of planning and decision-making. We didn't want the white protest to be just a SCEF thing. The value of a group like SCEF in a situation like this, we felt, was that it was mobile, could move fast, had a printing press handy, and had a few full-time people who could drop other things and act. But the turnout at City Hall had shown us that many white people in the city were concerned, and we felt we should not be making the basic decisions alone.

So that day we spent on the telephone inviting people to a meeting the next day—which happened to be Memorial Day and thus a holiday when no one would be working but certainly not in the mood for a picnic.

Meantime, that day (Wednesday), in response to the pressure from both the black and white communities, the city deescalated. They partially withdrew the Guard, lifted the curfew, let many of the prisoners out of jail, and granted the request of black militants that they be allowed to set up a marshal system to patrol their own streets. Things quieted down considerably in the West End—although that night tragedy struck as two black people were killed. One was a 14-year-old boy shot by a policeman; the other was a 19-year-old youth shot by a merchant. The youth was eating a fish sandwich in front of the store when he was slain.

Our meeting of whites was held the next afternoon in a church, and 70 people showed up—with a number of others expressing support who could not be there. The temporary chairman, a young Presbyterian minister, opened the meeting by saying we were meeting because a number of white people felt the need for a "radical response" to what was happening, that we were having "liberal" responses but we needed a "radical" one. The group got off on that foot—and continued in that direction.

The upshot of the meeting was an ad hoc organization that named itself the White Emergency Support Team (WEST), the stated purpose of which was to support the black community at this time. It was made clear that it was not to be a negotiating committee or a go-between, that its purpose was not to "quiet things down" but to try to bring influence to bear to see that Louisville faced its basic problems.

We set up three committees immediately: (1) a policy committee to meet right away and draw a policy statement to be mailed that night to those present and others seeking signatures that could be publicized; (2) an action committee that was given freedom to proceed with direct action, leafleting, picketing, and the like; (3) an information committee that would get the facts on how the rebellion started and its real causes to the community by all possible means—the press, radio and TV, and our own publications.

Part of our policy statement was borrowed almost verbatim from a statement issued by white people in Washington during the April uprisings there. If radical organizers and organizations keep in touch with each other, we would learn a good deal by sharing our experiences and become more effective by sharing our materials.

The policy committee also drew up and publicized a list of "immediate demands"—including the original ones made at City Hall, plus a demand that the policeman and merchant who had killed the black youths be charged with murder.

By Friday morning, the West End was quiet—and we thought WEST could settle down to a long-range task of educating the white community. But we had underestimated the will of the city administration to counterattack, its blindness in facing the real issues, and its determination to crush activists instead of solving problems.

On Friday afternoon, the City-County Crime Commission met and issued a blast. It ignored the basic social problems and recommended that "proper authorities" investigate an out-of-town black speaker at the original Monday night rally, the "role of antipoverty workers" in the disorders (some VISTAs had been active in WEST), and the role, "if any," of SCEF leaders in starting the riots. Meantime, the grand jury had met and brought charges of assault and battery against the black man who had been struck by a policeman—the incident that had produced the original protest against police brutality.

In other words, powerful people in the city had apparently decided to "blame the victims" for what had happened and to try to solve its problems by scapegoating. This is the traditional way of handling thorny problems in Louisville.

That night (Friday), police moved to implement this line. They arrested the out-of-town speaker mentioned by the Crime Commission and held him incommunicado until late Saturday morning. Then they picked up two other speakers at the Monday night rally, two young leaders of the militant Black Unity League of Kentucky (called BULK). A "court of inquiry" was hastily convened in police court for Saturday afternoon. Police charged that these three black people were plotting to dynamite oil refineries in the West End. They produced no evidence whatsoever to support these charges, but all three were jailed under a total of $175,000 bond.

WEST had got into operation Saturday morning as soon as we got word from the black community that a court of inquiry was to be held. Our action committee did a telephone campaign to get people to the courtroom. After the court hearing, we immediately set up a picket line at City Hall and issued a statement to the news media about scapegoating.

On Sunday, movement lawyers got a habeas corpus hearing in Circuit Court, attempting to free the three men. This failed. The hearing went on until 10 p.m. Immediately afterward, people from WEST, BULK, and other groups met at a West End church until after midnight to plan a counterattack. We decided that the main thing that must be done at that moment was to raise a voice in the community challenging the hysteria that was being built up by the scapegoating process—and to get the facts on what was happening to as many people as possible. We knew we could not depend on the commercial press to do this for us—even though the Louisville papers are better than most. So some of us stayed up all night and prepared a leaflet. The leaflet was headed "City Shifts Blame for Civil Disorders; Frames Black Leaders." The leaflet briefly stated the real causes of black rebellion, reviewed the facts of what had happened in Louisville, stated the circumstances of the arrest of the three black leaders, pointed out that this followed a national pattern of framing and jailing black militant leaders, and then said:

On June 1, in Louisville all of the court machinery and official apparatus sprang into action. Why? Because police said they had heard a rumor that black people planned to dynamite oil refineries.

Just four days before, police had shot into the homes of black people. Just three days before, two black people had been shot dead. This was no rumor; it was real. But no court of inquiry was convened, no official machinery sprang into action.

White Louisville must face the fact that this set of circumstances says one thing very clearly—that when white property appears to be threatened we do something about it, but when black lives are taken we do not. There followed the obvious specific demands.

In the next few days, WEST—mobilized by the action committee—distributed tens of thousands of copies of this leaflet—in downtown Louisville, in the courtrooms where hearings were being held, on campuses, at meetings throughout the city, by mailing to various lists. We also set up picket lines at City Hall and at the jail. The following weekend WEST, along with other groups in the black community and in the white one, set up a mass protest rally. A movement attorney from New York came and spoke about the national pattern of repression. Other speakers included local leaders—militant blacks, young and old; Muslims; and white activists. After the rally, many of the participants went to the home of the police-court judge to picket and attempt to see him. The meeting had been billed in the leaflet announcing it as a "rally against a police state," and it produced the greatest show of unity Louisville has seen in some time. The Steering Committee Against Repression, a coalition of Southern human rights groups, joined the local groups in sponsoring it and brought people a feeling of support from outside the community.

Meantime, other people in WEST were working on different levels. Some of them formed a more "respectable" delegation to City Hall—"respectable" not in the sense of who took part, as it was open to all, but in the sense of being made up of people who preferred not to picket or take part in direct action but who wanted to make a determined attempt to actually talk with the mayor. They did have a conference with the mayor and presented the WEST viewpoint. Other WEST people were contacting press representatives and giving them information on the real situation in the ghetto and a viewpoint they might not have otherwise had.

There is no doubt that within a week's time these efforts had had an impact on public opinion in this community. Newspaper articles and editorials were making note of the charge that the city was seeking scapegoats to avoid facing the real problems in the West End. The word "scapegoating" was getting into the popular vocabulary in Louisville—and at meetings throughout the city there were discussions as to whether this was what was happening. We believe this is testimony that if you speak the truth insistently, even in these times of hysteria, it *can* be heard.

After a week, bonds of the three "scapegoats" were reduced, and as this is written two have been released. The battle for truth is far from over, because the city is continuing its efforts to becloud the issues and to crush all who have challenged them. Also, the new Kentucky Un-American Activities Committee has been set up (KUAC—pronounced QUACK—we call it), and the governor has told them to look into the Louisville disorders. That's about all we need at this moment—those people dabbling in the serious social problems in this city.

However, for the time being we have at least slowed the steamroller of hysteria that was launched by the city in the wake of the uprising, and we have found that a voice of sanity can be heard. Temporarily at least we have built a little beachhead of resistance against the encroachment of a police state, a sort of liberated area. We will continue to build on this experience.

Meantime, WEST has started some long-range efforts. A legal committee has been set up; we raised money for an answering service, recruited seven lawyers each to be responsible for responding to calls one day a week, and made a mass distribution of a brochure "Know Your Rights" with a telephone number for people to call when they feel they are mistreated by police.

Also, we are preparing a brochure with pictures and information from interviews with shooting victims, documenting some of the things that happened during the rebellion.

In addition, a special committee is planning an information campaign in the poor-white areas of Louisville.

Meantime, too, other groups in the community have been doing other things. The local Religion and Race Council has been holding "truth sessions" each night at various churches in the white community where black speakers "tell it like it is" and things like the Kerner report are discussed. At the height of the rebellion, we found that while the Council of Churches telephone service functioned well as a "rumor center," it was not really able to be a service center for people in the West End—for example, people whose relatives were injured and needed to get through the curfew to care for them. Therefore, a start was made on a service center to be operated by a community organization within the West End. Since the disorders quieted so soon, this never really got into operation but would be able to, should the necessity arise again.

From our experience here, we are able to make these general suggestions to those who may be faced with similar crisis elsewhere:

1. Find out as much as you can about the experience of other communities. A report sent out by the Center for Emergency Support in Washington in April was invaluable to us. We didn't follow that model exactly, because circumstances here were different, but the ideas from Washington helped us. We have copies of the Washington report if you'd like to see it. We also have extra copies of this Louisville report. If other communities wish to share their experiences, we will help distribute them.

2. Don't underestimate what a few people who are ready to move can do. Only two or three people did the telephone campaign that gathered our first demonstration of white people. It could have been done by one person. The main thing is the will to act—rather than to spend time talking.

3. But don't forget either that many people who have not responded before will do so in a crisis. One of the most important things we did, even though it delayed action for a day, was to take the time necessary to gather together a larger group of people to share planning and decision-making. At a time like this, any sort of desire to dominate or creditmonger is fatal—we are in a life-and-death crisis and the point is to get the job done.

4. Assess the resources in your community, what groups already exist, and what they are doing. That way you won't waste time in a duplication of effort—but you may also find you'll have to do things we didn't have to

do here in Louisville. For example, in a community where no white groups are actively concerned with the ghetto crisis, an ad hoc group would need to do a number of things that other groups were doing in Louisville. If the Religion and Race Council had not already been planning discussion groups throughout the white community, our ad hoc groups should have tried to stimulate such meetings. It may seem more moderate than direct action—but it is essential to reach the unreached. If the Council of Churches had not been organized to provide some of the service functions needed during a rebellion (ministers at the jail, and the like) an ad hoc group would need to do this. In our own situation, because we did have other resources in the community, we were able to concentrate on public political positions and direct action—also very necessary and not likely to be done by more moderate groups.

5. Obviously you don't need to wait for a crisis to act in the white community. People usually do—unfortunately—but the educational work should be going on all the time. And efforts should be made to stimulate action against repression of black people *without* a crisis.

6. Once you are in the midst of a crisis, it is important to set up a mobile machinery—democratic and with as broad participation as possible in general policy-making, but able to act quickly when action is needed, without interminable board meetings and discussions. One way to do this is by seeking general agreement on basic approach and philosophy as West has done and is doing with its policy statement—then giving a small action committee the freedom to act within the bounds of that policy. For example, it was important here that people were willing to meet at midnight on a Sunday instead of waiting until morning and that some were willing to stay up all night to issue a crucial leaflet.

7. And finally, remember that we're in for a long struggle. You can build a beachhead in a week, as we did, but you can't win in that period of time— and the repressive forces hover on all sides. Saving America from a police state at this point in history will require the sustained and tireless efforts of all of us—and there will be times when we feel defeated—but we must keep on, on every front where we have maneuverability. The frightened people who are trying to settle our social problems by repression are many and powerful. They are playing for keeps and the stakes are high—involving no less than democracy itself and the future of all of us and of our children.

POSTSCRIPT

Two years later, Louisville's "Black Six" (three more black community leaders were indicted after the above case was written) who were charged with conspiring to destroy private property during disorders in May 1968 won a directed verdict of acquittal. On July 7, 1970, Circuit Judge S. Rush Nicholson said that the prosecution had failed to prove the charge of conspiracy against them. He instructed the jury to return a "not guilty" verdict after the prosecution closed its case.

The prosecution had asked for repeated delays in the trial—and at one point got it moved to rural Munfordville, Ky., after material charging the city with "scapegoating" was circulated widely in Louisville. It was moved back to Louisville after two white staff members of the Southern Conference Educational Fund (SCEF), Martha Allen and Mike Honey, sent a letter to everyone in the Munfordville phone book asking them to protest the trial. Honey and Allen were charged with jury tampering because of the letter, but have since been acquitted.

According to a SCEF communique, ". . . The Black Six case was won in the court of public opinion in Louisville at least a year ago—long before it came to trial in a court of law. The most important part of this, of course, was the support in the black community from the time of the first arrests and indictments. . . ."

Over the two years the White Emergency Support Team (WEST) did a great deal of work to reach sizeable sections of the white community. [*The original report was written in 1968 and the Postscript in 1970. SCEF has since dissolved but the work is carried on by other groups*] Ed.

Combating the Klan

Anne Braden

Generally, the organizing to combat the Klan that I have been involved in has conceived of itself as being more than just against the Klan. In every meeting that I have been to we begin by talking about the Klan and somebody always says, well, we can't just talk about the Klan—it's really racism that's the problem. And that's fine, but when somebody says that we shouldn't be concentrating on organizing against the Klan, I disagree with that. What I have seen happen is that people see the Klan on the rise again and it brings home to them that racism is not defeated. It shocks them. The Klan is so disreputable that organizing against it becomes sort of the opening wedge to get people to deal with racism in their communities on many levels. I think it has worked that way to a certain extent here in Louisville.

One time we heard it announced that David Duke, who was at that time a big Klan leader, was going to speak at a place out to the southwest of Louisville. That's an area where the Klan had once been active, and apparently they'd had an organization there all along, but it was not making itself too visible. Now they'd invited Duke to come and speak at this community center out there. A group of us decided we had to do something. We got in contact with all the organizations we could think of in town that would be opposed to the Klan: including church organizations, civil rights groups, women's organizations, the YWCA. We asked them to join in. At that time, Duke's faction of the Klan was trying to put forth this new and respectable image. He's very slick. He's the darling of the TV talk shows. He surprises people with his polished college-educated talk, not like the image of the old-fashioned Klansman. We thought that one thing that we needed to do was get out to people what he really stood for. Fortunately, there had been a good bit written on Duke by then including a whole section of a book called *The Klan* by Patsy Sims. She interviewed all the Klansmen and went to the rallies and knew what David Duke said at the rallies as opposed to what he said on TV. We got together a fact sheet organized in two columns: what David Duke's Klan says it stands for and what it really does stand for. Then we asked these other organizations to put their names on it with us as opposing Duke and we got a real good response. We got the YWCA, which is very good nationally but hadn't done much with it locally, and we got groups like the Catholic Commission on Justice and Peace and other church groups. I don't think we got any labor unions on that though we tried. Anyway, there were about twenty-four of those organizations that joined and then we had a demonstration, a peaceful picket line out in the front of where he was speaking. This turned out pretty well. We didn't get a lot of people because people were afraid—racists really run that part of the county. But we did get about seventy or eighty people, and that was more than the number who came out to hear Duke. This was a much lower turnout than he was used to getting. One of the guys who organized the rally said that more people would have come if it hadn't been for the picket line, and I'm glad he said it. Actually, I think it was just poor organizing on their part, or maybe a lack of interest, but it was nice that they gave us credit anyway.

In any case, the main thing was that we got this fact sheet circulated. We printed thousands of copies and we got people to take a stand against the Klan. The other thing that we did, because he reaches so many people through TV, was to contact all the TV stations beforehand. We said, if you are going to have that man on TV we want equal time. This discouraged one station from putting him on at all, but another one did put him on and gave us equal time. We had three people on there to counter what he had said. I think that you can use those equal time provisions and in this case it certainly helped us.

The coalition was dormant for a while, but then we heard that the Klan was going to have a big rally last September. So in the summer people began coming back together. We had maybe about thirty organizations in loose touch over the issue. We began planning a big counter-rally. It turned out that the Klan never actually had their rally, but the fact that they planned one gave us a chance to get organized. (I say "us," but I did not do nearly as much on this as other people here because I was away during a lot of this period.) We used our rally as a way of getting people to put their names on a statement—a very simple statement that said that we were opposed to the Klan and racism—a little bit more than that, but essentially that is all people were saying. Every organization in town worth anything, white and black, agreed to endorse that thing. The rally turned out very well; there were 600 or 700 people there and for the first time we really got a good bit of labor involvement, with speakers from some local unions.

I mentioned earlier that you get people together to talk about the Klan and it always leads to talk about what we can do about the more respectable forms of racism. After the big rally the group—they call themselves the Louisville Anti-Klan Coalition—began to look around to formulate an ongoing program. I think that in organizing around something like this there are two pretty obvious levels of organizing. One is that you need something public and visible. Something that lets people know, when they're sitting and wondering which side of the fence to jump on, that they have a place to go—that there are people who agree with them. That is why you do public things like the rally. That way you can hopefully recruit some people. Then there is the whole other thing which is sort of an educational job of reaching out to people who may very well not agree with you, or at least won't ever come to a rally. You have to figure out ways to reach these people. This group here has what they call an outreach committee. They borrowed a film on the Klan—there are several films on the Klan now—and in a very systematic way, they have called up church and community groups and said, "Can we come show this thing and have a discussion?" They get a lot of invitations that way. It isn't publicized a lot, but it is going on constantly.

As a way to reach out to people in the unions, they had an all-afternoon Saturday workshop on fighting racism in the workplace. They got C. P. Ellis as a speaker. He's an ex-Klansman who now is a union organizer in North Carolina, and he's a very interesting speaker because he tells you all the experiences he's been through and how he got from there to here. He's a very down-to-earth guy. They had a pretty good turnout and after Ellis spoke they broke down into small groups. People talked about things like why white workers needed to support black workers and what you could do in terms of not being pushed around on the job.

The Coalition is now planning a workshop for teachers and students in the schools, because there are some indications that junior Klans are being organized in the schools. The National Education Association and the Council on Interracial Books for children has prepared an excellent curriculum for junior and senior high school students on the history of the Klan and racism in this country.

I think there were some mistakes made here which I don't want to be too critical about, because I was not too much involved—I was out of town a lot right after the rally and I feel presumptuous criticizing. But I think it is probably something that happens in a lot of places. A lot of effort was put into that rally because it was an important statement to make to the community. Often when you put a lot of energy into something like that, people are sort of exhausted and you run the risk of losing the momentum that the rally gives you. After you get the people to take a public stand you really have to work to keep them involved and find something for them to do—put them on a committee, call them up and inform them of a meeting.

Sometimes that does not happen after a big event, but the ideal thing is that you pick up on the enthusiasm that the rally gives people and give them something else to do pretty quick.

The other debate which has come up here recently is that they had this very simple statement that people signed and endorsed. Some people got the notion that they should deepen that statement further, that it didn't give enough analysis of where racism was coming from and all that. And so we got to spending a lot of time drafting a new statement that was more of a political analysis of racism. All of it was probably true; but it seems to me that whenever you are trying to form a broad coalition that involves diverse groups, which you really have got to do if you're going to be effective, you have to keep your unity position as simple as possible. The more complex it gets, the more that people have to agree to, the more people you are going to lose. That debate is still going on here; they have not changed the statement and I think they probably will not. I think it would be a mistake because I think what would happen is that they might have a more developed statement and it might even be more correct, but they will lose people; whereas you can bring a lot of different people together around the basic question a simple thing opposing racism.

There's another issue that organizing against the Klan points up. And that's the way organizing at the local and at the national level tie together. There had been this horrible incident in Greensboro in which Klansmen and Nazis had killed five people who were members of the Communist Workers Party. People in our local Anti-Klan group—we had about 24 organizations in our coalition—were contacted and helped organize a couple of buses to go to Greensboro to protest. They were part of an enormous demonstration. In the course of this organizing, many people that we did not know before or very well got involved. People who had not been active in Louisville before were ready to continue to be active after that. When they rode to Greensboro on the bus and got to know people they came back to work with us. My feeling is that the local and national level organizing tie in together. Just organizing locally you can get pretty discouraged with what you accomplish in that it is so little, but if you get the feeling that you are part of this big movement it gives you a real boost. Organizing at the local and national level feeds back and forth.

POSTSCRIPT

The particular anti-Klan coalition described here no longer exists, although it has reappeared in new forms at least twice since, at times when Klan activity became visible in the community. This is what has happened in many places; people come together in an anti-Klan coaliton when there's a crisis, when the Klan is visible and active. As such organized activity counters the Klan drive and it becomes less visible, the coalitions disperse and people go back to activity in other things. But in

Louisville I think we gained something each time such a coalition formed, each time new people were reached and activated; there's a growing body of people we can go back to as new situations arise. I think every community needs an on-going, always active anti-racist organization, because racism is ever-present. In Louisville the Kentucky Alliance Against Racist & Political Repression plays that role.

CHAPTER 5

Community Workers in Service Agencies

Administrators and practioners in service agencies are very often involved in community work essential to agency survival and expansion, and necessary for fulfillment of their service objectives. The practioners in these cases are all dealing with the input of clients and community people in determining policies and procedures of the agencies. All of these cases were collected for the first edition of this book but are included here because the practice principles they illustrate are timeless.

In "A Settlement-House Staff Loses Its Building" the agency was faced with a crisis. Systematic input from the community was obtained concerning the needs of that community. With this input the agency was able to shift their domain in terms of (1) the social problems covered, (2) the populations served, and (3) the services rendered. The organizer contrasts his active, emotional participation with what he sees as the professional reserve and scientific objectivity advocated by other community organizers. What do you think of his style of relating to community people?

The administrator charged with setting up a new multiservice center also attempts to organize an area advisory committee. He finds that local leadership is very self-serving, and long-standing rival factions in the community vie for influence on the advisory committee. It is not unusual to be faced with rival factions or personal animosities when organizing a new group in the community. The organizer must use all the skills at his command to help the group overcome these difficulties. This organizer chose not to deal directly with these issues. What are some of the other strategies he might have used? In the end he feels he has failed because he has input only from the advisory committee, and they are not representative of the constituency his agency is being set up to serve. Do you think a more skillful organizer would have fared any better?

Most social agencies are faced with recruiting and training nonprofessional people for their boards. In "Leadership Training for Board Members" the director of volunteer services for a welfare council explains how he and his staff have attempted to be more responsive to the input of people from the committee his agency serves. Instead of having one big, window-dressing meeting, they had regional meetings to encourage face-to-face interaction among board members. The case illustrates a very real problem of welfare councils. One of the participants accuses the welfare council of not being responsive to the most critical need of the black community and not having black people properly represented on the board. In a very real sense the board received more of an education than they bargained for.

In "Mrs. Kaplan Speaks Up" a planner for a welfare council brings a group of "experts" together to start a process of planning a multiservice center of senior citizens in the center of town. They all agree that this is a good idea. Then Mrs. Kaplan, a senior citizen, who has been a volunteer for years, points out that older people need small neighborhood centers, not a large downtown center. The narrator, to his credit, is very responsive to her input and not only begins seriously planning along the lines she suggested but decides to have input from senior citizens in all the communities where centers are planned.

In the final case, the administrator of a narcotics program in a suburb finds that attempting to assist the addict through a service agency was doomed to failure. This is a very rare instance of an administrator of a direct-service agency actually choosing to phase out a service. The only hope he saw was to change the community's attitude toward addiction. He used all the resources at his command to influence community opinion. This included using unexpected help from the mayor. It also included phasing out a very informed and active citizen advisory committee in order to staff the mayor's task forces. Note the groups towards which the education efforts were targeted. Are these the same groups you would have chosen?

Building an Advisory Committee

I was a supervisor in the City Welfare Department before going on loan to the mayor's Human Resources Commission. My job was to set up a multiservice center in a mixed middle-income, working class area. In trying to organize local people into an advisory council, I found out that local leadership is jealous and self-serving. Grass-roots representation is hard to locate and harder still to get moving.

I had a conference with the Commission's program director in his office. I was to set up a community center that would promote a supermarket of social services. (There had been much beating of the chest by politicians about the program.) I was expected to more thoroughly acquaint the people with the available services. In that conference the program director gave me the impression that the local block club, church groups, and the like were grass roots in nature. He gave me the names of two people whom he thought to be powerful community leaders and springboards to effective action in the community. I was to organize an area advisory committee. He said little else. The conference was in fact very brief.

One other man, several years my junior, was also transferred from the Welfare Department to be my assistant in the area. We sent letters to all the groups in the area stating what we were in the process of planning for a multiservice center. We received many invitations to speak that we accepted as rapidly as we could. I thought that that was the best means available to familiarize the community with the services that would be offered through the center.

We had no physical facilities for the center. The people of the community were theoretically supposed to, and I believe expected to, have a hand in selection of the building. I soon realized, however, that this process would take too long. My assistant and I personally combed the area by car in search of a building that would be near the center of the target area, easily accessible by public transportation, and large enough to house the proposed services. After weeks of frustration, I finally chose one that is poorly located but of adequate size. We planned several storefront operations to correct the poor location of this building.

Shortly after the acquisition of the physical facility, I sent a letter to the block clubs in the area inviting them to attend a public planning meeting. During these weeks I also talked with the two people suggested by the Commission's program director: Mrs. Clark and Mrs. Coombs. Mrs. Clark assured me numerous times that she did not seek an official leadership position in the area advisory committee. She said she already had enough to do as president of the neighborhood association of block clubs. With this in mind and in an effort to convince the community that I was willing to place the leadership in their hands, I named Mrs. Clark as the temporary chairman for the meeting. As the meeting got underway, rather than talk about substantive issues as I had anticipated, she led the discussion to structure and organization. Mrs. Clark was nominated from the floor for the position of chairman of a "steering committee." She was quickly elected by a fairly large majority. A Mr. Wolfson and several other community people also received nominations. I sat on the stage dumbfounded and not sure of what to do as the events quickly followed one another. Later in that meeting several members of churches complained that the procedures used by Mrs. Clark were poor and unfair. I believe that Mr. Wolfson led in voicing these complaints.

Mrs. Clark's tactics in the meeting produced many ill feelings and represented a step backward for the Commission. Mrs. Coombs confided in me after the meeting that she felt betrayed by her friend Mrs. Clark. She said, however, that she had anticipated something of this sort. She maintained her relationship with Mrs. Clark and with the Commission, and was, in fact, elected vice chairman of the steering committee. At the meeting and after it I think that animosity toward Mrs. Clark oozed from many in the community. I felt that this animosity probably spread to me and the Commission because of my selection of her as meeting chairman. My presence on stage coupled with inactivity in the case of Mrs. Clark's tactics gave the impression to everyone in the meeting that we backed Mrs. Clark.

In the light of both this situation and my proven unfamiliarity with its petty politics and the like, I decided to back off for some time. In the one month before the next planned meeting of the steering committee, my assistant and I did accept speaking engagements from the block clubs, churches, and so on. We spoke at least once a day and sometimes as often as four or five times a day. There was nothing else we could do. We tried to disseminate accurate information about the program and sought to explore program possibilities with the area's residents.

In the week after that first meeting I also attempted to disassociate myself from Mrs. Clark in the eyes of the community. I wanted to make it clear that she was officially supported only by the organization of block clubs of which she was president. As chairman of a steering committee for the advisory committee for the center, she was to call meetings, nothing more. I did retain some contact with Mrs. Clark. More specifically, I accepted an invitation to speak at a meeting of her block club organization. At one point she also had me over for lunch. It became evident that she was not a very smooth operator and that she rather openly sought patronage. She wanted a staff position in the in-service training program of the new center. Mrs. Coombs and others in the community openly sought jobs.

A few days before the scheduled second meeting of the steering committee I met Mr. Wolfson on the street, totally by chance. I suggested that he might come to the scheduled meeting (simply because I sought as much community participation as possible). Mrs. Clark came late for the meeting. Early in the meeting, Mr. Wolfson asked me, from the floor, whether it was legally possible for the steering committee to transform itself into the advisory committee. I replied from my position in the audience that this was indeed possible. The idea, of course, appealed to all of those on the steering committee and Mr. Wolfson's motion quickly carried. Correct procedure dictated that a new chairman and so on should be elected. Mr. Wolfson was immediately nominated and elected to the position of chairman.

I learned later that Mr. Wolfson and Mrs. Clark were the leaders of rival factions in the block-club association. There was considerable personal rivalry between them as well. From the discussions after the meeting and from observations during the meeting, it also became evident that the community representatives on the steering committee were by and large rather middle class. Mrs. Clark, for example, had a good home, as did many others. I also realized that these people were very skillful in the use of parliamentary procedure.

In the regular monthly meeting of the advisory committee that followed, I attempted not to get too involved. I did not want to take sides. During the meetings of the advisory committee I sat in the audience and participated only to give official views on issues that arose. In a way, I played the role of a technical guest. During these months my administrative tasks multiplied immensely because of the assignment of regular civil-service personnel to the Center.

During these first months of operation, each community contact pressed home more firmly to me the realization that the block clubs were not as potent as my superiors had led me to believe. My feeling that the advisory committee did not reach the man in the street also grew. A month or two after Mr. Wolfson was elected, I explained to him in detail what I thought about lack of representation in the advisory committee. He concurred.

On my own initiative, I talked with school community agents in the area in an attempt to obtain a sampling of ADC and welfare recipients. The school community agents contacted a sampling of welfare recipients and invited them to participate in the advisory committee meetings. Twenty-one in all were contacted. Of these, only eight showed up at any of the meetings. All of them were very ill at ease. Four agreed to serve on the advisory committee. Only two ever came to later meetings. Only one ever opened his mouth. Inadequate representation on the advisory committee of the people we are supposed to be serving still stands as my major problem.

A few months after his election, it became evident that Mr. Wolfson had personality problems: at a minimum, it was evident that his motivations for assuming the chairmanship were something less than laudable. For example, after several meetings he began boasting of the fact that he was a public servant through his role and also boasting of the fact that his outside work yielded him an income of $12,000 per year. He also began making decisions without the consent of the advisory committee.

Mr. Wolfson came up for reelection in June of this year. I did nothing to influence the course of the election. I felt that he was OK and that his opponent was not too strong. I also felt that although Mr. Wolfson and his opponent, Mrs. Downs, were about equally qualified, Mr. Wolfson was more thoroughly versed in the matters of the community.

As it turned out, Mrs. Downs received a very substantial vote but did not win. Mr. Wolfson grew more militant almost immediately after he was reelected. At the next meeting he took the occasion to demand undefined powers for himself. He threatened to resign if he did not receive them. No one wanted him to resign.

Last week he came to the Center at about lunchtime with two people who needed service. Later he complained that the people had had to wait 45 minutes before they received attention. He failed to mention that one woman got the job she sought and that the other woman was unqualified for the specific job she sought. In private, Mr. Wolfson is still very agreeable. However, in public meetings he is a heller. He is not interested in solutions; he wants only to select issues and beat the desk with them.

A few days ago, Mr. Wolfson proposed to me that the community aides be rotated in order to further personal and professional roles. I pointed out to him that the aim of the Commission was public service and not professional growth of personnel. He persisted with a fury that has become characteristic of him. I finally suggested to him that if he wanted to pursue the matter further he should take it directly to the central office.

To my frustration, I find that as an administrator for the Commission I am dealing primarily with the area advisory committee and with the Commission personnel. I feel that I should be working personally (and through my staff) more directly with the grass roots of the area. However, I do not have enough people. The VISTA volunteers that we are scheduled to get this year may be a shot in the arm. They will be living in the area and are sufficiently idealistic to get a following. If these volunteers are not successful in engaging the grass roots, I have contemplated propagandizing every fifth person in the target area to make them aware that there is an advisory committee of which they can become a part. I have also contemplated trying to get key contact people on each block.

A Settlement-House Staff Loses Its Building

I was faced with a crisis. I had recently been notified by the church group that supports our settlement house that they were interested in continued support of our services, but not of the building. We were free to take over the building and finance it ourselves, or redirect our services in some other manner. In either case, the church would continue to provide us with staff funding. To be honest with you, I regarded the letter as a mixed blessing. The settlement house had been operating in this neighborhood for 40 years. The problems had changed and the traditional program that we still conducted seemed a far cry from the community's needs. There had been three police-community confrontations within the month and one bombing of a local retail merchant's store. The schools are bad and the whole area is very tense. Urban Renewal has never considered it a target. For some reason it's become a forgotten area.

My first response to the letter was, "Hell, they're giving these people the shaft again. We're going to stay in the building." When I cooled down, I realized that we had been too tied to the building, and that we had done too little in terms of moving out and handling real community problems. I shared the letter and my feelings with the board of directors. Of course, I first discussed it with a number of key board people, especially the chairman of the program committee. When the board met, they told me to do three things: (1) determine the problems in the area, (2) deter-mine those services that were critically needed and suggest how we ought to be involved in meeting those needs, and (3) answer the question about whether we needed the building to offer our services.

Now when I say that the board delegated this authority to me, I don't mean to imply I'm a passive guy. The program chairman and I thought these issues through pretty carefully. And I certainly wasn't going to do all the work. We involved all the board members, for example, in meetings with community and neighborhood groups. As most of the board people are not from the local area, I wanted them to get a feel for what the real problems were. We set up different kinds of meetings. We involved the "respectable" community leaders, the agency people, and some of the political leaders. We also asked to be invited to regular meetings of other community groups: neighborhood councils, welfare-rights organizations, churches, and so on. Some of them didn't even know we existed. But in each case, I told them of our dilemma, and that we wanted to find out what people thought the communi-ty's real needs were and if any of them could be met with the settlement-house program in the building. Or I would ask if our staff could be helpful in some other ways.

The board members present took good notes at each of these meetings. The program committee chairman and I had developed an inventory of things to look for. So when a board person took minutes, he only recorded those things that were significant.

After nine or ten of these meetings, we found certain themes emerging. People in the community needed (1) recreation and social services, (2) day care and preschool services, and (3) expert help in running organizations and all the pro-cesses that are involved in community organization. We shared these findings with our board and set up three task forces.

I worked with the CO task force. We tried to figure out how our staff could be helpful in pulling this community together. Several alternatives presented themselves.

Were we to form an organization of citizens or residents ourselves, or were we to help other groups get organized for whatever purpose they had in mind? Should we develop a community council of all the other organizations in the community, or should we hire ourselves out as consultants to groups and individuals that wanted to engage in social action on behalf of the community?

I had really thought hard about these issues. My model in working with my community is to be as articulate and to the point as I can. I don't necessarily throw out all the ideas. My people wouldn't stand for that. But I do say that if we are going to do this or that, then the consequences for us are that we are going to have to be willing to commit this or that other thing. In other words, I want them to see the consequences of their decisions. I am not one of these guys who holds off, cool and aloof.

My affiliation with the task force on day care and preschool services was primarily as supervisor of another staff member. After documenting needs for day care, they began negotiating with the antipoverty agency for a demonstration project. Our hope was that if we could get something started in this neighborhood, it could spread to a citywide project. Even if Head Start or the antipoverty programs couldn't fund us, we might at least start a citywide "mothers for day care" organization.

The recreation and social-services task force visited every local agency. The most important thing they found out was that services were fragmented, and that someone had to take the initiative in pulling services together in some integrated manner.

It's interesting how all three task forces pointed to the need for CO expertise. The board examined the findings of each of the three task forces and voted to accept eviction. It was a historic meeting. We decided that night to stop being a settlement house and to become an action agency. Our feedback from the church that supported us was positive. We knew we would have their continued support. We had some question about the welfare council, however, They provide us with 50 percent of our budget. I wondered what they might think of our becoming an action agency, concerned with organizing and planning. The council has been very jealous about its planning function. But they can't get down to the neighborhood level, and we were right there. It might take a little effort, but I was sure we could convince them that we were on the right track.

As a community organizer, I am very verbal and very honest about the way I feel about things. I guess I possess a certain charisma in the way I function. Once I get started, I can easily move a whole group. I usually see a direction in which I want to move and I can convince people that this is the way they ought to want to move as well. I know that this may not be good "process." It's just like "Mr. Charlie" walking into a neighborhood and telling the people how to function. But I try to listen and sense what people are feeling, and then I respond to what they feel. I guess I am manipulative, but I'm not sure whether being manipulative is good or bad. I can really listen to people, but unlike the caseworker, I become an extremely active and emotional participant in the whole process. I have feelings about what transpires and frequently express anger when I feel it. I have none of the professional reserve and scientific objectivity advocated by the profession. And people are candid in the way in which they express their thoughts to me. They can get angry at me and I can take it without hating them for it. I think it's healthy.

Leadership Training for Board Members

As director of volunteer services for the Welfare Council, the business of training new board members for our affiliate agencies falls into my lap. Our Board Member Institutes have been in operation now for some 25 years. As long as anyone can remember, these Institutes have been held on one day at a big hotel downtown. They have been well attended, accompanied by a great deal of fanfare. We have 235 member agencies. We get between four and five hundred people to attend.

If I had to describe their objectives, I would say, for the record, that these Institutes were established to enable new board members to better understand the problems of their community, to give them some new insights into the problems of social welfare, and to train them to do their jobs as volunteers more effectively. Off the record, however, I would have to tell you that the whole thing has degenerated into a big public-relations affair—a way of bolstering a new board member's ego, and making it look to the community as if the Council is doing a job. Actually, I can tell you, not much learning goes on.

I would say the Institute we had two years ago was a total failure. A big luncheon in a swanky hotel doesn't cut the ice anymore. Boards have changed a great deal during the last five years. You don't think of a Board member arriving in a chauffer-driven car in a mink coat anymore. A lot of our agencies have become decentralized. Many of them are reaching people from minority groups. Neighborhood people and service recipients are finding their ways onto agency boards.

You might be able to bring four or five hundred people from all our agencies into a single room, but you certainly can't get them to hear the same things from the same speaker anymore. Their backgrounds and their perspectives have changed. That's how it should be. If welfare is going to be a community function, then policy making has to be shared with every sector of the community.

Our Institutes have always been planned by a lay group, a subcommittee of the board of directors for the Community Council. In addition, I have an advisory committee that works directly with me—these are board people from our member agencies who have particular interest in the whole question of volunteers. I have a lot of discretion in choosing the advisory committee. Over the past few years, I have recruited people who represent minority groups and neighborhoods that have never had any voice in giving direction to Council affairs. Last year, I decided to have my advisory group meet together with the subcommittee of the board to plan the Institute.

The planning process was educational in itself. The really different points of view expressed, reflected quite a range of socioeconomic backgrounds. If nothing else, everyone agreed that there was something wrong with the Institutes and that somehow they had to be made more pertinent. We couldn't resolve the issue of content, but we did reach unanimity on breaking down into smaller regional Institutes. We conducted four of them in four parts of town, giving us a chance to meet in smaller groups. We hoped for more opportunity for discussion and fuller participation.

The big decision we had to make was whether to assign new Board members to Institutes based on the proximity to the agencies they represented. In essence this would segregate people by neighborhood or sections of the city. We decided not to. Our purpose for having regional Institutes, we decided, was not to serve regional interests but to encourage more face-to-face interaction between board members from all our agencies. Don't think we didn't have some resistance from within the Council. A lot of my colleagues thought I was being foolish. Several Council board members raised a big fuss. A lot of people wouldn't go to working-class neighborhoods. We lost some people (I guess you would call them the old guard), but we picked up a lot of new people. I had to push hard to get what I wanted, but I'm convinced it has been worth the effort. It actually worked out quite well. Board members related to each other not just as members of an audience but also as people who represented "community leadership," agency clientele, or constituencies such as neighborhood councils.

This year we decided to go the same route—regional Institutes. A good deal further along in our own consensus, we were able to think through some very imaginative program content. Before the Institutes actually took place, we had arranged field trips to poverty areas and to a variety of community agencies like the courts, a mental hospital, the welfare department, a family service agency, and the like. We wanted people to have a feel for what welfare was all about before they attended. But were we unprepared for what was to take place!

We planned a theme to focus on "urban problems." We wanted our members to understand and appreciate the need for public housing and good welfare programs, to understand why there seems to be an increasing movement towards decentralization of services and their control. We also wanted people to get a feel for the reasons behind the development of indigenous social movements.

At the first of our regional Board Institutes this year, a black participant stood up and challenged the main speaker. He said that white people did not understand the problems of blacks and that it was ludicrous for a white man to be standing at the podium talking about housing problems, poverty, and the need for better education, when in fact all we were doing was perpetuating our racist society with handout programs and palliative efforts that made no dent on the social structure. He was obviously intelligent and very articulate. He asked that we take a one-hour break in order for the black participants to caucus. The chairman opened up the issue to the floor. There were some heated feelings pro and con, mostly among the white members, for about 15 minutes. Finally someone said, "If the black participants want to have a black caucus, then let's have a white caucus."

I met with the white group. There seemed to be a lot of sympathy for the black perspective, but a good deal of uneasiness as well. Since no one was altogether sure what the black caucus was discussing, the white board members could do very little but share their confusions, air their guilt, or give verbal support to the needs of blacks for self-determination. I must tell you, I was not sure how to play my own role. I was hoping that Charles Patterson, a black member of our staff who went to the black caucus, was having less difficulty than I. It was a futile hope.

The black members decided to develop their own association within the Council. Without deciding on the name, they decided to elect temporary officers and to contact black board members from all the other agencies in town. They wanted to elect Charles as secretary because of his position as a staff member on a council, but he declined on the same grounds, although he later told me that he was really torn. He felt the blacks should have their own association. He told me that he felt he "belonged" to them, and that he felt he should be their staff person.

At the end of the hour, the black caucus issued a statement accusing the Welfare Council and the welfare agencies in this community of being racist and against the interests of black people. They demanded one third representation on the Council board (roughly the same proportion as there are blacks in the central city). They also called for a stoppage of all Board Member Institutes not planned with black people, or not in the interests of black people. Apologizing for the disruption, but explaining that it was long overdue, they marched out of the Institute, which they said was not for them.

The whites who were left discussed the issue for about two hours. It was a good discussion in that it cleared the air and opened up a lot of feelings. It was a poor discussion in that there were no blacks to whom we could relate.

All this happened three weeks ago. I'm not sure where we go next.

Mrs. Kaplan Speaks Up

As a planner for the Welfare Council, I work with a lot of city agencies. Because of my interest and my background, I have a lot of dealings with the school system and with the Parks and Recreation Department. For some time we had been concerned with the fact that so many senior citizens would hang around the downtown area aimlessly, with almost nothing to do. The small park near the Civic Center was full of older people. The Recreation Department offered a fairly good program, and the school system conducted a variety of evening adult-education courses in the area. Still, most of these people needed other kinds of professional services. A lot of the people who filled the park looked pretty desolate and lonely. I met with people from the school system and Recreation Department, and while both groups seemed interested, neither felt that they could commit additional funds or that they really had the jurisdiction to provide the kind of counseling services that were needed. People from both departments were willing to help me organize some other kind of service, however. I called a lot of the clergymen in the area and asked them if they had noticed the older people looking hopeless and helpless in the park. Most of them agreed that they had been troubled by this fact for some time. I invited those interested to become part of a group that might perhaps be able to set up a store front with all kinds of professional help for the senior citizens who lived or frequented the downtown area.

At an initial discussion meeting, we pulled together 25 or 26 people to talk about the issues. I invited Professor Clark and Dean Nosechal of the School of Social Work. Both had made studies of the needs of senior adults in this city, and had concluded that one of the top priorities was the development of a multiservice center for older people in the downtown area. Professor Clark talked to the group about his findings. Now get this scene.

Everything is going along well. I am beginning to get a nice glow of satisfaction. Professor Clark is really detailed in his recommendations, and the clergymen and some of the downtown business people there are nodding in agreement that something needs to be done. Then Mrs. Kaplan, a senior citizen who had heard about the meeting, gets up and starts talking.

She looks at me and she says, "Mr. Melan, I don't want to hurt your feelings. You spent a lot of time getting this group together and it's wonderful. But, you do not need a downtown center for older people in this city. What you do need are small neighborhood centers where a lot of older people live and which they can walk to. Those people who need the care the most do not have transportation money and do not come downtown. What's more, these people do not come out in bad weather and you do not see them hanging around the park in the winter. Where are they to go? The people in the park come down here two months out of the year. True, a few of us live downtown, but most of the people who come downtown are not the people who need services. These senior citizens come downtown to shop or go to the theater and they're not going to use the storefront that you're talking about."

You know I'll never forget how I felt. My first reaction was to be angry at her because the experts, I mean everything I had based the calling of this group together on, had been leading us to designing a new program downtown. Then here in the flash of a pan and out of the mouth of a person who was not a professional, who had not been working as a volunteer for years, and who had never conducted a study of senior adults, the rug was pulled straight out from under my feet. I think I was speechless for a moment, but I did a lot of quick thinking. I said, "You know you're absolutely right. You're absolutely right. I think I've been wrong and I am grateful to you for this suggestion." I wasn't even sure exactly what I was going to say until I said it.

You know, as a result of her comments, we gave up the idea of a downtown center. We are now working very closely with the city redevelopment authority, with each of the major Protestant churches, and with one of the local Catholic parishes. It didn't take us long to find out that there were hundreds of people on Old Age Assistance or on Social Security and that there were few agencies serving the neighborhoods in which they lived.

We are in the process now of trying to get funded to set up a couple of pilot demonstration projects in three of the census tracts. Now the easiest thing to do would be just to get the money, find some buildings, and open up some storefronts. But that's not the way we are going to go about doing it. I think Mrs. Kaplan taught me something. We are going to go about it the long, hard way. We are going to talk to senior adults in each of the neighborhoods, and find out what they really think they need. Then we're going to go out and find a top-notch administrator to head up the program. If possible, we are going to find a retired person who can do the job, and get him to train some other older people as neighborhood aides to locate those in trouble and in need of help. What we're talking about is a senior adult service center made up of senior adults and for senior adults. I have a feeling we are going to not only find people in need, but also lots of people with things to offer and no outlet. Why just think of senior adults as people who have nothing but "needs"? After all, they weren't senior adults all their lives.

Killing It and Making It: The Evolution of a Narcotics Program

WE CHANGE THE FUNCTION OF THE CENTER

Finally, we were unencumbered by groups that were incapable or unwilling to assume responsibility for the program. I did not anticipate that we would be able to achieve miraculous things in this town. I said to myself that I would give it the old college try to see if the intervention of an agency could do something about addiction in a suburban community. I knew that it had not in Los Angeles. I thought that suburbia might be different, but I found that it is not—the problem of addiction in suburbia is no different from the problems of addiction in Los Angeles.

About two and a half years after the project started we had done nothing to stem the tide of addiction. We were forced to ask ourselves what we should do. The attempt to assist the addict through an agency was doomed to failure. We had two alternatives. One was to continue as we were doing—assuring salaries to our staff. The other was to close out the agency. We almost did. I felt that we should not use public funds to maintain staff. I felt that we were bound to close out the agency unless we could make a valid case in its defense. We were just patching up a few people at tremendous cost.

At this point we called in two top people from the New York Medical Center to advise us. They pointed out that there were important things that had to be done. They identified for us how the community was creating addiction. It is a long story. Suffice it to say that it's true. If a great deal of the social fabric is not changed, including the legal structure, you won't get any place with addiction. Even though I'm a community organizer, I had become so involved in directing an agency that I failed to realize that addiction was not a problem of the addict. It was a problem *for* the addict, and *of* society.

OK, the experts helped us see that. But we did not know what to do about it. One possibility was to document the structural and social causes of addiction. If we could do that, at least this community might be able to recognize how it was creating the problem. An effective study and follow-up program might have big payoff for other communities as well.

I wasn't sure where to start until I thought of Betty Vendeaux, a reporter and sometimes T.V. commentator on health and welfare problems. I had met her when I first came to town. Five other people and I had given panel presentations on the problems of addiction, and she approached me with the thought that the whole show was worth a story. I didn't go for it. I like to work behind the scenes. I hate big spreads that promise more than you can produce. Besides, the newspapers usually give a very bad press to volatile issues like drug addiction. At that time, I had completely avoided her.

Now I called her, and asked if she was still interested in addiction. I reminded her that she had wanted to do a story once, and told her I was glad she didn't. We had not been very successful. Now, I told her, we were moving into a project that would document the origins of addiction but would only be successful if it included community education. She was still interested. I told her I would let her do the story, if she underwent an educational program. We had recently instituted a six-session community-education program on narcotics. She agreed. Then I told Betty that she would have to let me see the final copy on everything to be released. I especially wanted her to concentrate on narcotics and addiction. I wanted very little in the papers about the Narcotics Center. Community education, not agency publicity, was the issue. Again, she agreed.

After she had undergone the training program and had several talks with me, she arranged an interview with the mayor. The mayor actually wound up interviewing her. He literally peppered her with questions about what was going on in addiction. She emphasized that he should contact the Center. "After all," she said, "it is here."

Then she urged me repeatedly to go talk with the mayor. I didn't want to get involved in politics. Political involvement is what destroyed treatment of addiction in Los Angeles. I saw no reason to play this game of frivolities in this city.

Finally, I did speak with him and found him to be a completely different breed of guy. In effect, he said that he would like to do something with what we had learned. In no uncertain terms, he stated that we could have the weight of his office if we would advise him on how we wanted it used. Frankly, I would have liked to not get involved—I would have liked to just sit back and write a book. Obviously, as a professional, I could not do that—I had to take the opportunity before me.

The completely accidental focus of the mayor's interest permitted us to do more than merely articulate the variables that caused addiction. A health-oriented mayor who agrees to keep it out of politics and spearhead a task force—you simply can't walk away from it. It is a very big undertaking. From a selfish viewpoint I would have preferred to quietly sit back, but the fact that we could do something with our research was the point at which I knew the project could move.

At this time, we had a pretty good advisory committee going. You remember, this is what had become of the original Center board. The advisory committee was broken up into several viable subgroups. They were each made up of different types: school personnel, public health workers, employers and personnel managers, social-agency types, and the like. All these people entered training programs. Once the professionals were trained, we trained lay people and added them to the subcommittees. At first, we had expected the training and establishment of semiautonomous subunits by function or field to be an end in itself. Each one could use its new knowledge to effectuate changes in its own field.

This approach worked for a while. Then came the pressure from the mayor's office. He wanted us to set up task forces to study and recommend programs for the elimination of addiction or for its treatment on a central and coordinated basis. I felt that the opportunity was great. But we did not have the manpower to keep up our work with the function-field subcommittees of our advisory committee and to staff the mayor's task forces at the same time. We had to make a choice. Something had to give. We decided to let the advisory committee and its functional-field subcommittees go. It was a hard decision. When you are a community organizer, you hate to let a viable structure fall apart.

Working with the mayor, we changed our approach somewhat. We focussed only on the people who had enough influence to change the community's posture towards addiction. Some were people we identified as well-known community influentials. Others were the key administrators or decision-makers in the relevant organizations. Actually, our work with the advisory committee and our educational efforts and training programs bore fruit at this point. We were well known and had already been in contact with many of the people we were now trying to influence anew.

We aimed our efforts at the following:

1. The coordinating agencies, such as the welfare council in the voluntary arena and city and state governments in the public arena.

2. The relevant caretaker services, such as the welfare department, vocational rehabilitation, family-service agencies, recreation, or group-service groups.
3. Community leadership (the power structure)—often we involved the wives of powerful men, knowing that their family names committed the husbands.
4. The general community—in essence we said that if you want to combat the problem, you have to be sympathetic, patient and understanding—like bring an addict home for supper—I mean it.
5. The schools.
6. T.V., the newspapers, the local radio station—Betty took charge of this.

It is hard to tell, but I think we are on our way to something important.

LOOKING BACK

Often, CO projects develop from completely accidental events. Often the only credit that community organizers can take is that they saw a hot opportunity go by and grabbed it. Many of the neat reports of community organizers do not reflect this; they make it appear calculated. However, more often than not, the CO worker moves with a situation rather than having control over it.

In this project, we started out with an attempt to help the addict through an agency. After a few years we were ready to quit. Then we aimed toward research and extensive documentation of the fact that addiction is an adaption to the environment. From here we moved to the formation of an educational task force from the structure of the advisory committee (previously the Center board). This educational task force was seen at the time to be an end goal in itself, and then, completely by accident, the mayor came along and in effect asked us if we wanted to get action on our new-found knowledge.

I think I like the way things are going. I can't take credit for them. I didn't plan way in advance for things to turn out this way. I guess you could say my staff and I set the stage for certain things to happen. The good community organizer is the guy who can spot an opportunity and take it. He has to be willing to give up a pet project, or even something he has invested a lot of himself in. You've got to take yourself seriously as a professional, but you can't be too concerned about yourself personally. Ego has no part in this business. Sometimes you just have to know how to admit failure. Lots of times you can't do a thing right. You have to know when to stay and when to get out.

6

Tenant Organizing

Since the mid 1960s, organizers have increasingly directed their attention to problems related to housing. The concern is easy to understand. Most organizing with low-income groups has been neighborhood based, and neighborhood conditions are intimately interrelated with housing. Over the years, tenant organizing has become very sophisticated. A wealth of experience has been accumulated and the cases in this chapter necessarily reflect only a small part of it. Still, some of the most important arenas of tenant organizing are represented in these cases—organizing public housing tenants, fighting displacement, organizing a tenant union, a rent strike, a rent control initiative campaign, and a fight against arson.

Lawrence Grossman prepared the materials on "Organizing Tenants in Low-Income Public Housing." This case is from the first edition and was written during the 1960s, but these exact situations exist today and the case is quite applicable to current conditions. Some of the federal regulations have changed, but the organizing principles are as timely as ever.

This case is distinctive in its description of the analytic and conceptual steps the organizers undertook in formulating their objectives, their strategies, and their tactics. They systematically selected a "core committee" of residents. Their decision to intervene manipulatively in the tenant decision-making process was also based on careful analysis. One may quarrel with their analysis of the situation and with their handling of some of the issues, but one cannot find fault with their efforts to be critical at every stage in the organizing process.

San Francisco's International Hotel is a case that is very complex; in fact, the struggle lasted for 10 years. It is narrated here by Chester Hartman, a very astute housing planner and an activist with many years experience. One of the central housing battles going on in cities all over the country is over the displacement of low- and moderate-income residents, a large proportion of whom are people of color. That the organizing effort in this case was sustained for such a long time is testament to the depth of feeling people have about this issue as well as the fact that San Francisco has a long history of protracted struggles around Third World issues. The fact that the tenants of the hotel were elderly as well as militant also added to their appeal as a cause to rally around.

From an organizer's perspective there are a number of issues that are instructive. Hartman cites as an issue the lack of adequate planning for tactics that might have proved more effective the night that the residents were evicted from the hotel. He feels that a more actively militant resistance to the eviction could have embarrassed the City's liberal administration—and that even the threat of physical resistance, by posing the specter of a pitched battle, might have prevented the evictions. There was also the possibility that people would have been hurt.

Hartman points to several innovations for dealing with issues of displacement that this case illustrates. One was the attempt to have the city take over the hotel by eminent domain and then sell it back to the tenants. In most instances eminent domain is used to displace low-income tenants and turn the property over to people developing it for profit. In this instance they were forcing the city to take the property from developers for the benefit of the low-income tenants. While there was controversy over this "buy back" proposal because of how costly it would be for the tenants, it did serve as a consciousness-raising device. After considering the weaknesses of the buy-back proposal, people were then able to formulate plans whereby the city would have ultimate responsibility for the property while the tenants lived there with rents they could afford. This did not happen. However, Hartman points out that using every tactic to delay eviction and attempting to force the City to take financial responsibility for housing of low-income residents is important. This is part of a long-range strategy for dealing with the dilemma that the private housing market is no longer able to satisfy the housing needs of low- and moderate-income people.

"The Rent Strike as a Political Weapon," although dealing with different short-range issues such as building tenant unions and winning rent strikes, is at bottom also about making the government responsible for owning and maintaining housing that low- and moderate-income people can afford. Jane Benedict describes *In Rem* housing in New York City, a device whereby the city takes over property on rent strike and then leases it to tenants at rents they can afford. The Metropolitan Housing Council has been in the forefront of the struggle for *In Rem* housing. It is seen as one skirmish in the struggle to get the government to take responsibility for the housing needs of lower-income residents.

In this case, a rent strike campaign is described on a step-by-step basis. Rent strikes are legal in New York. The expertise of the experienced organizers appears to be very necessary to guide tenants through the whole rent strike process as there are many pitfalls along the way. If the strike is not done properly tenants can be evicted. From Benedict's description, what do you think are the necessary skills and knowledge the organizers must possess? She also sees rent strikes as a means of organizing a stable united tenants' movement in order to solve the housing problems for lower-income people.

David Scondras takes us through the history of a Boston-based antiarson campaign. Even before he worked on the arson issue he was an experienced community organizer. He started working on the issue out of a deep sense of moral outrage over the deaths of children stemming from what appeared to be an arson-for-profit scheme in his own community. The case is instructive because he describes an organizing process that takes us from proving arson in a particular neighborhood to developing statewide legislation, to becoming an advisor to organizers in other cities fighting arson, and then developing a citywide strategy for dealing with arson. It is most unusual to find an organizer who can effectively work at all of these levels.

He obviously brought a lot of organizing as well as analytical skills to this task. Among these skills was the ability to bring people together into an organization that could turn out numbers at critical junctures. Another was a very skillful use of the media for imaginative publicity. Scondras was also able to do some serious investigative research and developed a theory of who was responsible for the fires. His theory proved so accurate that it was able to predict where subsequent fires would occur. It was also important that he understood who among the responsible officials in the city and state governments was most likely to attempt to put a stop to the arson.

Finally, Scondras reflects on how his thinking changed as he delved further into the problem of arson. He also analyzes some of the weaknesses in their organizing strategy. He now sees the problem of arson in much broader terms—as one of control of resources by working-class people. At the time of the interview he was attempting to develop a broad working-class coalition around this issue. Most good organizers change over the course of an organizing campaign: their understanding of the issues they are dealing with deepens and consequently their organizing strategies change.

When Scondras began working on the arson question it was as an outraged community activist. He was subsequently able to form a company and not only hire other organizers but to make his own living fighting arson. It is not unheard of that community activists become full-time professional organizers but it is relatively rare.

Chester Hartman's "Running a Rent Control Initiative" campaign was written as one part of a postmortem dialogue on lessons to be learned from the defeat of a rent control initiative in San Francisco. His article was written in response to the claim by a group of housing activists that a more sharply defined, decentralized, and grass-roots campaign could have brought victory. Hartman argues that it was chiefly the city council's passage of a weak alternative rent control law that determined the outcome of the initiative campaign, by enabling opponents to claim that a new law was "unnecessary."

The overall validity of Hartman's contention is perhaps less interesting than the insights his article contains about the problems that will crop up in coalitions. Hartman recognized that differences will almost inevitably flare up in coalitions. The task of a good organizer in this situation is to keep the differences from turning into acrimony. The idea of a coalition is to multiply the effectiveness of each group taking part, but if relations within the coalition become badly poisoned its ability to work for the shared goal will be sharply diminished.

All too often, organizers will go on to their next campaign without fully taking stock of what they have just been through. Hartman's analysis of the rent control drive illustrates the kind of process that has to take place if lessons are to be drawn from organizing campaigns that have failed.

Organizing Tenants in Low-Income Public Housing

Lawrence Grossman[1]

ON ORGANIZING PERSPECTIVE

As an organizer approaching a much violated or disenfranchised population, you can either "play-it-by-ear," doing whatever seems to work at any given time, or begin by consciously facing the implications of your intervention. As students and faculty at a graduate school of social work, all with some organizing experience, we chose the latter route.

Our intervention strategy flowed directly out of the analysis of society that brought us to organizing in the first place. More specifically, our action design emerged from an analysis and understanding of the problems being faced by the people we chose to organize. Self-determination of the target population was of major concern to us. But self-determination without leadership by a cadre of organizers, we knew, had resulted in the deteriorated social conditions that we faced at the start of our program. We were not going to be passive.

---

[1]Prepared especially for the first edition of this book.

In order to test out our assumptions, we decided to organize a large, sprawling low-income housing project in Brooklyn. We selected this particular housing project because of its far-ranging reputation as one of the worst places to live in the entire city. Persistent thefts and muggings, urine in the hallways, and a recent rape in an elevator resulted in the tenants not answering knocks on their doors after 3:00 p.m. More than half the apartments were occupied by single-parent families. There was a pervasive sense of hopelessness. The locked doors not only kept people out, but also added to the feelings of those inside that there was no exit.

This case history is the result of our early decision to think through each of our actions and each of our decisions before and after the fact.

We began by just hanging around benches talking to mothers with their youngsters, picking up ideas as to what they thought was wrong with the project and what they wanted to change, but it was obvious that we were compromising our original intent. We had to know the population better to be able to work out our design, but each such effort caused us to be perceived a certain way by the people, in advance of our reasoned presentation of ourselves. Our initial contacts also partially committed us to some relationship with the contacts.

In our first meeting with the housing project's manager, in which we discussed our self-help concepts, he suggested the names of twelve tenants. These, he said, would be good material for a tenants group. After brief interviews with seven of them, it was clear to us that any organization built through these individuals would not be action-oriented.

At this point, we ceased our organizing contacts, and took two days for stock-taking and a work-up of the population.

ANALYSIS OF THE SOCIAL SCENE

We believed that:

1. As a consequence of their residence in this particular project, the tenants shared exposure to a particular set of social conditions.
2. The nature of these conditions had relevance for the life choices and life styles of every tenant.
3. Every tenant had to find some way of adapting to these conditions.
4. The social milieu of this housing project created pressures inimical to the maintenance of self-respect on the part of an individual tenant, inhibiting any achievement of community or general well-being among the tenants as a collectivity.

With regard to this last point, we felt that the following environmental features mitigated against self-esteem and self-respect.

1. *Managerial Monopolization of Power.* There was an elaborate set of rules and regulations governing such tenant behavior as walking on the grass in front of

one's own home, hanging towels out of windows, sink overflow, making noise at night, and riding bicycles in the project. There were multiple criteria for eviction and income levels. The manager acted as a "legal guardian" towards the tenants. He could enter apartments at will. He had wide discretionary powers in interpreting, changing, and enforcing rules. He had a set of "discretionary" fines at his command that he used when he wished. Tenants had no legal recourse.

2. *Managerial Monopolization of Knowledge.* Not only were there myriad rules, but the exact nature of these rules was kept a secret from the tenant. Many of the infractions that brought fines were not listed anywhere, but fell within the manager's "judgmentary" powers. A tenant could not challenge "laws" that he did not clearly know. There was wide differentiation in the manner in which different tenants were treated by management, but there was not enough circulation of knowledge among tenants to establish this. There was no orientation process to adequately prepare the new tenant for living within the project. Half-understandings and tenant isolation began the moment residence began. There was a further imbalance in knowledge in the accumulation of personal information on each tenant in the manager's files. Any contacts the tenant had with a city agency, for example, resulted in material being sent to the manager. There was no reciprocal knowledge in the tenants' hands of management's activities. The manager also used knowledge gained from tenant informing on tenant. In such a "Kafkaesque" environment, the bewildered individual came to feel quite helpless before the vast resources of the manager. There was a case of a tenant breaking a neighborhood store window. The owner came to the manager to complain. The manager fined the tenant, and the tenant paid the fine without even knowing it had nothing to do with project life.

3. *Lack of Tenant Access to the Decision-Making Power.* The manager was a distant authority. Behind him he had the shadowy omnipotence of the state legislature and City Housing Commission, both sources entirely beyond the reach of the individual tenant. The manager stood behind his receptionist, housing assistants, assistant manager, and secretary, all people with power to close off entry to the manager, but no real power to make basic decisions in the manager's place. If a tenant could gain an audience with the manager, he would have nothing to offer him in the way of bargaining material to barter a compromise. The individual tenant was completely vulnerable.

4. *Prisonlike Uniformity and Monotony of Housing Units.* All apartments were painted in one drab color.

5. *Societal Perception of Tenants.* The project has been written up in the newspapers as a bed of crime, filth, and corruption. Tenants felt a stigma from the project's reputation, this being added to the general stigma of being low-income and black in a national culture that respected neither.

6. *Breakdown of Relations with Housing Police.* The management and the housing police were under separate administrative control, and they did not cooperate. The tenant suffered from the lack of reciprocal responsibility. The manager sometimes charged a fee for a tenant's calling the police. Tenants thought the police were doing the charging, and this, combined with the slowness and erratic quality of police response, caused tenants to be afraid to use their own legitimate means of protection.

7. *Tenant Informing as a Control Measure.* The manager put very little responsibility in the hands of his assistants and so relied little on information they gave him. With his lack of trust of the police, he had come to encourage tenant-informing as a control measure. This further separated and degraded tenants.

Uncertainty, even more than exemplary punishment, is a keystone of terror. In order to survive in this environment the tenants developed styles of behavior in response to power and status deprivations. The basic types of adaptation were as follows.

1. *Anonymity and Apathy.* A large group of the tenants came to *accept* the situation as it was. They retreated into passivity under the overwhelming nature of the threats and pressures. Their greatest success was in avoiding being noticed, avoiding fines, avoiding eviction, and avoiding trouble. Their basic way of minimizing the constant pain of unjust deprivation was to "believe" in its "deservedness." They came to incorporate second-class citizenry, pessimism, and fear into their overall self-image. They had little belief in themselves.

2. *Hostility and Anger at the Management.* There were fewer tenants maintaining this adaptation than the first. It was hard to continue anger when there were no outlets for carrying it through. Most of the people who remained angry carried their hostility as a secondary strain beneath one of their other adaptations. Open, conscious anger could not be maintained because it kept the deprivation wounds open and reinforced the individual's awareness of his inability to do anything about it. Anger thus became diffuse and undirected towards what was hurting the tenants most—a momentary response that could not seriously contest the circumstances of their lives.

3. *Manipulative, Operating, Cynical "Roll with the Punch" and "Get Yours" Adaptation.* Other people developed a "cool self" and a "worldly self." They cynically participated in a whole number of procedures to which they gave no emotional significance. They gave authority what it wanted, kept out of trouble, and manipulated all they could for small, petty gains. They gloried in victories like cheating the manager out of a few dollars or having an auto while on relief. By minimizing the uniqueness of pain they minimized their deprivations. Implying that this was the usual way people lived, they denied any emotional significance in the struggle between manager and tenant. In fact, they came to deny the emotional significance of most of their activities.

4. *Upward Striving—Identification with Authority.* Those tenants who informed on fellow tenants were a striking example of this type. Informing for petty personal advantage, they also succeeded in separating themselves from the masses of people in the project. Cherishing any exceptions that were made for them, they eagerly sought contacts with authority as entry point to an upper-class world. In effect, they acknowledged the severe nature of the limitations on dignity in the project, but tried to deny that they suffered such limitations. They were harder on the other tenants than the manager himself.

People who adapted by retreating (type 1), by becoming cynical (type 3), or by identifying with the repressive authority (type 4) were themselves enemies of the community. The apathetic feared the exposure and commitment of "community." The cynical rejected commitment and reciprocal responsibility. The last refused to identify with the community for fear that such identification would symbolize all they despised in their life circumstances.

Four other conditions interfered with the development of community. These were *rootlessness,* which came from the fact that added income could bring eviction, and thus inhibited motivation to build and strive; *isolation* from the surrounding communities, on a physical as well as a cultural basis; *managerial perception of tenants* as control problem, which resulted in minimal efforts to keep the grounds in top shape and repair appliances rapidly; and the *initial strangeness* of all the people, who had been uprooted from somewhere else and moved into this strange new world.

LAYING OUT PROGRAMMATIC OBJECTIVES

Based on this analysis, we defined our general or broad objectives as follows.

1. The development of a powerful tenants' self-interest organization.
2. A systematic restructuring of the destructive features in the milieu (through the tenant associations' choice of targets for action, for example, forcing the manager to negotiate and to publish the rules, and the bridging of isolation).
3. Through a style of fighting such issues that emphasized the uses of power, the development of political and democratic skills to facilitate the emergence of dignity and the kind of communal interaction that would support self-esteem.

STARTING THE TENANTS ORGANIZATION

Our selection of members for the "tenants association" we decided to create was based on our understanding of that combination of tenant types most likely to result in an action-oriented group. Our concern was that it survive over time, and that it have potential for relatively democratic interaction.

We decided to get a group of 10 to 12 together at the start, of which we hoped that 2 would be of the anger-adaptation type, 2 of the "identified with aggressor" type but less deeply "identified," and the rest from the "apathetic" group. We expected that many of the apparent "apathetics" would soon turn out to be angry people or level-headed people ready, given a viable means, to do something about conditions. We wanted some of the success and energy of the least obnoxious "identifiers" at the start.

We met with 11 women—2 "identifiers" from the manager's original list and 9 from among those we had met on the benches around the project. Of these, six were "apathetics," one was "angry," and two did not fit neatly into our classification scheme. Only one organizer was present. We wanted it to be clear that this was to be a tenants' organization.

RECRUITING A LEADERSHIP CORE FOR AN ACTION ORGANIZATION

We brought these women together by telling them that "they had come up with so many good ideas, that we thought it was a good idea to bring them together so as to figure out which things might come first."

It was an interesting meeting. The tenants, perhaps because of experience, showed very little confidence in their ability to effectuate change. The organizer, by contrast, effused a good bit of confidence.

During the course of the meeting, the organizer made appointments to see each participant in her own apartment, asking each to invite other residents from their own and adjacent floors. We used this tactic because we knew that the easiest way to have members drop out is by not having anything for them to do.

We also felt that these meetings were essential if we hoped to spread the word about an open meeting we planned for a short time later. Heavy attendance at the opening meeting was essential if we were to impress the manager with our strength. We hoped, also, to recruit more angry and committed people to our core. Meetings took place around stairwells.

Tenants and organizers rang doorbells. There were approximately 12 apartments on each floor. Counting the floors above and below the one the tenant lived on, this meant that 36 families were contacted. If no one answered, a slip was left under the door indicating that there was to be a meeting in the hall in 20 minutes. At the end of 20 minutes doorbells were rung again to remind people to come.

Approximately 20 to 25 people congregated around each stairwell. They were in housecoats, carrying children. The tenant who had been to the first meeting would introduce the organizer as someone who would talk about "our association."

These were very successful meetings. Word of the association spread effectively. Our first open meeting had over 300 in attendance. We also found five new active recruits for the "core"—one of whom was an "angry," two of whom were partly "identified" and partly other things, but very competent at organizational tasks, and two of whom were really "untypeable," somewhat apathetic but also quite ready to work to change things if a strong organization was presented to them. Two of these five were males, the first men in the core group. The act of standing up in front of their neighbors and introducing the worker also bound the original women more closely to the organization, as it caused them to be identified as a key part of it by their neighbors.

ORGANIZING ACTIVITIES

We had approached the manager before attempting any organizing because we had assumed that our presence would soon be noted anyway. Our approach had been aimed at developing communication channels, reassuring some of his fears, and establishing our clear independence. We understood his position towards a possible association as ambivalent—it certainly might make for a better housing project community (nothing could really make it worse, even from his point of view; he was a young hotshot manager, fairly new to the project, sent there to improve it). On the other hand, a "runaway" tenants' association over which he had no control was the one thing a manager feared most. We certainly meant the association to ultimately be "runaway"—beyond his control—but not runaway in the sense that it would be beyond the possibility of rational negotiation. We emphasized the rational-negotiation part in discussions with him and left his vanity to complete the task of reassurance that the association would not get "out of hand."

We traded tactical strokes with him, gaining a slight advantage. Prior to the first open meeting, we discussed his possible roles with him. We relayed to him three issues that concerned the core committee, one of which involved a request for a bicycle path, and asked him to prepare answers on them. He agreed to. We also agreed that there would not be a wide-open question-and-answer period at this meeting, to avoid its deteriorating into the kind of gripe session that would make the members feel either frightened or frustrated.

We arranged that this first large meeting would take place in a room a little smaller than the ideal size for the number we hoped for. Over 300 tenants came to a room that ordinarily held around 200. The manager was somewhat intimidated upon his arrival, and at that moment accepted the fact that he would have to negotiate with this organization, at least for a short while.

The manager reacted at the meeting itself, however, by going back on some of the agreements that had been determined with the organizers during their earlier discussion, and presented some of the issues in a manner that implied that he had always been working for their solution; in fact, he would have done nothing had not the tenants pressed the issues. He also barged into a question-and-answer session that broke the meeting up with diffused frustration.

These changes in his presentation had either been planned, or were a consequence of our having intimidated him. They had some immediate small success in taking some of the steam away from the tenants, but the lasting impact of the meeting in the minds of the tenants was the picture of the manager sweating to keep up with them, in front of a room where their members overwhelmed him.

The manager and the organizers retained a successful, guarded relationship with each other throughout the entire organizing period. The manager felt more dependent on the organizers than we did on him. He saw us as something of a safety valve or buffer—another level of possible negotiation and possible compromise.

Once a strong tenants' association was a fait accompli, he needed us more than we needed him, and it was easy to maintain complete independence of him while still receiving information and a number of concessions. Both sides paid some attention to preserving communication lines with each other.

Programmatic goals were selected with great care at all points of the organizing process.

There were three basic types of program issues attacked by the group. These aimed at the following.

1. Ameliorative changes.
2. Significant structural changes.
3. Symbolic changes.

At the start all victories have symbolic as well as substantive significance.

It was necessary to aim for small, likely successes at the start. The "apathetics" would have fallen back into pessimism and the "identified" into formalism, if we had not proved that the organization had potency.

A number of early programmatic victories included the following.

1. The manager's accession to weekly negotiative meetings with a committee of four tenants.
2. The waiving of the rule about bike riding and the promise of a bike path for the future (later fulfilled).
3. The publication of the rules and regulations presumably governing tenant-manager relations.
4. The discontinuing of favors given for tenants informing on tenants.
5. An agreement that an explicit rationale would be given for every proposed tenant fine.

The major extended "short term" objective was the winning of a traffic light. Without it, a park and a middle-income neighborhood across the street were inaccessible. After repeated letters to the traffic commissioner, we received contradictory responses (one saying "we cannot respond to your request until we do a traffic survey," and another received just prior to the first saying "we have done a traffic engineering survey and the street does not justify a light"), and were able to exploit the situation through a liberal newspaper that requested an explanation from the traffic commissioner. At this point he conceded the light. We had won a first victory!

There were no early program failures. There were, however, a number of internal struggles over program issues. These struggles generally resolved themselves into struggles between "identifier" types and other tenants. In most cases, the organizers openly threw their weight behind the non-"identified" tenants, as we believed that the organization no longer needed the identified types. They could either adapt to the new philosophy or get out.

The five issues around which there were differences between groups of tenants were the conviction that:

1. Children were the major cause of trouble in the project and something should be done about their hanging around hallways in the afternoon.
2. The fine for extra calls for the exterminator should be dropped because the roaches were not immune to it.
3. We should write the Governor to veto a Welfare Residence Bill.
4. We should pressure the manager to stop giving favors to informants.
5. Since a successful new start was being made, the name of the project should be changed.

The tenants who were still actively identified with authority voted as follows:

1. Yes on doing something about the children.
2. No on dropping fines.
3. No on writing the Governor.
4. No on putting tenant pressure on the manager.
5. Yes on changing the Project name.

The other tenants generally took opposite positions.

All of the decisions except the one on cockroach fines went *against* the "identifiers."

The cockroach fine was continued because the organizer working with the Health Committee had difficulty either confronting its membership or turning to other organizers for help. He let the Committee make a decision that he should have prevented.

Some tenants had brought the request to the Health Committee. This was the only committee that was dominated by "identifiers." The organizers had been slow to notice this. It should have been obvious. What kinds of people are usually attracted to "keeping things clean"? These same tenants had punitive attitudes toward their dirtier brethren. They saw themselves as dispensing rulings for the "good of the people," rather than as representing the people. They saw fines as a just deterrent for dirty apartments.

The issue around changing the name of the project was particularly gratifying to the organizers. The manager had suggested the possibility as a public-relations move by changing the housing project's name. The firmness of some of the original apathetics *against* such a move, their burgeoning dignity and pride in their project, was a sharply satisfying experience. Instead of changing the name of the project, they voted to have a big celebration over winning the traffic light, and invited three big-name baseball players (one black, one Cuban, and one white) to join them.

Later in the organization's history, the tenants became involved in the surrounding neighborhoods, and the association becoming a major part of an area council.

EVALUATION AND ANALYSIS

There were a number of heated and prolonged discussions among the organizers relating to the degree of our interventions appropriate to our objectives. What types of decision-making structures should we strive to develop within the organization?

Our goals for the organization included giving it an action orientation, building tenant skills and confidence, assuring a respect for democracy, and priming effective and democratically-oriented leaders in anticipation of our withdrawal. These objectives had some contradictory implications. The "apathetics" were a problem in terms of general participation and the "authority-oriented" ones a problem in terms of democratic participation. The "apathetics" required quick movement on issues to maintain their confidence, while the "authority-oriented" ones could manipulate fast movement into a strengthening of their nondemocratic style. The fewer people who participated in decisions, the faster they went. The "authority-oriented" ones also used slower processes to entrench formalism. Some insisted on intricate procedures that supported their greater experience, and upon which they built up their power. For these reasons, the organizers decided to keep full control of the association for the first seven months of its operation. We forestalled any elections during that period.

We were afraid that early elections would have resulted in control by the "identifiers." We used every means to build up some of the non-authority-oriented talent that was emerging. We put them on the committee that met with the manager. Thus they controlled information and at least seemed powerful. We mentioned their names whenever possible.

We maintained an action focus rather than a formal or organizational focus in a variety of ways. We only called large open meetings, for example, when there was something large to be done. We made sure that certain larger policy decisions were struggled through by as many members as was possible prior to the open meetings.

The issue of tenant informing was used as a direct teaching tool and as pressure against the "identifiers." We stimulated a number of discussions around the subject. At first the identifiers argued against approaching the manager on this subject on grounds of its "triviality," and then on the basis of its "lack of feasibility." The organizers manipulated such discussions so as to force the informers to publicly denounce the "principle of informing." By the end of these discussions, it was clear to the informers that they had to quit their informing behavior or quit the organization. One did drop out; the rest adapted.

As a counterbalance against our generally aggressive role, we made a strong point of never going with the tenants when they met with the manager. This was a way of signifying our essential respect for their own accountability. They lived in the Project, not we. We discussed what happened with the manager when they wished to, but after the first two visits, never prompted such discussions ourselves.

The dilemma concerning our intervention and their independence was strikingly exhibited at election time.

Among the serious candidates for the chairmanship, the three most active women seemed to be:

1. A clear "identifier" type with significant organizational experience, who had done much of the letter writing on the traffic-light campaign.
2. A younger, moderate "identifier" type who chaired the Health Committee.
3. A bright young nonidentifier, non-"any type," who usually spoke for the group that met with the manager.

The organizers were rooting for the third. We had primed her by putting her in the position of reporting on the meetings with the manager. She was clearly the most politically intelligent and flexible of the candidates, with a real appreciation for other people. Candidate No. 2 was acceptable to us, but Candidate No. 1 was not. We were sure that her relative rigidity would kill off the organization.

When the time came for nominations, at a "core group" meeting, a surprise occurred. A man was the first nominated. He was as much of an "identifier" as No. 1, but considerably less hard working.

The organizer present took this nomination as in part a tribute to his own maleness, and in part a falling back on old images of authority. He acted against it in whatever ways he could improvise. He suggested that the man in question had "Boy Scout meetings on Tuesday nights, didn't he? Well the chairman could not afford to miss meetings. Maybe someone else should assume the role first."

The group responded positively to the rather blatant manipulating, probably out of a degree of gratitude towards and confidence in the organizer who had performed it. They then went on to bypass woman No. 1 and tentatively suggest No. 2 (whom they rightly sensed was more to the organizers' liking than No. 1). Sensing the tentativeness and having already gone this far, the organizer went one step further and mumbled something about No. 2 already being chairman of the Health Committee (which she would gladly have given up for the chance to chair the entire organization). They chose No. 3.

This behavior was consistent with the approach of the organizing team, even though it had an improvisational character. The organizer faced the dilemma of organizational effectiveness versus self-determination, by choosing effectiveness in such a way that it would engender greater self-determination over the long run. No. 3 was the one candidate whom no outsider (the organizer included) could possibly push around successfully.

At the close of one year of organizing, there remained a fairly powerful tenant organization with 387 family membership, 4 active committees, and a reliable core of 20 to 23 hard workers.

As organizers, we attempted quite sincerely to rationalize our actions before the fact rather than after, and in the main succeeded more than is usual. The tenants usually knew exactly what the organizers were after, particularly when it affected them directly. They *let* the organizers "manipulate" them at times because they wanted to be "manipulated" into a successful organization. They were also testing our skill, and thus "using" us.

This does not in any way obviate the organizer's need to know what and how he is doing; it merely takes the tenants out of a one-dimensional aspect and validates their subjectivity. A clumsy organizer would still fail out of clumsiness, and an incorrect analysis would probably lead to a stillborn organization.

San Francisco's International Hotel: Case Study of a Turf Struggle*

Chester Hartman†

Few local land-use controversies in recent times have had the duration or notoriety that have characterized the battle over San Francisco's International Hotel. It has lasted ten years and is far from over; it saw the City's sheriff at first go to jail for contempt of court rather than carry out a court-ordered eviction; and it then saw 2,000 people facing 400 cops and sheriff's deputies when the eviction action finally came down. This article attempts to analyze what has been won and lost so far, the reasons the fight for the Hotel took on the dimensions it did, and what lessons there are in it for future struggles of this type.

"Turf," or land-use, struggles are a prototype of class warfare in urban areas. Economically and politically powerful forces seek to displace occupants of land not being put to its "highest and best use." The rules of the capitalist economic system and its various enforcers in the political and legal arenas act to carry out that transformation, usually in a relatively swift and quiet way. The financial and social

*From *Radical America*, Vol. 12, No. 3 (May–June, 1978) pp. 47–58.

†I should make clear my own relation to the struggle described here. I was involved in many ways: as frequent demonstrator; as a regular reporter of the story for *Common Sense,* a Bay Area radical newspaper; as a housing consultant who helped draw up and negotiate around the tenants' substitute plan described in the text for City ownership and subsidization of the Hotel; and as a member of the Northern California Alliance, one of the left political organizations involved in the latter stages of the fight for the Hotel.

costs of that change generally are borne by those least able to bear them. These costs take the form of higher rents, other living/moving costs, and disrupted lives and social patterns. When change in land-use occurs under government auspices (as in the urban renewal and highway programs), there are now a set of protections and financial aids, still far from adequate and won after hard fights and much suffering. But where no direct government action or funding is involved—your classical "free market" real estate deal—those unfortunate enough to be in the path of "progress" have no rights or benefits whatsoever. They are entitled to no more than a timely eviction notice (usually from 3 to 30 days, depending on the state and circumstances).

On occasion, such attempts at displacement-replacement meet resistance. People don't always go quietly. Outside support then develops. Creative and effective oppositional strategies and tactics may be employed. The political and legal system can be forced to act in a more humanely responsive fashion. The results of such struggles are delay, widespread exposure of the way in which the system operates, sometimes some victories.

In San Francisco, as in many other cities, the housing crisis is becoming the central issue, and likely the main organizing issue, not only for low-income people but for moderate- and middle-income people as well. Speculation is driving prices and rents out of sight; there is no rent control; housing and neighborhoods are being lost to developers; rehabilitation efforts turn out to be a subtle form of bulldozing people out of their neighborhoods, the new, elegantly named "gentrification process." The I-Hotel struggle embodied these concerns. It was seen as a way of saving needed low-rent housing, driving back the developers, protecting a Third World community. The issue was framed by residents and supporters as property-profit rights vs. housing-human rights. The struggle succeeded in communicating this to the people of San Francisco. The eviction drama itself—graphically and extensively publicized, not only in the Bay Area but nationally (Walter Cronkite, the *Washington Post, NY Times, Baltimore Sun, LA Times,* etc.—in many cases on the front page)—was portrayed not merely as a "human interest story" but in terms of the basic political conflict that produced it.

THE HISTORY

To run through the bare bones of the story:

The International Hotel is a three-story, 155-room residential hotel, located in downtown San Francisco, at the seam between the expanding financial district and Chinatown. It is one of the few remnants of a once-flourishing Manilatown, now the site of banks, corporate headquarters, office buildings, trendy shops, and all the other edificial undergirding of an expanding capitalist economy. Manilatown hardly has any separate reality now and its residents really form a corner of the adjacent Chinatown community. The Hotel has the poor luck to be located on the wrong side of Kearny St., the financial district side rather than the Chinatown side. As the city grew into Wall Street West with World War II and the rampant Asian military and trade activity of the next three decades, the market for downtown real estate boomed.

In the Fall of 1968, a local real estate magnate and politico, Walter Shorenstein, told the tenants to be gone by Jan. 1, 1969. At the time 196 people were living there, mostly middle-aged or elderly, with a few younger residents. Over half were Filipino, and many of the rest were Chinese. Almost all were male and poor, living on pensions and social security or part-time wages. Those who worked were for the most part cooks, busboys and waiters in local restaurants or maintenance workers in hospitals. Some were supporting families who remained in the Philippines. The population structure of the Hotel reflected the country's racist immigration laws, which limited entry of women and children, while encouraging the male laborers who worked the fields, mines and ships. Those who had worked and still worked as seamen used the Hotel as their permanent homes, often paying the rent on their rooms while they were away or storing their possessions at the Hotel. Like many such "hotels" in downtown areas of San Francisco and other cities, the International Hotel functioned as a micro-community, providing an important social nexus and support system for those who lived there. While the number of residents steadily dwindled over the next decade, due to knowledge that the building was under threat of demolition, the basic character of the resident population remained the same.

Aided by the United Filipino Association and others, the tenants decided to resist and after a few months forced Shorenstein to give them a three-year lease. Their counter-offensive weapon was publicly to embarrass Shorenstein, a Parks & Recreation Commissioner appointed by Mayor Joseph Alioto and head of the local Humphrey for President Committee (picketing a dinner Shorenstein was hosting for Hubert was probably the most effective single tactic.) The lease was a pretty repulsive one—tenants had to pay property taxes and repair costs, plus a hefty net rental to Shorenstein—but it bought three years, made the I-Hotel into a major public issue, and established the International Hotel Tenants Association (IHTA) as the controlling body for the Hotel and the continuing struggle. Following expiration of the lease Shorenstein decided to bow out and sold the Hotel to the Four Seas Investment Corp., a Hong Kong- and Thai-based company eager to expatriate its capital out of an "unstable" Thailand after overthrow of the Thai military dictatorship. It reportedly bought the property sight unseen and perhaps illegally; Four Seas is now being investigated by the US Customs Service and the Thai government to see if this capital import violated those countries' laws. (The large-scale role of foreign investment in US cities is just being recognized. In a recent *New Yorker* article on the Hotel, Calvin Trillin pointed out the relationship between prices for luxury buildings in Manhattan and such factors as economic instability in Italy, terrorism in W. Germany and the growth of Eurocommunism. He facetiously suggested that in pursuit of self-interest the New Yorkers who control this real estate might consider switching their charitable contributions from the *NY Times'* Neediest Cases to the Italian Communist Party).

Four Seas then spent some three years trying to empty the building (at the same time picking up several other adjacent properties to make a more attractive development parcel). Tenant resistance took the form of lengthy legal proceedings and simple refusal to move: as squatting actions the world over have shown, property laws assume everyone will cooperate in the system. All the while the issue was becoming bigger and bigger within the city.

Regular demonstrations were held, with hundreds, at times thousands, of people. No local issue in decades had drawn crowds as large and as repeatedly. In July, 1976, a court finally ordered the eviction—a directed verdict in the face of a hung jury. Various stays were then obtained, the most dramatic being on Jan. 17, 1977, just 12 hours before a combined Police-Sheriffs Dept. strike force was to descend on the Hotel. A week before a crowd of several hundred people, hastily assembled via the supporters' efficient telephone tree, had successfully prevented Sheriff's deputies from posting eviction notices. January 12 and 16 had seen mass demonstrations of 3,000 and 5,000 people, respectively, in front of the Hotel. The court gave as its reason for the Jan. 17 stay an affidavit by Police Chief Charles Gain that he had "reliable reports" of automatic weapons on the Hotel roof and gasoline stored for firebombings. But everyone knew the "reports" were sheer lies, a face-saving device for the legal system, concocted by a City government that did not want to risk an unpopular and possibly bloody police action as in the 1934 General Strike. It was a heady, although temporary victory for people power. Another important factor was liberal Sheriff Richard Hongisto's publicly-stated reluctance to carry out the eviction, which eventually landed him five days in jail for contempt of court. (Judge Ira Brown, who had directed the eviction, termed Hongisto's refusal "the greatest threat to every court in the country.")

The next few months were spent in battle with the courts. Under great pressure, the City in late 1976 had agreed to a "solution" to the problem: the Housing Authority would purchase the Hotel through its eminent domain powers, then re-sell it to the IHTA for permanent low-rent housing. The governing Board of Supervisors agreed to lend the Housing Authority $1.3 million to cover the purchase; the Housing Authority in December held the necessary public hearings, and in January filed its taking action. But in May the courts threw the tenants another curve ball: a judge ruled the Housing Authority could not take property from a private owner in order to transfer it to another private owner. While astute observers of the urban scene will recognize that that's what redevelopment agencies do all the time, it seems the courts will give this taking power the widest latitude when land is taken from the poor to be given to the rich (i.e., urban renewal), but such use of eminent domain powers becomes illegal when a housing authority tries to reverse that direction. The matter has been appealed (with a decision still months off), but the courts insisted that the eviction order be carried out, the appeals process notwithstanding.

The tenants made one last-minute try to force the City to intervene effectively: a plan they submitted to Mayor George Moscone in early July for permanent Housing Authority ownership of the Hotel, with tenant management. That would have bypassed the legal problems, plus some severe financial problems the tenants realized were inherent in the original "buyback plan," which they themselves had put forth. The economics of buying and renovating the Hotel were such that resultant rents would have been way beyond the reach of low-income tenants. In part, this was because the "fair market value" the Housing Authority (and later the tenants) would have had to pay to Four Seas had risen in three years from $850,000 (the price Four Seas paid Shorenstein) to $1.3 million. With possibly several hundred thousand dollars worth of renovation needed, there was no way room rents could remain in the $50–55 range. The tenants' new plan would have required an annual City subsidy along the order of $50,000—which seemed a small sum to preserve 155 well-located units—and put forth an important political principle of City responsibility for meeting housing needs of its low-income people. Unfortunately, however, Moscone was having no part of this concept of government responsibility, particularly in light of the city's financial difficulties, and rejected the plan outright.

As a result, the eviction went ahead on the morning of August 4, 1977, beginning at 3 a.m. Two thousand supporters came down to form a human barricade around the Hotel. Four hundred police and sheriff's deputies, backed by firetrucks, horses and all the paraphernalia of the state's brute force, clubbed their way through the crowd, seized the rooftop with aid of aerial ladders, battered down doors and windows, and over the next four hours removed about 50 remaining residents plus 100 or so supporters inside the building. It was brief, brutal and effective.

The issue did not die with removal of the tenants. A fight still is underway to save and restore the building, or perhaps salvage only the site and build new public housing on it, maybe even retake the entire block for the Chinatown-Manilatown community. Although Four Seas is in possession of the I-Hotel, a City "stop work" order has prevented them from demolishing it, pending the outcome of a court action on the status of their apparently expired demolition permit. (Establishing that the permit has expired would lead to long delays, in obtaining a new permit, preparing an environmental impact report, etc.). Incredibly, Four Seas twice tried to demolish the building illegally, simply by showing up with bulldozers early in the morning. Quick action by supporters and police stopped the bulldozers, but not before a big chunk was chewed out of a back wall on the second attempt, adding to the extensive damage done by police and sheriffs during the eviction action. In March both Four Seas and its bulldozer driver pleaded nolo contedere to five misdemeanor counts arising from the illegal bulldozing and received a $500 fine, two years' probation, and, for the bulldozer operator, 15 days in jail. The district attorney's vigorous prosecution action can be traced to steady pressure by tenants and supporters. The original "buyback" plan still is alive in the form of the court appeal on the Housing Authority's eminent domain action. A voter opinion statement on the tenants' alternative plan for City ownership was placed on the Nov. 8 ballot (by a Supervisor opposed to it) and lost 2–1, voters being scared by the exaggerated price tag assigned by the Controller.

Perhaps the most promising new hope is the two grants the IHTA and two more mainstream Chinatown housing groups have just received to study possibilities of using the entire block the Hotel sits on for the community's housing and service needs. The original grant came from the National Trust for Historic Preservation, and supplementary funding came from the City's Commission on the Aging, putting the imprimatur of important federal and local bodies on the study. Endorsement letters from Mayor Moscone, the Supervisor who represents the district in which the Hotel is located, and Sen. Frank Church of the Special Committee on Aging, all represented important political support for the study, which will be undertaken by two of the area's leading architecture and planning firms, chosen by the tenants. The hope is to use the feasibility study as a political organizing process as well, with a view to seeing how the entire block can be restored to the community rather than incorporated into the expanding financial district. Both renovation and new construction will be explored, and it is possible that the most reasonable solution at this point will be to replace the Hotel with a larger low-rent housing development. It will be some time before the final chapter of the I-Hotel story is written, and whether the "bottom line" is victory or defeat remains to be seen.

THE POLITICAL FORCES INVOLVED

The Hotel tenants and their organization, the IHTA, were at all times the center of the struggle. But in fact their leadership and the level of the group's activism shifted considerably over the course of the decade. The age, infirmity and English language problems of many of the tenants limited their participation and ability to lead the struggle. But enormous deference was paid to their expressed desires and views as these emerged in individual conversations and group meetings. Until the mid-1970s leadership of the IHTA was with one or two residents who managed the Hotel and in practice were quite despotic, suppressing any real participation or dissent by other tenants. The move toward broader participation and democratization of the Tenants Association came largely as a result of the re-involvement of several younger Filipino activists who had originally been around during the 1968–72 period and now were members of KDP (the Union of Democratic Filipinos). The elected chairperson of the IHTA since 1976 was in fact a KDP activist living at the Hotel.

The question of leadership and a political center to the struggle was complicated enormously by the fact that the IHTA was only one of three major tenants groups within the hotel building. The street level spaces (residential rooms were on the second and third floors) were occupied by several stores, community services and organizations. Two of the downstairs organizations occupying extensive spaces were the Asian Community Center (ACC) and the Chinese Progressive Association (CPA). The former, a.k.a. the Workers Committee to Fight for the International Hotel and Victory Building (an adjacent parcel also owned by Four Seas) is linked to the Revolutionary Communist Party (RCP). The latter is linked to the Maoist I Wor Kuen (IWK) group and is the key element in what was known as the I-Hotel Support Committee, which included other progressive groups and individuals in the Bay Area. (Many other supporters identified themselves more directly with the IHTA). All three tenant groups obviously had material bases in the Hotel struggle, although the upstairs residential tenants were the most widely identified and supported tenant group. Tensions among all three groups were usually quite high, particularly as two other Bay Area left organizations—KDP and the Northern California Alliance (NCA)—were closely associated with the IHTA. Each group had a specific view of the struggle, how it ought to be carried out, and its relation to a broader revolutionary analysis. Needless to say, each group also felt an enormous stake in its particular role in the outcome of the struggle, in terms of credit for a victory and hoped for hegemony with the Bay Area left.

Running through the composition, positions, tensions among the various tenants and support groups over the last three years would require a separate article several times the length of this one. In practice, the existence of this large and confusing cast of characters, each of whom had some legitimacy, meant that often there were several voices speaking on behalf of, and different tactics used in the name of, the "tenants." The general public and many of the less "inside," non-affiliated supporters—who were by far the majority to show up at large demonstrations—had little knowledge of the internal politics of the situation. Confrontational tactics against the Mayor and other public officials used by one or another of the downstairs groups (who had major political differences with one another, the Workers Committee-RCP-ACC faction putting out the line that the struggle was essentially a class struggle, the Support Committee-IWK-CPA faction's line being that it was basically a Third World Issue, representing national oppression) often worked at cross-purposes with the IHTA's tactics. One striking example was the placement of the I-Hotel issue on last November's ballot. The IHTA and its supporters initially regarded the proposition as a trap, a "no-win" situation, and upon hearing rumors that some supervisors were thinking of placing it on the ballot phoned one of the more friendly Supervisors to register their protest, only to be told by the befuddled man that he thought they wanted it on the ballot; it turned out that the Workers Committee on its own had concluded that such a ballot proposition would be a good idea and was lobbying strongly for it (in the name of "the tenants"). There have also been points at which some of the left organizations subordinated the I-Hotel fight to what they regarded as more pressing, organizationally-determined needs, such as KDP's shift of personpower toward other struggles involving Filipinos (the defense of Filipina Narciso and Leonora Perez, the two Filipina nurses convicted of killing patients in an Ann Arbor hospital, and the anti-Marcos campaign in the Philippines) and NCA's sudden withdrawal from the Hotel following defeat of the Nov. 8 ballot proposition when it went into an "internal period" to deal with political differences within the organization.

The presence of the Hotel's downstairs Marxist-Leninist organizations served to limit the support the struggle received from the Chinatown area itself, as the political stances and past tactics of some of these Asian youth groups have alienated large parts of the surrounding community, where they are well known. A further effect was to limit the City administration's support for the struggle, which in some quarters was regarded as essentially a leftists' cause, rather than a true community issue.

By contrast, however, the wider group of supporters from San Francisco, Berkeley, Oakland and other nearby communities seemed for the most part unaware of and uninvolved in these more sectarian concerns. The intense ideological and tactical fights that underlay such questions as when, where and for what purpose demonstrations were called, what chants were used at demonstrations, what line was put forth in literature, etc., all were questions that seemed to have little bearing on those who actually showed up and otherwise acted to support the Hotel tenants. It is likely that a very high proportion of supporters were unaware of the distinctions and differences among the various tenant groups.

The outpouring of support for the I-Hotel is probably explained in large part by factors that already have been alluded to, but are worth summarizing. The Third World working class tenancy of the Hotel clearly was a major factor, in a highly politicized city with a large and varied Third World population and a long history of issues involving Third World struggles, domestically and internationally. The fact that the tenants were elderly and clearly in need of outside assistance, yet at the same time determined and militant, also was important. And the cumulative long-term nature of the struggle, with its periodic victories and delays, in itself provided an incentive to support the Hotel; there was a feeling that victory was possible, especially given the accession of a new liberal city government in November of 1975. "When I arrived in San Francisco in 1974," remarked one activist, "the I-Hotel already had a legendary quality."

The limits of a liberal city government also were well revealed in the I-Hotel fight. George Moscone is a typical liberal mayor. Richard Hongisto was extraordinary, as sheriffs go. Both did some good things. Moscone twisted the arms of a reluctant Board of Supervisors to eke out the $1.3 million loan to the Housing Authority; Hongisto initially refused to evict and publicly mouthed some brave words, such as "laws in our society are written to protect people with property and money." But in the end both chose to serve that system, to protect people with property and money. Moscone would not accept the tenants' new plan and institute a new eminent domain action for permanent City ownership of the Hotel, the only act that would have definitively called off the eviction threat, even though the required subsidy was small and readily available from a no longer needed allocation of the hotel tax. Hongisto not only led the eviction, but participated in such a vicious way (sledgehammering down doors, threatening to order press and medical people out of the building when they remonstrated against his techniques) that one wondered whether his previous acts and words had any real meaning.

EVICTION NIGHT TACTICS

The mass demonstrations mounted around the Hotel played an important role in raising public consciousness about the issue, pressuring the City government (and courts), and politicizing both the demonstrators and tenants. Important questions can be raised about eviction night tactics, however. The entire sequence of events, starting around 10 p.m. when the call went out (triggered by informants in the Sheriff's office) that ''this was the night''; through the hours of waiting, chanting, dry-run arm linking, amplified reports on the progress of the approaching army (''they've left the Civic Center,'' ''they're moving down Broadway''); watching the slow parade-like arrival of motorcycles, police-bearing buses, ambulances, firetrucks, paddy wagons, blue-and-whites; being clubbed, jabbed and pushed around for a few minutes before retreating; watching the axes and sledgehammers batter down the doors as we shouted and chanted from across the street; seeing people led and carried out of the building over the next four hours—it all had a surreal quality, like a prearranged script working itself out. Partly because of the age of the tenants and the expressed desires of at least some of them, the plan was to not resist beyond a certain point and not to resist in ways that would incur extreme police violence. But it seems no real consideration had been given to using those 2,000 people in a way that might result in really stopping the eviction. The 400 sheriffs, deputies and police were extremely well-supervised and controlled, all in all (there were a few instances of ''exuberance'' and loss of control, but considering the situation, history and potential, it was a pretty unbloody affair). Police Chief Gain oversaw and commanded the outside operation from an 8th floor command post in the adjacent Holiday Inn, the Sheriff and Undersheriff themselves were in full control of the inside operation. The political risks of the situation, not only for these men but for the City administration, were immense. The whole world, or at least the whole country, was in fact watching, via its reporters and t.v. cameras. It was most likely not a situation in which those in charge would have chosen to carry out the eviction no matter what kind or degree of force had to be used; rather, the force was finely tuned and in control.

And yet the crowd of demonstrators, their leaders and organizers seemed not at all to consider any kind of scenario that might have led the Police Chief, Sheriff and Mayor to decide to retreat, in order to avoid the unacceptable political consequences of unrestrained brute force. The crowd of 2,000 was in no way accoutered or otherwise prepared by instructions or training to hold out for longer than a few symbolic minutes; leaders with bullhorns in fact exhorted everyone to retreat within a short time after the police clubs and horses started in in earnest. Whether this is the "normal" reaction of a predominantly middle-class-background, largely white crowd, or there simply was no concept that things could be different, everyone did their expected thing, and despite this huge turnout the outcome was never in doubt. A friend told me of a film he saw of Japanese resistance to an airport expansion scheme, in which demonstrators wore protective equipment corresponding to that worn by the police, were highly disciplined, used creative, well-thought-out, well-rehearsed tactics, fought back, and made it a real battle. Their intention and plan was to resist effectively, to stop something.

There's no question that the police have the armaments to win such a battle, where there is one of them for only five of us; but there is every likelihood that the politics and control in such a situation put a strict clamp on how far they will be allowed to go, how many and whom they will be allowed to injure. What would have been the political consequences of forcing this pitched battle and the pathetic scene of burly sheriffs escorting elderly Filipinos out onto the street to continue into the morning rush hour, as tens of thousands of commuters came into a totally tied up downtown battlefield? Our eviction night showing was profoundly depressing, not so much because we lost, but because it was set up so that there was no way we could do anything but lose. And the "lessons" to the public, to the police, to ourselves, are clear: we are a paper tiger.

Much of this criticism of eviction night tactics can be traced to the lack of a unified leadership in the I-Hotel struggle, which in turn stemmed from the central involvement of several distinct political groupings who disagreed with each other violently on many levels. A set of bitter accusatory papers was circulated within and to the various left formations analyzing eviction night, but relating perceived errors to the long-standing, broader history of disagreements. The Support Committee accused the Workers Committee of disrupting security plans during the eviction action, of abandoning the human barricades and attempting to persuade demonstrators to disperse. The Workers Committee in response said it regarded the eviction night demonstration as a futile gesture, doomed to fail, and that in contradistinction to the Support Committee it had sought to prevent the eviction attempt from coming about at all. Regardless of the comparative merits of the two attacks, it is clear that there was no unified strategy and set of tactics regarding how to handle the eviction attempt, and that most of the 2,000 persons there to protect the building and tenants were very confused by the conflicting directives they were given. That rare opportunity offered by the presence of thousands of persons prepared militantly to defend something they believe in was poorly utilized. And although it is difficult to make the case concretely in the space of this report, it seems at least plausible that a clearer overall sense of strategy, more unified leadership and better-planned tactics over the year and a half before eviction night might have prevented the August 4 eviction from ever being attempted and might have given tenants and supporters a clear victory.

SOME INNOVATIVE TACTICS

Some of the political tactics used in trying to save the Hotel may have wider applicability. Several months before the eviction supporters succeeded in having the Hotel listed on the National Register of Historic Places (a secondary level landmark status). Interestingly, the designation derived not from architectural considerations but from the Hotel's role in Filipino immigration history. Rebuilt after the 1906 Earthquake, the International Hotel had for decades housed, in communal fashion, low-paid Filipino and Chinese workers. While this designation did not prevent the eviction, it nonetheless has potential importance, because the designation means an environmental impact report will have to be filed, should Four Seas have to get a new demolition permit, and that process can provide important delays and political leverage. Additionally, the new feasibility study grant—which eventually may provide the best hope for taking back the building and site—is available only because of the National Register status.

The eminent domain action is perhaps the most important innovative step in the struggle to make the city government more responsive. The power to take private land is truly a potent, potentially radical tool. To date cities have used it primarily in a regressive way, often cloaked in "public interest" or "public welfare" rhetoric— replacing "slums" with a convention center or new office buildings is good for the city's economy, creates jobs and tax revenues, and that benefits everyone. I know of no other instance in the United States in modern times when a city government has attempted to use its eminent domain powers to take land away from a wealthy developer for retention as low-rent housing. (The fact that the developer is foreign, with no ties to the city's power structure, may have made this easier). While there has been considerable after-the-fact criticism of the original IHTA "buyback plan" by some in the organized left for its financial unworkability and incorrect political perspective—that it placed responsibility for providing housing on low-income people themselves, rather than on the government—in retrospect there was no way that eminent domain action would have been embraced by the City had it not been regarded as just a temporary means of getting the property away from Four Seas and into the tenants' hands. The Board of Supervisors put up the $1.3 million only on the condition that it was short-term loan to the Housing Authority, the actual taking agency. The Housing Authority went through with all the complex taking procedures only because it regarded its involvement as temporary; it never was willing to own or manage the Hotel. The movement from the old "buyback plan" to the newer concept of using City eminent domain powers and City subsidies, thereby placing with the City ultimate financial responsibility for ownership and maintenance, was an important progression in people's consciousness, albeit not a

step the City seems willing to take. But any ultimate outcome of the I-Hotel struggle
that is based on taking the Hotel away from Four Seas by eminent domain—no
matter how jerryrigged the financing scheme is for making sure the units would
remain as low-income housing—would be a truly progressive gain and one that
might be repeated in San Francisco and other cities. Even if a plan led to the I-Hotel
being demolished and new federally-financed public housing erected in its place,
the solution would be a model to follow elsewhere. (While in some ways not as
attractive a solution, it would provide more, larger, newer, and better units).

In more recent months, following the August eviction and the November
defeat of the ballot proposition on the I-Hotel, cooperation among the various
groups central to the struggle has markedly increased. One supporter attributes this,
correctly I believe, to the weakened position of the struggle; if any victory is still to
be salvaged, unity will be essential. While the struggle appeared strong, prior to the
eviction, with chance of a clear-cut, dramatic victory, the various groups regarded
leadership and "the correct line" as extremely important. The recent involvement
of the two more mainstream Chinatown housing groups, as co-sponsors with the
IHTA of the feasibility study for the Hotel block, is a significant development, both
in representing support from the Chinatown community and eventually involving
the City administration more closely in finding a solution to the neighborhood's
housing problems. At the same time, the IHTA itself has declined considerably.
Half of the former tenants have relocated in a hotel seven blocks away (the rest are
scattered about), and while the Association continues to meet attendance is poor and
leadership uncertain. The new feasibility study can represent going on the offensive
by developing community support for an imaginative plan to recapture an area
several times as large as the Hotel site, through a combination of public and private
programs. Where the leadership will come from for this effort is at the moment
unclear. And whether such a development will again lead to sectarian warfare, lack
of a unified strategy, and inability to reach out to the immediate surrounding
community remains to be seen.

Running a Rent Control Initiative Campaign*

Chester Hartman

*The analysis of San Francisco's November 1979 rent control (Prop. R) campaign by the
Renters Alliance (RA) in Shelterforce #19 raises some extremely important issues about
housing and electoral politics. Their analysis proceeds from, and to an extent continues, a
heavy internal split that occurred during the campaign between some of the "housing*

*From *Shelterforce*, Vol. 6, No. 1 (February, 1981), pp. 6–7.

groups'' and the vast majority of others in the San Franciscans for Affordable Housing (SFAH) coalition. I think it is important to talk about this kind of tension and the issues that led to it, because it seems to have arisen in similar campaigns elsewhere. Carrying on such a discussion is not easy, in part because, as one of the major actors in that campaign and in the ensuing conflicts, I hardly can claim objectivity, in part because it is necessary at many places to separate out the issues raised by the RA from the particulars of the Prop. R. campaign as they have described them. But—particularly since over a year has passed since the events described—I think I can state what the problem was in a way that would find basic agreement from all parties.

The Prop. R campaign was an intentional effort from the outset to build a broad based left-liberal coalition to pass a comprehensive and strong piece of housing reform legislation. That move stemmed directly from the November, 1978 Proposition U campaign. Prop. U was an initiative requiring landlords to return to their tenants any Proposition 13 property tax windfalls they received. The Prop. U campaign was run by a small group of housing activists (the Renters Alliance, as the group subsequently renamed itself) and it lost 47% to 53%.

The seriousness of the city's housing conditions and the expression of interest in the housing issue by a range of left-of-center non-housing groups made it seem possible to forge a broad-based coalition made up of labor, church groups, gay groups, neighborhood organizations, the Democratic Party, and others that could pass something more comprehensive than just rent control. (Prop. R also included controls on evictions, speculation, and condo conversion, as well as aids for homeowners and several programs to increase the housing supply). The fifty member coalition was formed quickly and smoothly, and spent the first four months of 1979 drafting and holding community hearings on a comprehensive piece of housing reform legislation. Everyone in the coalition agreed it was an exciting, effective process.

Around May of 1979, at the end of the drafting process and the beginning of the signature drive to put the initiative ordinance on the ballot, the split began to appear. Some Renters Alliance members, plus some other housing groups complained that the coalition was dominated by non-housing groups and that the campaign techniques for the Prop. R campaign were not "grassrootsy" enough. A decision not to hire one of their members as campaign coordinator seemed to be what finally pulled things apart.

The campaign from that point on was characterized by a good deal of internal conflict, which emerged on every conceivable issue and vote and was extremely unpleasant for everyone.

I think the story of the Prop. R campaign is worth telling because of the complex issues that it raises concerning running campaigns and working in coalitions.

In running a housing reform initiative campaign, the question of relations with other campaigns is very important. In our case, there were simultaneously races for the mayor's seat and other citywide offices and six of the eleven supervisorial seats, plus 18 other voter propositions, one of which—the anti-highrise initiative—split our membership (the neighborhood-oriented groups strongly opposed the Manhattanization of San Francisco, while the labor unions responded negatively to what they saw as a threat to jobs). We had to tread a thin and cautious line on these parallel campaigns, in order to maintain our coalition and our focus on the issue that brought us temporarily together.

We made a basic policy decision as a coalition not to formally endorse any other campaign (candidate or issue), while allowing individual coalition members complete freedom to act as they chose with respect to other campaigns. This seems to me a correct policy, probably the only workable one given a broad coalition and a variety of other matters simultaneously on the ballot. But what do we do about coalition members who are strongly tied to a candidate who supports our issue? Are they forbidden as a group from working for that candidate?

The issue is easier when the reform group decides from the outset to run an interlocked issue-candidate slate, as was successfully done in Santa Monica: the rent control and city council campaigns were essentially one. Where conditions are appropriate for this kind of joint strategy, it clearly works: there is more efficient use of resources, and if you win, you win big. Santa Monica seemed to offer optimum conditions for this joint strategy: a very high (80%) proportion of renters, a sophisticated and highly motivated electorate, high quality candidates and leadership, and a reasonably well-funded campaign.

Just beyond the issue of endorsement is the question of cooperative relations with other campaigns. I believe this is an important distinction, both for public consumption and in terms of internal campaign dynamics. Endorsement is a mistake in my view unless one takes it a step further into a unified issue-candidate campaign, like in Santa Monica. Cooperative working relations are both necessary and desirable, in large part because of scarcity of resources. For instance, campaigns can cooperate on door-to-door leafletting, which is very time consuming yet critical for campaigns of our type that cannot raise sufficient funds to do citywide mailings.

Take a city the size of San Francisco, with about 300,000 households. To mail something (bulk rate) to each household requires over $25,000 in postage, apart from the costs of buying and using mailing lists and the labor involved in hand addressing that many pieces. The cost would have been well over half our entire campaign budget—thus ruling out such a mailing. By contrast, the real estate forces opposing Prop. R did twelve targeted mailings, averaging out to about three pieces per household.

It would take about 2,000 person hours to cover the city of San Francisco. It's obviously a highly attractive proposition to work out a "you carry my literature, I'll carry yours" arrangement with some other friendly campaign. For virtually the same labor input you double your outreach capacity. (If the door-to-door work involves personal contact, the issue is very different: I am referring here only to door-to-door literature drops).

The guidelines I would suggest here are simple: make maximum use of these cooperative arrangements for door-to-door literature drops (I don't think they're appropriate in other areas of campaign work); make sure they are fully discussed and agreed to within the coalition (with either consensus or an extraordinary majority needed to approve each arrangement—strong political or moral objections from member groups should be respected); and make it clear that any individual or organization who has objections to carrying literature of a specific other campaign, even after a coalition-wide decision has been made, is under no pressure to do so.

The RA analysis unfortunately doesn't help clarify this important issue of relations with other campaigns. They state that "SFAH therefore dropped its independent stance, but made the mistake of endorsing and working for the Democratic Party 'slate' instead of for genuinely progressive propositions and candidates which would have strong appeal to the supporters of Prop. R.'' But that's a total misstatement of fact. SFAH never departed from its original non-endorsement policy. What we did (and what the RA statement presumably refers to) was to cooperate with the Democratic County Central Committee (a key member of our coalition) on the Party's election-eve "door hanger" slate card. Our Campaign Steering Committee decided to provide some of the volunteer labor in pasting polling place information on these cards and distributing them, in exchange for the Party covering all costs of the operation and giving the Yes on R endorsement an extremely prominent place on the card. That's obviously very different from endorsement.

SHOULD SMALL LANDLORDS BE EXEMPTED?

Let me turn to some of the other issues raised in the Renters Alliance analysis. Exempting small landlords from controls is a very important question. Every campaign will have to wrestle with this issue. I believe the Renters Alliance assertion that exemption of two and three unit owner occupied structures from Prop. R's controls "boomeranged" and caused 80–90% of exempted tenants (12,000 out of about 200,000 renter households) to vote against Prop. R or not at all is simplistic and incorrect. (The 80–90% figure is sheer guesswork in any case—no polls were taken on this subgroup).

Some tenants who spoke at the hearings pushed for a law which covered all landlords. But even in a city with 70% renters, as is true in San Francisco, tenants represent a minority of actual voters. A recent Census Bureau study of the November, 1978 election shows that 59% of all homeowners voted, compared with 28% of all renters. And not all tenants, sad to say, vote for rent controls. The Renters Alliance notes that SFAH heeded the weaker mandate of the public opinion poll we took over the voice of tenants expressed at our neighborhood hearings. Of course we did. This random sampling poll was of the entire electorate, not the specially motivated group who came to our hearings, and it is the entire electorate who votes on such issues.

The RA analysis also notes that the coalition paid particular attention to pressure from some union officals in the coalition on this exemption issue. The union most strongly advocating exemptions was the largely Black Longshoremen's & Warehousemen's Union, many of whose well-paid members are small landlords (one of the contradictions and ironies of the working class in capitalist America). That indeed is one of the prices one pays for being part of a coalition, and we knew from the outset that such compromises might have to be made.

The real issue is not compromises *per se,* but the content of each individual point. With respect to this one, I can only conclude with the observation that the three most recent winning rent control campaigns—Santa Monica, Baltimore and Berkeley—*all* exempted small owner-occupied buildings. With some reluctance, I agreed with that exemption in Prop. R and think it is the sound strategy (one can always work to strengthen an ordinance once passed.)

BUILDING A MULTIRACIAL CAMPAIGN

The issue of how to create and run a multiracial campaign around housing reforms is one we never solved, as the RA analysis points out. Nor did the 1978 Prop. U campaign solve that problem, and the Renters Alliance (with one exception) was itself an all-white organization.

On the face of it, housing reform is a natural for Third World communities. Yet we have the irony of San Francisco's Black community having almost no citywide progressive leadership. A group called the Black Leadership Forum actually came out against Prop. R. The city's only Black supervisor, elected under the old citywide system, is an open proponent of reactionary causes, including his leadership of the successful special election last August that rescinded the district representation system.

Attractive literature by the No on R Campaign, stressing that under rent control housing would become more scarce and Blacks would be at an even greater competitive disadvantage, and reproducing the *Amsterdam News'* damaging anti-rent control editorial, all were powerful obstacles to overcome. Add to this the generally low registration and turnout rates in Black and other minority communities in San Francisco, plus the fact that its housing movement is white dominated, and the situation gets even more difficult. Everyone knew it was a problem in the campaign, lots of efforts (including having a Black campaign co-chair) were made to do something about it—although probably not enough—and no one had any good answers.

CAMPAIGN ORGANIZATION:
GRASSROOTS OR CENTRALIZED

The core critique in the RA analysis is the centralized campaign vs. grassroots organizing theme, which speaks to both campaign organization and campaign tactics. It is a critical question. But the RA analysis ignores the low voter turnout among renters and claims that the well financed ($700,000) and vicious campaign waged by the real estate industry are "superficial" explanations for Prop. R's defeat. The RA analysis focuses instead on the issue of a centralized campaign. What most others would regard as the real reason Prop. R lost so badly was that four months before Election Day, the Supervisors passed both a weak rent control and moderate condominium conversion control ordinance.

This unanimous Board action (outright reactionaries and real estate types on the Board actually voted for it) did what it was intended to do: led a substantial portion of the electorate to buy the argument—central to the No on R campaign—that the city already has acted to remedy the problem, and that people should give the new laws a chance to work. It is the kind of move by the power structure that is virtually impossible to foresee or prevent. And while it is effective as an undermining strategy, it also represents a victory of sorts.

Correct analyses of why political campaigns win and lose are terribly important as guides for future action. I don't think the RA position that we lost because Prop. R "failed to build on the strengths of the grass roots movement that almost won a hastily organized Prop. U in 1978 . . ." (emphasis in original), while downplaying or ignoring the other factors mentioned, sheds the kind of light that can illuminate future efforts.

My own position on the centralized campaign vs. grassroots organizing issue is that it is a false issue; that any effective campaign (not only in terms of winning but in terms of building for the future) should and must have both; and further that there always will be a tension between the two modes that is not so terrible. That tension will come from the inevitable competition for scarce resources (staff time, money, etc.) and on occasions from the clash of long-term (movement building) vs. short-term (campaign winning) goals. It seems obvious to me that the best way to build a movement is through concrete, important victories, and the best way to lose those short-term gains is by not having a base to protect and advance them.

On the question of how the centralization vs. decentralization issue affects campaign tactics, it is a fact of life in American politics that lots of money has to be put into media work (even if the air time itself is free under the Fairness Doctrine, production costs for professionally-done ads—and it's crazy not to use the free time to best advantage—are very high.) Housing activists should not be put off by "slick" media work and consultants, as long as the political content of the final product is progressive and helpful to movement-building.

The clearest example of the benefits of good media work was the recent Prop. 10 victory in California: the overwhelming defeat of the landlords' anti-rent control initiative was probably due primarily to the superb t.v. spots, featuring Henry Fonda, Jack Lemmon and Ralph Nader, which effectively drove home the theme of fraudulence. Production costs of the ads took about half the total campaign budget. Had the landlords' slick well-heeled statewide media campaign not been effectively countered by a slick media campaign on our side, Prop. 10 would have nullified meaningful rent control and most tenant activism in California for years to come.

The need for centralized direction of a campaign seems evident: campaign themes, tactics, literature, fund-raising and spending all must be consistent and under collective control. This of course does not mean things cannot be done in a decentralized manner, just that decentralized work must be centrally coordinated and approved.

Tensions will of course arise here. A good example is around decentralized raising and spending of money. In the Prop. R campaign the city's most progressive and well-organized district initially pressed for financial autonomy. The campaign executive committee took an opposing view: that while district efforts to raise money and print literature were to be encouraged, excessive autonomy in this sphere presented dangers to the campaign. First, hasty or unsophisticated approaches by district people to potential large donors who happened to live in their area might produce a $25 contribution, when a $100 or $500 contribution was possible with proper care and feeding of the donor. Second, a policy of allowing district groups to raise and spend money autonomously probably would lead to a situation where lots of money was being raised and spent in a district which likely would turn out heavily for us anyway. While it was easier to raise money in progressive districts, it may be more important to spend it in other areas: districts with high renter populations where money is hard to raise (lower income and minority areas) and/or high turnout districts where people will vote out of their self-interest as renters. The point is that an overall campaign perspective should guide the spending of money.

Such problems and tensions between the central office and district groups should not disguise the enormous difficulties of building district organizations within the housing movement. Here I feel the RA analysis errs, by blaming the failure to build such groupings on excessive centralism in the campaign and attention to media work. Centralism and media work, as I have argued, are necessary in such a campaign, and—regardless of that necessity—there are huge difficulties in involving people in sustained housing work and building a housing movement.

To sum up, the kinds of tensions the RA describes are inevitable and are not fatal or even necessarily damaging to a campaign effort. The real problem is how to organize people. We didn't do it in Prop. U or in Prop. R. The housing movement isn't so good at this generally. Renters Alliance says "If large numbers of tenants were organized in district committees it would have significantly changed the balance of power in SFAH." Obviously. And that would have been desirable. But they weren't, and the reasons for this general weakness in the housing movement have to be probed clearly and honestly if they are to be overcome.

Until the day we build that Big Housing Movement in the Sky we're going to be highly dependent on coalitions and working relations with other left-liberal groups. They are not going to be as knowledgeable about housing as we are, will not have the same history of housing work, may not have the staying power in the housing field we would like them to have. They are likely to have other, more dominant concerns (labor unions are going to be primarily interested in the workplace, gay groups in gay rights, neighborhood groups in local issues other than housing, and so on). My point is that although many of the dangers of coalition politics the Renters Alliance describes are there and must be struggled with, we can't be arrogant with the non-housing groups we work with, can't guilt-trip them, must understand we're playing in a somewhat different ball park when we enter coalition politics, that different organizations have different political goals even though we're together for the moment on the question of housing reform.

This seems to be one important lesson from the internal dissension within the Prop. R campaign. Parts of the housing movement have a tendency toward purism, idealism or ultra-leftism.

What began in San Francisco as a harmonious and for several months extraordinarily successful effort at coalition politics ended with much enmity. The effort cannot be regarded as useless by any means: it did, as a fall-out, produce rent and condo conversion controls in San Francisco, measures that doubtless will be strengthened as the shortcomings of weak controls become clear. But neither San Franciscans for Affordable Housing nor the Renters Alliance is an effectively functioning organization now. Even with our election loss, I'm not sure that had to be. One of the important lessons to study about the Prop. R campaign, then, is the relationship of housing organizations and the housing movement to broader movements for social change and other special interest and general purpose left-liberal groups. This 3-part dialogue about the Prop. R campaign in *Shelterforce* perhaps adds something to an understanding of these issues.

The Rent Strike as a Political Weapon

Jane Benedict

I'm the chairwoman of the Metropolitan Council on Housing, which is twenty-two years old. We got started on the issue of rent control, but we've spread so that we cover the waterfront—every kind of housing, every kind of tenant. We'll organize anyone who wants to be organized. We have branches in all five boroughs of New York, and we have about ten thousand individual members.

We do everything we can to reach people. We distribute literature, we have demonstrations, we have a monthly newspaper, we're sometimes on radio or TV. We're delighted to get any publicity that can creep into our rather unfriendly press, so that people will know there *is* a citywide tenant union.

By now we're well enough known that we get members not by marching from one building to another saying "Come see us," but by people coming to us on their own. Let me paint how it goes. Let's take the Harlem branch as an example. It has a weekly meeting on Tuesday nights. It runs its branch so that at six o'clock at night it opens the doors of a community room in a particular development. This is publicized in our paper. On the back of our paper there is a directory of a regular schedule for every single branch. And it doesn't change except for the most dire emergencies. So people know and they come and they get up in the meeting and they say, "Look, I'm living in this building on Lenox Avenue, and we haven't any heat and we haven't any hot water." Organizing goes on all year round. But the worst situation is no heat. That is the most dire. It's brutal, it's barbaric. They say, "What can you do?" Well, the answer is, "We'd like you first of all to join Met Council." We explain what the dues are, which are fifteen dollars a year, or if they're not working, it's eight dollars. "You show your good faith and your seriousness by joining and go back and get others. Or bring them to the regular meeting of the branch and we'll discuss here what can be done." We will go to a meeting in a building, but only after tenants have shown that they're really serious about it. We don't just go and make empty speeches. We're far too busy and there aren't that many people to cover that many buildings in all of New York City unless this group shows it really means it. So either there is a meeting on the premises in the building, in the hallway if it isn't too big a building, in somebody's apartment, or in the branch itself on the regular meeting night. And the alternatives are put down. "Look—you've got a landlord that's paying no attention to you. You've got no heat or hot water. Why don't you organize a rent strike?" There really isn't much of any other answer in a situation like that, where the landlord's paying no attention to the building.

What's a rent strike? Well, having joined Met Council, then you set up a committee with a chairperson and a treasurer and two or three other people. And this is our way of putting aside money. Each month you will get a bank check or a bank money order, or if you have a private checking account you get a certified check. You make out a check for the amount of the rent to yourself. Mary Jones will make out a check to Mary Jones and she'll sign it. The check will be fully made out on the front, but not endorsed on the back because once it's endorsed it's negotiable. And we don't want anyone handling that money but the person who is really to endorse it, the tenant. So Mary Jones makes out this check fully on the front. She doesn't make it out to Met Council. We don't want the money. We don't touch it. She doesn't make it out to a tenant association. She doesn't make it out to the landlord, God forbid. She makes it out to herself. Someone or a committee, depending on the size of the building, collects all those checks at the beginning of the month. And two people, who are selected by the group, go and rent a safe deposit box in a local bank. It's usually twenty dollars or so a year. And into that box monthly go the checks. The treasurer keeps a very simple accounting. It doesn't take a professional and it doesn't take a middle-class person. It simply takes somebody who can read and write to put down the names of the people, the apartment number, the amount of the rent, and the date it goes into the box. Any tenant on rent strike can look at that book. Any tenant not on rent strike cannot look at the book. It's only for the people on rent strike.

Now, where we organize a rent strike, we tell the people to make a list of everything that's wrong in the building. In the public areas of the building first of all. There's no heat, there's no hot water, the roof is leaking, the hallway is never swept, there isn't any superintendent—whatever is wrong. Then make a list of what's wrong in every apartment of people who are on rent strike. Not the people who are not—we fight like a union, only for people who are part of the union. No union worth its salt goes and settles grievances for people who are not members of the union, although everybody will benefit from the overall gains. Now, in the buildings that are taken over by the city, that rent strike may have started under the landlord. And the building may have been taken over for non-payment of taxes later. But we say to the tenants, "Go right on with your rent strike. When the city comes around and says, 'We want the rent,' just make it clear you're on rent strike. Because nothing has happened in the building to make it any better."

In New York there is a type of housing which represents a rent strike taken to a higher level. It's something called *In Rem* housing, which is a legal term in Latin which I translate as "in the thing." It refers to buildings that have been taken over by the City for nonpayment of real estate taxes. Right now there are twenty-six of these buildings organized by Met Council, and we do a lot of work with the tenants in these buildings.

The present city administration is headed by Ed Koch, the mayor, who is pro-landlord, pro-banker, not a friend of tenants in any way. But the housing administrators who have to deal with these buildings that have been taken for nonpayment of taxes have to deal with the realities of the situation. They cannot collect the rent unless they offer the tenants something in return. So in these twenty-six buildings where the landlord got out because of rent strikes, the City has offered what it calls an interim lease. It lasts for eleven months and it's called interim because the hope of Mayor Koch is that either the tenants will buy the building or some slumlord will. We don't want either of those things to happen. We don't want the tenants to buy the building. We want them to run the building, to get help from the City in certain repairs that they can't afford, but for the City to hold the title. Now that is an experiment—a new departure for us and for everybody else. And we are just renewing the leases for the fourth year. We did not consider alternatives to this because we have a fairly basic feeling about what housing ought to be in this miserable world that we've living in.

About fifteen years ago we developed a philosophy of what we call "housing in the public domain," that we want the tenants to control the buildings but the title to remain vested in government. We feel strongly about this—that it's not to the advantage of the tenants to own the building. They then pay the taxes, and we see no reason why they *should* pay taxes, particularly for these old hulks. It is years of neglect through non-repair and non-maintenance that has brought the buildings to this condition. So we say that the tenants should run the building, set the policy for the rents (which they indeed are doing), and put every cent of that money back into the building. And when the rents are not enough to cover certain basic repairs like a new furnace or a new roof or new plumbing, the tenants can demand that the City, State, or Federal government—which has done injury to the tenants through years of inaction—step in and make those repairs.

We don't make deals behind the backs of the tenants, we deal with the city only with the tenants present. We don't have private conferences, any of us. We're very careful about that. No union—and we are a tenant union—that talks privately to management is trusted by its members, and with good reason. We don't do that. On the day-to-day basis, this has been very tough. The Koch administration is very tough, and they'd like to see these buildings sold. We'd rather the city remain in a situation of legal responsibility where we can put pressure on them.

One thing I should make clear about rent strikes is that they aren't at all limited to this *In Rem* housing. We've been organizing rent strikes for many, many years, not as an end in itself but as a means to collective bargaining. A means of trying to get the landlord to make certain repairs and give certain services, which he should be giving anyway and he isn't. That's how rent strikes get started. And the method of starting the rent strike is the same, no matter if the title is in the City, or in a private landlord, or in some sort of management association. The pattern is all the same. We explain to tenants from the beginning that they cannot be evicted if they follow the procedure that we insist upon, that we will not work with a rent strike otherwise. That the money be in the safe deposit box, or if they're making repairs in the building, that it is in a minimal bank account a little at a time. The reason that we do this is so that every penny is accounted for.

Let's say just one tenant gets a dispossess. A dispossess is the popular term. It's called a notice of petition. And it means the landlord is petitioning the court for the right to evict Mary Jones because she hasn't paid her rent. If there's only one dispossess, let's say in a building of thirty apartments, we say, everybody should go. Now that's frequently a hardship, because people are on jobs and there are many people who if they don't turn up on their jobs would be fired. Everybody should go to court. Everybody possible should go with that one person to court to show that this is a group action. Because frequently what happens in court is really horse trading. It's called bargaining but it's really horse trading. The judge will say, "Why don't the two sides go outside and try to get together?" And a show of strength on the tenants' part really puts you in a better position to negotiate.

An organizer who has been working with the tenants goes with the tenants to court and negotiates together with the tenants wherever they have to negotiate— whether it's a little airless conference room in the court house, or out in the corridor, or wherever. And frequently a stipulation is drawn up which is on record with the court that the landlord will do X, Y, Z and at a given point the tenants will give this much money. Sometimes, in fact, there are negotiations without rent strike. We're not dying to organize rent strikes. They're a tremendous amount of work—both for the organization, the Met Council, the organizer and for the people who live there. So that if we can get a landlord to negotiate without a rent strike, that's fine.

We don't have an absolute blueprint. The only absolute we have is that if you're going to work with us, you'll have to join. You'll have to help carry the freight. The other thing is that if we have a rent strike it has got to follow the pattern we've set down in order that nobody get evicted and that money suddenly not be there. Because a tenant ordered by the court to pay rent who hasn't got the money will be evicted.

Let me sum up. The use of the rent strike as a political weapon is very important. A rent strike is comparable to a labor strike. It is a militant form of doing something but it isn't an end in itself. It is simply a weapon. Now the problem is to take these flare-ups and use them to keep an organization stable and united. A rent strike isn't a bandaid that you put on today and once the wound heals you shed it in the wastebasket. You have got to have a united movement to combat fundamental housing problems and achieve long range goals. Nobody thinks that "housing in the public domain" is going to take place tomorrow or the day after tomorrow. *In Rem* housing is a very important experiment in self determination. This opportunity has never existed before and we must wage a constant battle to hold on to it.

Stopping Arson

David Scondras

In the fall of 1976 a five-year-old boy was killed in a fire on Symphony Road, in the Fenway section of Boston. The people who lived on that street were a really assorted group in terms of jobs, income, life-style, sexual preference, race, and everything else, though most were low-income. But that fire brought them all to a kind of psychological breaking point. It was the seventeenth fire on that one street from 1974 to 1976, and this time a child was dead. It was clear in everyone's mind that something was terribly wrong.

Some people decided to leave but others were locked in. Some of them didn't have any other housing available to them; some couldn't get out for financial reasons, others for health reasons, and so on. These people were the most terrified people because they wanted to leave but they couldn't—and yet they didn't feel competent to do anything about the situation. A fairly large group of people, about twenty, decided on the night that the five-year-old was killed that they had had enough of this. They decided that they were going to put an end to it.

The situation was easy to define. The buildings were burning down, people were being killed, the fires were progressing up the street and people knew that the fires were being deliberately set. But it wasn't clear who was setting them, who was responsible, or what could be done about it.

When facing that kind of an issue, it was obvious to us that the first thing to do was to get people together. A few of us—about five or six—had been organizing in the Fenway area since 1971. We had built a food cooperative, a playground, a daycare center, a health center, a housing cooperative, a local newspaper. We knew that it was quite important at that very moment to get people together because if we did not do that, people would feel even more helpless and terrified. The other reason was that whatever we did, it would require a lot of cooperation on the part of a lot of people. How do you get that kind of cooperation without a base to work from? At the meeting that night we made a decision to hold a larger meeting. This is usually the first decision made when organizing. In preparing for the second meeting we arranged for Mel King to come—we needed an authority figure and he's a very popular state representative. It was also important that he's black. We were white organizers, but that community was multi-racial and we had a lot of friends who were blacks. That meeting was terrific. We had up to about thirty people there, and we devised a strategy.

We began by listing what we wanted to see happen. We had nine demands. We wanted an investigation by the Attorney General of the state as to who was burning the buildings down. We had reached a conclusion by doing a lot of property research that the fires were being set in order to get insurance money. It was arson for profit. Consequently, we were convinced that certain other key buildings were going to be burned down. These buildings were owned by the same type of people, in the same economic situation. All the telltale signs were there. Small fires had begun already; these were fires to scare people out of the buildings. Vacancies were going up. Cash flow problems were severe. There were court orders to do a lot of repairs, and we knew the owners did not have the money. Add all those things together, and we were convinced there were going to be more fires.

To make a long story short, we devised a theory. We put down all the history of the property that had been burned down, on window shades. In fact, they were my window shades. And when anybody came by we could pull down the window shades and show them to people. We listed the transactions for each property and you could see for each building that a lot of money was made. We identified the people who were involved in these buildings.

There were a whole series of problems facing the group. One was the fact that the Fire Department said there wasn't any arson on Symphony Road. The official word was therefore that we were wrong at best, crazy at worst. Sometimes there were intimations that the fires *had* been set—but by people like us. One city official said Symphony Road was filled with homosexuals, pimps, prostitutes, and drug addicts, and that's why there was a problem. The mayor's office was no help at all.

Kevin White was in his third term, and his administration was notable for its inertia. If things got done it was for cosmetic reasons. His office didn't listen to us and didn't care about the fires.

We had to shake something loose, so we managed to get the City Council to hold a public hearing. This was a chance to get our case before the media. We got about 400 people through leaflets, door knocking, talking to people, and telephone chains. Also, we used a kind of Catch 22. When you tell people the City Council members will come, you get a mob scene. And when you tell the City Council members that a lot of people are going to come, they will be there. Of course, the starting time you give the news media is thirty minutes before the time you tell everyone else. While the reporters are waiting for the people to show up, you have a chance to explain to them what's going on. They would come up with terrible stuff if we didn't have some lead time to briefly explain what was going on.

We never got any legislation through the City Council, but that hearing was a big success in terms of the number of people who came. We took everybody's name and phone number and tried to create a network throughout the neighborhood. We formed a new neighborhood organization, the Symphony Tenants Organizing Project or STOP. All of our literature started carrying a logo with a hand that said "STOP."

We were angry but not really surprised that we didn't get anywhere with the city government. All along, we figured our best hope was to get the state Attorney General's office into the case. Publicity was bound to help, and we did everything we could to spotlight the city's inaction. Once we smuggled our way into their art exhibition. One of the artists who was presenting an exhibit was a person named Jim Jones. He came to us and said he wanted to help us in some way. So we worked with him to make a blown-up photograph of a burning building with letters documenting the city's failure to deal with it. We sneaked the photo underneath a big sheet that was to be unveiled at the opening of the exhibition.

We also had a lot of support from some of the Boston weeklies, which kept the issue in the air. One reporter, Mark Zanger, did a lot of investigative writing and research that was especially helpful.

Eventually a meeting was set up between Mel King, STOP representatives, Attorney General Frank Bellotti and some aides, and the media. We gave the Attorney General every piece of evidence that we had.

We also had Governor Dukakis show up at our house at 8:00 one morning. We'd invited him to come and see what was going on, and he came. We pulled down the window shades and showed him one shade at a time to let him see the pattern of the fires. He was impressed. He assigned some assistants to work with us on drafting a bill to stop arson for profit. He also told the state fire marshall to deal with the immediate situation—which didn't really happen, but at least it was encouraging to get the kind of high-level recognition of our problem that Dukakis gave us.

At the same time, the local organization needed continual work. We had everything from pot-luck dinners to bake sales along with organizational meetings. We also managed to get VISTA slots eventually, but that took a while.

Everything came together for us in the fall of 1977, when thirty-three people were indicted. All of them were white, all of them were suburbanites, all of them were middle-aged. They were real estate brokers, lawyers, that sort of thing; one was an ex-detective from the fire marshall's office and one was a fire chief. In other words, the low-income people who live on the street and were continually being accused of the crime were the exact antithesis of the people who were ultimately indicted.

The arrests made a national scandal, partly because of the type of people who were arrested and partly because we had been using the media all along as a vehicle to get attention. Anyway, the accusations we were making went way beyond Symphony Road. This kind of crime was happening all around the country. And no one was doing anything about it. We had people flying in from Chicago, we had the *New York Times* there, the *Washington Post*. ABC News started putting together an hour-long special on our case, which it took six months to film.

This was the sort of publicity that rarely comes to a community organizing group, and we decided to take advantage of it. We pushed hard in the state legislature for an anti-arson bill, and after a year we got it through. We had to drop some sections because the insurance industry lobbied heavily against them, but we got a compromise version passed and it was the first comprehensive state anti-arson law in the history of the U.S. Governor Dukakis signed it in October 1978 on the edge of a playground that we had built. Lots of people were there, and the media in full force. It was a mob scene and we decided, "Why stop there?" So we didn't stop. We got a Boston Congressman to file a bill in Congress, which we're still fighting for. We started a company called Urban Educational Systems. It hired quite a few activists who formed a team of people. We have dealt with arson from New York to San Francisco to Chicago to New Orleans and most of the places in between, and we still are. We're still working in Boston, though. That's the one place where we can do something more than give advice.

Our focus in Boston shifted in two directions. One, we began to realize from our research that the banking industry was the central problem, not so much the insurance industry. The second thing we began to realize was that people needed to understand the issue in depth. So we began a series of teaching programs. We developed two slide shows, a movie, and a presentation which we put on in neighborhoods across the city. We wanted to explain the connection between banks, mortgage practices, insurance companies, fires in the neighborhoods, and abandoned houses. We are working to form alliances between different community groups, around the issue of housing.

Right now we are converting the effort to fight arson into a broader working-class coalition organized around the whole issue of control of resources. That's behind the arson problem in the first place and that is our goal. Originally, in STOP, I think we were parochial. We restricted ourselves, but then we jumped directly from our neighborhood to the state government and directly to the federal government. We discovered the city very late. If I were to do it again, I would have sent out people to other neighborhoods to do the same kind of research and to try to start other groups and form a citywide body. And I think we should have been less scared than we were of reaching out to working-class neighborhoods like East Boston and Charlestown that are nearly all-white. We were assuming that racism would make them support our enemies, not us. So we didn't want to get near them, and we only found out much later that we can work with them.

7

Women and Organizing

In this chapter we explore the role of women as organizers—particularly as organizers of other women. As in other organizing arenas in this book we can only touch on some of the more important issues. The cases deal with what has come to be known as a functional community—a group of people who share a common interest, not just physical space as in neighborhood organizing. I have chosen women as a functional group in this chapter because the women's movement is enormous and vibrant and women organizers are raising in very self-conscious ways a number of special issues concerning their roles.

First, Meg Campbell poetically reflects on her inner struggle to reconcile her roles as a woman and as an organizer. She feels as if she is moving through uncharted territory and worries about her ability to fulfill her obligations as an organizer while pregnant. She is also afraid that as an organizer she will be forced to express a side of her personality that is seen as "unfeminine." She concludes that the dual role of women as organizers has yet to be fully explored.*

What is new in this situation is not the fact that women are acting as organizers, or even that they are organizing for their own rights—that has been happening

---

*I met Meg Campbell three years after she wrote this article. She had two children then and was living in rural New Hampshire with her husband. Both she and her husband were still organizing, and doing it very effectively. In a sense she was answering her own question by the way she was living her life.

for generations. What is new is the widespread challenging of sex roles in a way that includes the questioning of "male" and "female" personality types. It is now recognized that to be a good organizer one must be able to be not only adversarial and combative but sensitive and caring.

The second selection deals with cleavages—differences of class, race, and sexual preference issues that can become issues for women working and living in shelters for battered women. While there is a fine line between organizing and service work in the battered women's movement, the issues raised in this selection are critical in any organizing work. If they are not recognized and dealt with they can lead to tremendous tensions and the failure to achieve even minimal goals in any organizing effort. Dealing with these issues is a difficult, painful individual process. Organizers must be willing to confront these issues in their own lives and must try to help the people they are working with to deal constructively with these issues as well.

Next, Lois Ahrens describes a feminist cooperative for battered women. The case is instructive because a major organizing strategy of the feminist movement has been the development of self-help groups. Feminist ideology has been the basis for the form these self-help groups have taken. It is believed that empowerment for women will come from a nonhierarchical structure and from collective decision making in these groups. The cooperative for battered women described in this case was gradually transformed from such a group into a traditional social service institution. Ahrens analyzes why this happened and gives specific suggestions for how this might be avoided by other feminist self-help groups.

There are literally thousands of self-help groups in the United States. One of their defining characteristics is that they involve mutual sharing, support, and advice giving, usually without the help of outside experts or professionals. In many cases the groups had their origin in a belief that professionals cannot be trusted, or that at best they are incapable of providing the necessary help. Of course there are instances where professionals have helped initiate self-help groups or may be called on at certain points in a group's development for the specific expertise they may have to offer. As can be seen from this case, the timing and appropriateness of professional activity within the self-help framework presents dilemmas that are not easy to solve. What do you think are appropriate roles for professionals and/or "professional" community organizers within a feminist self-help framework?

Women for Sobriety is a national organization founded by Jean Kirkpatrick. It operates on the self-help model and is specifically geared to the needs of women alcoholics. Kirkpatrick founded the organization because she perceived that AA was not meeting the needs of women. Among the problems she encountered were a constant comparison with AA, a lack of funds, and the inability of women to work together cooperatively. She ascribes the latter problems to "cultural training" and "cultural forces" that make it difficult for women to work together.

The case provides a contrast to the previous organizing effort. The organizer is interested in a single issue—alcoholism—and the organization does not run on feminist principles. In fact most of the power seems to be in the hands of the organization's founder. Do you think the problems of commitment, jealousy, and backbiting could have been avoided if the group had had a feminist ideology and an attempt had been made to organize in a more collective manner?

Jessica Shubow describes the Women's Pentagon Action. She contrasts its strategy, tactics, and ideology with what some feminists call a male model of organizing. In her view, the purpose of the Pentagon action was not to win specific gains but to contribute to an overall process of transforming society by exposing patriarchal attitudes that permeate at all levels. In addition, the demonstration had the goal of developing feelings of empowerment in an ever-growing number of women. Very creative tactics were developed that enabled women to express their feelings collectively and thereby to feel more powerful. She also describes the deliberate attempt by planners of the Pentagon action to take up many issues simultaneously.

This case raises a number of organizing issues. Do you think the collective expression of feelings does lead to empowerment? Do you think there is a distinction between "feeling good," recruiting people to a movement, and having a political effect? How would you evaluate the simultaneous dealing with many disparate issues?

In the last selection, Andrea Aiello describes the organizing she has done for an annual march called Take Back the Night, held for several years in Boston as well as other cities in the late 1970s and early 1980s. These demonstrations have sought to confront publicly the problem that women are often afraid to move about at night. By involving thousands of women in a collective expression of their anger and determination, they have sought to help empower women to walk at night without fear. The organizing for the march involved cultural outreach, publicity as well as attempting to contact women not ordinarily recruited. She is honest about the difficulties that organizers in her neighborhood had in recruiting black women and older women. In discussing her hopes for future Take Back the Night marches, she sets forth a broad range of goals that she thinks the organizers could address. Many people would consider these goals too broad.

Women as Organizers[1]

Meg Campbell

I feel I'm chasing a dolphin trying to write an article on Women as Organizers; she eludes me and draws me further and further into the deep.

Back on the shore I easily dismissed the old arguments. They are so self-serving and short-sighted, I scarcely like to dignify them by reply. What can one say to a person who fails to recognize that human beings are born into this world of two parents, father and mother, and that both have responsibility in child-rearing? Not that justice and equality are common! Negligent fathers are more the rule than the exception; but the injustice ought then to be saddled on the men, not the women. It's pure rubbish to say that women can't be organizers because they have to stay home and raise children.

I blithely assert that, and dive into the water. But I must be honest. I am six months pregnant, and I do not swim as fast as I used to. I roll onto my back to pause for a moment to think. I'm glad I'm not in the middle of an organizing drive. The thought overwhelms me. The prospect of knocking 1000 doors, right now, makes me shake my ahead. "Ah-hah! Are *they* right? Can a pregnant person organize? Is this just an omen of the years ahead?" So the doubts surface, little undercurrents at first, fighting yourself from within. You must be still, and listen. Your organizing voice will have her say.

AM I AN ORGANIZER?

"Wait a minute. They don't knock on 1000 doors, and they call themselves organizers. And even organizers who do organizing drives pace themselves. Besides, it's not even my job to knock on doors, but to train other organizers. Does that make me *not* an organizer? Have I moved into this training job because one can't organize and have kids (literally, have them, physically carry them)? Am I an organizer?"

Over my head by six feet of water, it's striking that I even ask myself that question. I've found, from my various travels and informal polls, that it's a question that women in this business, though, do ask themselves quite a bit; and a question men in the business, rarely ask themselves, even those men who, in my opinion, are *not* organizers, but something else. (Usually leaders or advocates, but they are convinced they are organizers.) Perhaps we hold the profession in too great esteem, and are overly hesitant to see ourselves in the role. Perhaps we have too rigid a conception of "The Organizer" in our mind, and knowing ourselves as well as we do, know we can't measure up to a supposed ideal of stoicism, brilliance and

[1]From *Just Economics: The Magazine for Organizers*, Vol. 6, No. 2 (April, 1978), p. 8. This magazine is now entitled *The Organizer* and is published by The Institute for Social Justice.

charisma. No matter that the men can't either, with a bit of swaggering and bragging, some give the impression they are organizers. They tell us so. Not all, of course. We look to people's work, not what they say, and performance and style emerge. We take a deep breath. There are women there, not so many as we'd like, not nearly as many as there should be, but they are there. With their colleagues, they've left those name-dropping, dashing fellows in the dust. (I imagine they're still haggling over theory!)

Performance and style. Those were the words which chased away my initial fear that I could not be both—organizer and woman. As with any fear, once it's quelled, it appears almost silly. To be afraid of the dark; we smile now, the memory of quaking fright long ago dissipated. To be afraid that organizing might change my personality at the very root, where I am a woman? That being tough as an organizer might mean losing my ability to be tender? Or, more fundamentally, that being competitive, and ambitious and a fighter might make me less attractive, less magnetic as it were, as a woman? That one could only be a woman organizer if one were willing to lead an essentially solitary life? That the work of personal relationships—ah well, that was "women's work," and it must be abandoned if one was to devote oneself to being an organizer?

Those questions used to pound at me. I was slow to realize that no man could reassure me, I had to reassure myself, just by traversing the territory, and charting it as I went. Other women on nearby paths were a tremendous help. We all yearned for more company. Promised we would keep our eyes back and ahead, encourage newcomers, coax those on the sidelines to step out. When the old blush of self-confidence returned, it was easy again to share lessons with the men; we were all learning.

ORGANIZING OURSELVES

Possible then to be pregnant and organize? Yes, for pregnancy only makes the lessons any organizer should know more obvious. One can never do everything at once, and one must be impeccably well-organized herself (or himself) to organize others. It is essential to feel the urgency of organizing—time is precious; yet look how wide the ocean spans we hope to cross. Might we not be good enough organizers to organize our lives in such a way that we may take children with us on our journey?

I don't say it idly. It will mean schedules and division of responsibilities at any given moment. It will take organizing!

But you see what I mean about the dolphin? Here I am rambling on all about myself, when there are countless other resolutions women have worked out for themselves to these questions. And more men are honestly probing their lives, and their assumptions, and learning to take up their slack of these responsibilities; that is hopeful.

I shall stick with steady strokes. In years to come, I may know this dolphin well enough to be able to write about her, to explain her sounds and movements to anyone on land; to say with certainty, "Thus and so is a fact" about Women as Organizers. The time seems a long way off.

Race, Class and Sexual Preference in the Battered Women's Movement*

ISSUES OF RACE, CLASS AND SEXUAL PREFERENCE

The explosive issues of race, class and sexual preference often come up in our day-to-day work with battered women. They are difficult to deal with because confronting these issues forces us to look at how we've been oppressed as well as how we oppress others. Many women, particularly white women, have never been taught to think or talk about our lives from a political perspective; and though women of color and many white working class women are taught early in life that the system works against them because of their race or class, they also have not seen their status as women as a political issue. What do "politics" have to do with battered women? Everything. Simply put, "politics" is dealing with power: who has it, who doesn't, and why.

All forms of violence against women thrive because we live in a world where white men have power ("the possession of control, authority or influence over others; the ability to act or produce an effect"). There are many groups of people who gain benefits from their positions (economic, social, cultural, religious), whether they use those consciously and intentionally or not. These benefits constitute privilege and are denied to those who don't fit into the powerful and/or privileged groups. Men have privilege to greater and lesser degrees depending on color, class and/or cultural background; heterosexual people have privilege; white people have privilege; middle and upper class people have privilege; people with no physical difficulties ("disabilities") have privilege.

Men of any class or race have power and privileges in their relationships to individual women; i.e., the societal sanction to beat women, the right to coerce or force women to have sex and the expectation that women will emotionally and physically take care of men. Some people have privilege with regard to one aspect of their lives and lack of privilege with regard to another. For example, a working class married woman has the privilege to talk openly about her family life and her relationship with her husband, whereas a middle class lesbian has more economic freedom, but not the privilege to discuss her life openly.

The institutionalized exertion by these groups of their power and privilege are called sexism, heterosexism, racism and classism. Battering of women by men exists in this context, in a system which is based on groups of people gaining and holding power at others' expense.

---

*Abridged from *For Shelter and Beyond: An Educational Manual For Working With Women Who Are Battered* produced by The Massachusetts Coalition of Battered Women Service Groups.

Because the battered women's movement is political and will effect social change, each of us working in our shelters and projects needs to take responsibility to learn about oppression, to confront our feelings about it and make a commitment to change. We are all limited by racism, classism, heterosexism, ageism and other forms of oppression. We are denied access to other cultures and to opportunity for growth. How can we be a safe place for all women if we don't look collectively and individually at the ways we are oppressed? We will grow from knowing about each other's experience without feeling guilty about who we are. The only way to effect change on a large scale is to start with ourselves and come to understand who we are as individuals and then to look at the whole system which allows and even sanctions battering and all forms of violence against women.

It is important to address these issues as they arise in our work, not because we want to stress differences, but because we each need to be able to understand and deal with women's experiences which differ from our own. If we don't have an understanding of these issues, they will continue to divide us and prevent us from joining together and building on the experiences that we as women have in common. We can build on our acknowledgement and acceptance of our differences and diversity along with our acknowledgement of our commonality.

Although we recognize that issues of race, class and sexual preference arise between battered women and the men who abuse them, that is not our focus here. The following section specifically concerns the issues of race, class and sexual preference and how these arise between women working and living in shelters.

—*Jane Weiss*

Class Differences in Battered Women's Programs

Conflicts arising from class backgrounds, privileges and expectations sometimes occur between staff members, between staff and battered women, and between battered women using our programs. As women committed to working toward a violence-free, unoppressive society, we all have a responsibility to fight classism and other forms of domination in ourselves and others. It is particularly important for those of us who have the privileges and power of the middle class to deal with our attitudes and prejudices about class differences. Those of us who gain from society's class structure can easily perpetuate it by refusing to recognize our privileges. Most of us were brought up on the American dream: anyone who works long and hard enough will become a success. People with privileges and power (i.e., white men) choose to keep this myth alive because it prevents them from feeling guilty about their privileges, and encourages working class people and people of color to look to themselves rather than a capitalist society for the reason that they don't have the same privileges and possessions. Being aware of and sensitive to class differences and middle class privileges can be the first step in working on this issue; however, we need to act based on this knowledge to prevent classism in our groups by staff and women using the programs.

It may be helpful to consider some examples of classism and how to deal with it as a staffer. Some middle class staffers make insensitive and hurtful remarks to less privileged women using our programs. A middle class woman might not understand how a working class battered woman might see relocating within or outside of the state as impossible. She may not appreciate how financially difficult or even impossible it would be, how scary it might be for someone who has done little or no traveling, or how uprooted the woman would feel without her own support network. Another example of a classist and insensitive remark is a staffer telling a battered woman that she should just hire herself a good lawyer. The blatant disregard for the woman's financial limitations is obvious, but the more subtle disregard for her experiential limitations is just as harmful. Women with economic privilege and professional connections should think before trying to support a working class woman by counseling her to do something that is beyond her means. Telling a working class woman that it's better to buy "good" (expensive) clothes and shoes for her children because they last longer, or that she should dress better when she goes to court (she may not own "good" clothes) can be very classist, in that it disregards a woman's economic ability and judges her according to middle class standards.

Staffers talking about month-long vacations, long distance trips, etc., can also be alienating for working class women, especially if they are coming out of violent and restrictive relationships. In the same way, values about food, such as vegetarianism, or about lifestyle, such as collective living, can also be alienating to working class and low income women, who may perceive suggestions of food or lifestyle as judgmental. (Vegetables are expensive and vegetarian diets are non-traditional in this society; many working-class women have never lived outside a nuclear family, never lived in college dormitories or other group households, and therefore collective living is quite foreign.) While it's useful for women in our programs to hear about different lifestyles, options and ways of thinking, it's important that staff be careful not to talk about such things in a judgmental or hurtful way.

While many women seeking help from battered women's groups are working class, middle class women also turn to us for support and refuge because their privileges have been severely limited by the abusive men they have left. Most middle class women using our groups, upon leaving their abusers, have lost access to the money and resources which were controlled by their husbands, and many are scared to death of their sudden insecurity. Although they may have other resources not available to working class women, it will take time for them to recognize this. Especially in a shelter, conflicts often arise between middle class and working class residents, and can escalate into full-scale battles. By watching for conflicts and making women deal with them right away, we can begin to prevent conflicts from escalating into such painful and oppressive incidents. Class issues in shelters, like cultural and racial issues, often arise in the context of food, childrearing and housekeeping, all of which require women's cooperation in a shelter.

Most of us clean our houses, cook our meals and raise our children remarkably like our mothers did; and you can't tell a woman that her mother was dead wrong about all that. Since we probably can agree that there is no perfect way to do any of these things, the most we can hope to do is to share our different experiences and learn from each other. Two women arguing about whether dinner should be meat or beans, fish or casserole, can get involved in a shouting match about what is better.

A similar battle can arise when a middle class woman tries to impose her standards on a working class woman. For instance, she might suggest buying juice for the children rather than Kool-ade, or health bread instead of Wonder Bread. The working class mother in this situation can feel defensive about what she's been giving her kids, and even resentful toward the other woman who can afford to buy more expensive food. Clearly it is more often the high price that discourages working class women from buying juice rather than ignorance about nutrition or lack of concern. If the middle class woman recognized this, she would be less likely to make such suggestions or at least wouldn't raise them as criticisms of the other mother. If a situation like this turns into an argument, a staffer should interrupt the argument and try to get the women to talk and to listen to each other. Because of the emotional nature of the argument, they might need an objective person to help them work it out. The staffer can try to get each woman to tell her side of the story, and to listen to the other woman without interrupting. Each should explain what she felt. Once they've listened to each other, it may be easier for them to get past "my way is better than yours" and closer to "why I feel the way I do about this." Talking to each other about why they do things differently and sharing experiences could bring the women closer together and they might learn about dealing with conflicts and differences and about appreciating the experiences of other women.

Aside from having to interrupt arguments we should be encouraging women who use our programs to reach out to women of all class backgrounds, to share their differing experiences as well as their common ones. As women, most of us were raised to think of others first; thus it shouldn't be so difficult for us to be open to each other and understanding of differences. We have a great deal to learn from each other.

There are no easy or short-term solutions to classism; the issue is a difficult one to recognize and address. By becoming more sensitive to and aware of class differences, however, we may begin to appreciate the positive exchanges that can occur. Sharing our experiences, we can enrich each others' lives and make things better for our children. We live in a society that encourages divisions of all kinds—class, racial, cultural and sexual. Challenging such divisiveness is part of our work toward ending woman abuse. We must be committed to changing not only our outward behavior and language, but also our inward feelings and value judgments. We can help each other do this, and become stronger and closer as we learn from each other.

—*Chris Butler, with help from*
Mary Quinn, Renae Scott and Gail Sullivan

SOME THOUGHTS ON RACISM

What I'd like to do in this article is to tell some of my thoughts on race and racism and some of the experiences I've had being who I am—a Black feminist, lesbian activist.

This article will be a sort of patchwork with separate pieces held together by a common thread. I've decided to write it this way both because it seems easier for me than writing a more conventionally organized essay and also because I want to begin to break away from these traditional forms.

*   *   *

I have the feeling that no one understands, that no one white understands our daily experiences. As I wrote the previous sentence I tried to think of an example. I didn't have to go any further back than this morning. On my way to work I passed an older woman on the street and when I looked at her she frowned. I assumed it was because I am Black. What's really important about this assumption is that it's *always* valid on some level. It's never far-fetched for Black people to assume that negative treatment by a white person is the result of racism. No one white understands what it means to have this a constant valid assumption in our lives.

*   *   *

I've wondered whether we're able to identify with white women's experiences because we see ourselves as women as well as Black, because we see white women as human like ourselves, women like ourselves, not "other," because we're raised to be "bicultural"—we *have* to be—because we've had contact with white women all of our lives.

It's impossible, I think to be a Black person in this country and not be deeply aware of white people. Part of our awareness is knowledge we need to survive. Very few Black people actually have no contact with whites and even those who have little contact are constantly bombarded with whiteness. There's lots of propaganda in this culture for the normality of, the rightness of whiteness, just as there's a lot of propaganda for the normality of heterosexuality.

White women, on the other hand, can grow up without ever having seen or known a Black person until they're adults. This is what it can mean to be a member of the majority race in a racist country. Even if white women have had early relationships with Blacks, I wonder how authentic they were, how honest and free. I'm thinking of the classic stories some upper class white women tell of their families' Black servants. At the same time that most white children are learning to relate to other people, they are *not* relating to Black people. So white women who're trying to learn to relate to Black women are faced with a basic kind of task much after they have gone through other basic development. I'm not saying that women can't grow after a certain age. Of course I believe that is part of what it means for us to be feminists. But it's much harder. There are so many years of living pulling against it. It's hard because it requires the courage to make one's self vulnerable and also because there's almost no help out there. No guides because this is something the society does not want done. It goes totally against the grain.

*   *   *

As Black feminists we are constantly being asked to legitimate feminist activities by our participation. At a recent academic conference I was the only Third World woman among feminist panelists. I was the only woman whose talk *focused* on women of color. I am furious that white women think they've dealt with Black women and with racism by giving me the responsibility of speaking for and about Black women. It's overwhelming to me and it's tokenism. What I want white women to do is to *include* Black women and other Third World women explicitly, *by name* in their work whether it be on medical abuse, lesbian artists or quiltmaking. What I want is that white women include Black women in their psyches, minds, hearts, their political analyses and political work. My sense of where most white women are on this is that they allude to Third World women but they do not feel competent to do more than that. And sometimes it doesn't occur to them to do even that. White women who are serious about fighting racism must get to the place where not only do they mention Black women but are also able to respectfully talk about what our presence means.

*   *   *

Somehow white women have got to recall what they *already* know about racism, about being racist. They *were* taught it and they've got to bring it up out of their memories and look at it and talk about it.

*   *   *

Another task that Black feminists are often asked to do by white feminists is to explain racism. Writing this article is like that. I feel that I've been explaining myself as a Black person and explaining racism all of my life. I sometimes get so angry and tired being surrounded by white women at workshops, meetings or parties who're looking to me for answers. Yet the context of feminism makes it seem worth trying again and writing feels more personally gratifying, not such a psychic drain.

Confronting racism is terrifying work. I've caught glimpses of how terrifying in my recent attempts to confront my own anti-Semitism. It requires constant commitment and deep and growing honesty. It's got to be done if this movement is to survive.

—Beverly Smith
First appeared in Aegis: Magazine on
Ending Violence Against Women

RACISM: A WHITE ISSUE

I've written and re-written this article only to find that because I am still only in the early stages of seriously examining my own racism and the racism in the battered women's movement, I am unable to articulate much of what I think needs to be said. I grew up in a home where my father believed and preached the natural superiority of whites. Because his racism was so blatant, it was easy for me to reject his ideas during the civil rights movement of the 1960's. Marching with Father Groppi for open housing in Milwaukee, sending my babysitting money to Martin Luther King and making sure that I always went to confession to the black priest in our lily-white parish were all signs to me that I had rejected the racist philosophy my father taught and had joined with the Third World people in their struggle for liberation.

As I began to get involved in neighborhood organizing and especially in the battered women's program, I watched Blacks and Indians accuse white feminist women of racism. Certainly, they didn't mean me—I had marched in Milwaukee. I too was oppressed by the white male. So when I heard women of color speaking of white privileges, I mentally inserted the word "male"; "white male privileges."

I viewed the anger of women of color toward my white sisters as a cop out. We are the most vulnerable to this anger, we listened and tried to adjust. It seemed to me that because it is much easier for them to confront us than the racist system or the men in their communities who give no support to their participation in women's issues, we are the most aggressively confronted.

I also defended the decision making process we used in developing grassroots organizations as totally open to all women. In response to complaints of exclusionary practices, special care is always taken to notify minority organizations and women of color of conferences, planning meetings, job openings and workshops.

Gradually, I began to realize the tremendous gap between my rhetoric about solidarity with third world women and my gut feelings.

I began talking to a Black friend of mine, Ella Gross, about how sick I was getting of the whole issue. Ella, in her normal blunt direct way, told me that I was sick of it because I didn't want to go past adjusting my behavior to recognizing my racism. In the many many hours I spent talking to Ella, I began to see how white women ignored the need to re-examine the traditional white rigid methods of decision making, priority setting and implementing decisions. Our way of including women of color was to send out notices. We never came to the business table as equals. Women of color join us on our terms.

I started seeing the similarities of how men have excluded the participation of women in their work through *Roberts Rules of Order,* encouraging us to set up subcommittees to discuss our problems but never seeing sexism as their problem. It became clear that in many ways I act the same way toward women of color, supporting them in dealing with their issues. Similar to liberal men's recognition of the oppression of women, I recognized the oppression of Third World people but never understood that I personally had anything to gain by the elimination of racism. While I fully understand how sexism dehumanizes men, it never crossed my mind that my racism must somehow dehumanize me.

As white women, we continually expect women of color to bring us to an understanding of our racism. White women rarely meet to collectively examine our attitudes, our actions and most importantly, our resistance to change. The oppression of men toward women is in so many ways parallel to the oppression of women of color. Asking a Black, Indian or Chicana woman to define racism for us or to lay the historical background of Third World people's experience in this country is what allows us to continue our resistance to change. The history of racism in this country is white history, we know it, it is the story of our parents, grandparents and ourselves. Why do we call upon those who have suffered the injustice of that history to explain it to us?

Knowing that we grew up in a society permeated with the belief that white values, culture, and life-style is superior, we can assume that regardless of our rejection of the concept we still act out of that socialization. The same anger and frustrations that as women we have in dealing with men whose sexism is subtle, not blatant, is the frustration and anger women of color must feel toward us. The same helpless feeling we have in trying to expose that subtle sexism must be the feelings of women of color in working with us. I have sat through hundreds of meetings with men, constantly raising issues about women's involvement or the effects of decisions on women, and felt totally frustrated knowing that to them I'm being petty, my issues are relatively unimportant to the business at hand, my comments resented. I always end up either feeling crazy or absolutely enraged thinking that they are deliberately acting dumb. I'm now beginning to realize that in many cases men do not understand because they have never committed themselves to understanding and by understanding, choose to share their power. The lessons we've learned so well as women must be the basis for our understanding of ourselves as oppressive to the Third World women we work with.

We must acknowledge what we think we have to lose by this understanding and find what we have to gain by eliminating our racism. We must believe that racism causes us to be less human and work toward humanizing ourselves.

It seems that much of our resistance to change comes from being angry at women of color. There are many times that white women are put in a real bind so that no matter what we do we are accused of being racist. There are times when racism is inappropriately used as an issue when the disagreements are clearly philosophical. But those, often very legitimate, resentments we have cannot become a justification for perpetuating our racism. The confusion we feel about when and how this movement is racist will not be cleared up until we understand racism as our issue and our responsibility and begin addressing it among ourselves rather than depending totally on Third World women to raise and clarify the issue for us.

—*Ellen Pence*
first appeared in Aegis: Magazine on
Ending Violence Against Women

RACE AND THE SHELTER MOVEMENT

In our struggle to open shelters, to stay open and to provide safety for battered women, we constantly make choices that determine the priorities of our projects. There is always one more thing to do—a meeting, a crisis, a class to help us learn how to run the shelter more effectively, and a wide variety of issues with which to deal.

In some shelters, people feel there is no need to deal with race, race issues or racism. As a Third World woman I feel this is a mistake. Even if there are apparently no visible Third World women in your community, that is no excuse. Often Third World women are part of white women's experience but work in invisible jobs such as factories, laundries, as houseworkers and babysitters.

Has adequate outreach been done to alert Third World women to your shelter? Has your staff been sensitized around race issues and language barriers? Racism takes various forms. It could involve out and out remarks about different kinds of food, values and communities, or more subtle ones. And both are devastating to the woman on the receiving end. Racism can and does affect the running of shelters. For example, when you define and develop what you consider to be the most necessary services to meet a battered woman's most basic needs, do you consider some bilingual staff members to be a basic necessity? Do non-English speaking women know about your shelter and can they get the same information and support once they come, as English speaking women?

In our shelter, our biggest discussions have been around how different cultures view discipline. Some women would rather talk out discipline problems, discuss, talk it out with their children. Other women feel spankings are the only way to discipline. Compound this problem with white and Black women in a shelter on different sides of the issue—and you've got a Big Problem, because they all have to live there in the house with the differences.

The next biggest issue has been around food. Who cooks with grease (shortening, lard, etc.)? Who doesn't and why? Do we have to have beans again? Or, that food looks, tastes funny—without ever eating it or tasting it.

Women often spoil their kids—never allowing them or themselves to experience other people's food, culture, etc. Music—what radio station is listened to in the shelter? Is it soft rock, semi-classical? Is *Soul,* Black Music, really that *loud?*

Do the surroundings—pictures, books, magazines, etc., reflect other women's experiences? Do books reflect multi-racial children—just as you would have them be non-sexist? I'm sure you would look for non-sexist books—look for non-racist books in the process as well.

Have groups come in to do training around Race? Deal with it now before you have to—before it becomes a problem in your shelter. There are ways you can expose your shelter community to the issues of Race and Racism. Encourage women to meet with and talk to Third World women. Learn about Third World women's lives through literature. Black women have always known about white women's lives. What do you know and how do you feel about Third World women?

In urban areas our battle is constant—never being able to put it lower on the priority scale. You may think, isn't life for a battered woman overwhelming enough, leaving the battering situation? Do we have to put that on her head too? I think *yes*. We in the shelters are about *change*—changing each woman's life—and the world she will be in after leaving the shelter will be different also. She may work outside the home for the first time in her life, and Third World women may work in the same workplace. It's a start to learn about other people's lives, and at some point women realize there is a commonality in their lives, i.e., leaving the battering situations, and support can be gotten from that alone.

It is important to understand Racism and its effects as you understand the sexist way in which we as women grow up. It is also important to understand the benefits and reinforcement the society as a whole receives from Racism, and how it affects us. It divides us as women and the guilt immobilizes us so that we cannot cross the line. Women—cross over the barrier—Dare to be different!!

—Renae Scott
originally appeared in Aegis: Magazine on
Ending Violence Against Women

Homophobia in the Shelter/Service Group

The subject of lesbianism might become a very hot issue, especially in a shelter. For many women, this experience marks the first time that they will be in a group living situation with all women. A woman might, for the first time, be openly expressing her anger toward men and hearing the same from other women. She could also be coming from a situation where her batterer accused her of being a lesbian or discouraged her from getting help from women's groups by calling them "a bunch of lesbians." In the shelter, she will see women taking power in their lives and will probably begin to feel close to some women. These experiences and feelings of fear and confusion might trigger the automatic homophobic responses that we all have been taught. A woman could feel the need to project her feelings on to other residents or staff in the shelter. A woman or a group of women could, by words and action, alienate another woman who is, or is thought to be, a lesbian. A constant topic of discussion might become trying to figure out who on the staff is a lesbian.

Homophobic comments are sometimes used in the context of women giving support to each other. One woman could assure another that she shouldn't worry, that just because she left her husband doesn't mean that she's a lesbian. Another example is of a battered woman hugging a staffer, then pulling away saying with nervous laughter, "People will think we're a couple of lesbians."

Whether the incidents and attitudes come out of fear, confusion or lack of information, they can be disruptive and make it very difficult to maintain a sense of unity and safety for all women.

It is important that there be on-going internal discussions and workshops on the subjects of homophobia and lesbianism before a blow-up or crisis develops. It is also important to interrupt the remarks as they happen. When interrupting comments, the most important thing is to get the woman to talk about what she sees as the meaning behind the words she is using. Because sex and sexuality are taboo subjects anyway, it is often hard for women to be comfortable enough to talk about their attitudes. When someone is trying to deal with her negative feelings (such as anger, hurt, fear) about someone else by using words like "fag" or "lezzie" as insults, the first thing that she needs to do is to be able to express her feelings more directly without using those words. After the feelings have subsided, information to contradict the myths and stereotypes can be provided.

Because it is so hurtful for a lesbian to have to hear unconscious comments that label her as "sick," "evil," or "disgusting," she should not be put in the position of always being the one to say something about the homophobia. Part of every staffer's responsibility is to make a safe space for all women, and to interrupt attitudes that could be harmful to any woman.

It is not necessary for either lesbian or non-lesbian women to reveal their sexual identities in the situations that require some information about lesbianism. In fact, it might be a good consciousness-raising experience for a heterosexual woman to *not* qualify her remarks with an "I'm straight, but . . ." introduction. In this situation, where she might be labelled a lesbian, she will be able to feel some of the fear and anxiety that lesbians face every day.

When a woman first arrives, it is important that you tell her that this is (or tries to be) a safe, supportive place for *all* women of different races and cultures, including lesbians on staff and using the services.

Children and Homophobia

Children can reflect homophobic attitudes by calling each other or other people "fag" or "queer." Childcare workers can strategize about how to talk with kids about homosexuality and homophobia in a way they can understand. An information session could be planned that would include examples of how people are different and what that means.

If a mother is concerned about her children being "exposed" to lesbians and gay male childcare workers, there are usually some myths that are causing her fears. One common one is that lesbians and gay men molest children. The reality is that over 90% of the molestation of children is done to young girls by heterosexual males. It is a sad fact that children run the highest risk of molestation in their own homes. Another myth is that children will be influenced to grow up to be homosexual if they are around lesbians and gay men. First, a woman might need to talk about her fears if that really did happen. Second, it's important to point out that no one really knows what "causes" homosexuality or heterosexuality. Most lesbians and gay men grew up exposed to exclusively heterosexual life styles, yet somehow managed to find the way that they needed to be in their lives.

Homophobia in the Community

The fact that our organizations are based on the principle of women helping women and that we help women escape from violent men makes our organization a likely target for homophobia. While doing community outreach, public speaking, meeting with local officials or representatives from other agencies, we could run up against attitudes and comments that need to be challenged or confronted. It is harder, however, to deal with rumors and indirect comments.

Some common homophobic comments are: "Oh, that group is just a bunch of lesbians," or, "the lesbians at that place molest the women that come to them for help." These comments produce anxiety in us because women we want to reach might be afraid to come to us; our community might not support us; and our funding could be jeopardized. The most important thing in dealing with these fears is to be prepared and not to run scared by trying to prove that there aren't any lesbians in the staff, or by reacting personally to the accusations.

Homophobia has very little relation to the quality of work we do with battered women. People who are "lesbian-baiting" are not really interested in the services we provide. They are reacting out of a fear of seeing women take power together or are enjoying the products of some voyeuristic fantasy about lesbians and sexuality. In either case, it is important to maintain the attitude that homophobia is the problem, not homosexuality. Confront people's worst fears about lesbians. Have they ever actually known of a woman being molested by a lesbian? Give people the information that you have about homophobia with an attitude similar to the one you have in explaining violence against women. Once again, lesbians should not be blamed for or expected to deal with the oppressive attitudes. If homophobia can scare our organizations out of supporting lesbians or taking a stand on an issue, then it has done what it was created to do.

—M. Smith

Battered Women's Refuges: Feminist Cooperatives vs. Social Service Institutions*

Lois Ahrens

Refuges for battered women, like rape crisis centers, seem to be undergoing a transformation throughout the United States from feminist, nonhierarchical, community-based organizations to institutionalized social service agencies. The shelter in Austin, Texas provides a typical example of this transformation. As someone who witnessed this process as part of the original Coalition on Battered Women which formed in Austin, Texas in November 1976, and later as one of the shelter's two staff people first hired in May 1977, I have had a long association with the Center, from planning to implementation stages. This experience may help feminists working with battered women avoid the pitfalls we faced.

When we began in November 1976, we were a coalition of twenty women who represented a feminist counseling collective, a women and alcoholism task force, a Chicano group, nurses, social workers, grant writers, a women's center, the local mental health agency, and women who had themselves been battered or who had come from families where mothers or sisters had been battered. We represented a diversity of agencies, ages, ethnicities, and ideologies. Though our differences were abundant, our common goal kept us striving to have everyone's concerns heard. We spent hundreds of hours talking about what we wanted the goals of the group to be because we felt that process to be crucial to creating a non-bureaucratic organization. Through discussion it appeared that we all believed hierarchical models are oppressive to all people, and have historically been especially so to minorities and to women, in particular, battered women. Because of this conviction we believed that the structure of refuges for women should be models for collective work. Each individual should have her own area of expertise and that work should be done in a collaborative manner. We argued that this method would allow for personal growth for staff members and also serve as a model to women living in the Center by showing that women can work together cooperatively, without bosses.

Further, the group ostensibly agreed that when we create bureaucracies each worker's role in the shelter becomes more specialized and fragmented. Such specialization leads to individual involvement in only one area and creates a familiar syndrome. First, workers begin to feel less responsibility and involvement with the entire program. They begin to view work as a 'job', lacking political purpose. Second, the individual worker feels less empowered and less capable of working as peers with women who come to the refuge. Women are transformed into 'clients' to

*From *Radical America*, Vol. 14, No. 3 (May–June, 1980), pp. 41–47.

be routed from one desk or department to another (and nowhere viewed as complex individuals). In this scheme everyone suffers and feminist hopes for new models of support are dashed.

PHASE ONE: THE FORMATIVE STAGE

In the beginning, our group was singly-focused, and functioned in a collective and task-oriented fashion. At the time, there seemed to be general agreement on issues such as the value of a feminist perspective in the shelter, the inclusion of lesbians as visible members of the collective, and the need for workers and residents in the shelter to share in decision-making and leadership. We viewed ourselves as a collective, and a very successful one. Our Center opened in June 1977, funded by county and private mental health funds.

PHASE TWO: SIGNIFICANT CHANGES

Soon after the shelter opened, the twenty coalition members agreed to form a twelve-member Coordinating Committee. The coalition agreed that a smaller number of women was needed to meet more frequently to direct the actual workings of the new Center. They elected twelve of their group according to how much time and energy each could devote to a Coordinating Committee. Three different things began to happen at that point. First, two of the Committee members became paid staff people. Staff was working approximately eighty hours a week and therefore had greater and greater knowledge of the shelter operations. Other Coordinating Committee members began to feel threatened by this shift and started treating the staff as 'paid help'. Simultaneously, many Coordinating Committee members chose not to work directly in the shelter. A division grew between members with day-to-day knowledge of shelter happenings and those who became more divorced from the daily realities faced by paid and nonpaid staff. Secondly, many of the original Coalition members who identified themselves as radical feminists became involved in other projects instead of continuing with the Center. They felt they had worked to establish the shelter, but were not interested in committing time to its daily operation. This created a definite tilt in ideological perspective on the Coordinating Committee and a significant lessening of support for the few remaining radical feminists. Third, the Center for Battered Women began its own process of incorporating as a nonprofit, tax-exempt organization.

PHASE THREE: BOARD DEVELOPMENT

Until that point we operated under the tax-exempt status of the Austin Wc ɔ n's Center. Six months after the Austin Center for Battered Women began i‹ wn incorporation process, elections were held to choose a board of directors. Unfortunately, the first board was not representative of the community. Ballots were sent to those on the mailing list and to all those who had participated in volunteer training. Individuals who merely "expressed interest in the issue of battered women" composed one part of the electorate. Women volunteered to run for directors. This loose system allowed board members to be selected who had had no previous contact with the Center or whose knowledge of the Center was only through friends of the incumbent board members. Volunteers in the shelter were already working overtime, and most could not be convinced of the necessity of volunteer representation on the board. The majority of volunteers had had little or no previous experience as volunteers or as board members, since they were former battered women who were divorced, working full-time jobs, and caring for their children. Most felt their primary interest was in working directly with battered women in the shelter, not in serving on a board.

This vague and unrepresentative election allowed for board members to be elected who represented no community or group, making them responsible or responsive to no one but themselves. This problem grew when two minority women (both volunteers with a community base), feeling overlooked and misunderstood, resigned from the board. The board, rather than address the issues raised by their resignations or call new elections, replaced them by appointing two personal friends, an Anglo male lawyer and an Anglo woman.

The staff viewed this as a consolidation of power by the board, and challenged the appointment rather than election of new board members. The staff protested a number of issues. First, no attempt was made to fill the vacancies with other Black and Chicano women involved with the shelter. Second, the board was not addressing the issues the two women had raised. Third, there had been no precedent for having men on the board. The staff indicated to the board that it was essential for them to examine their own racism and the Center's credibility in the Black and Chicano communities. Further, we were concerned that the replacement board members had no ties to the daily operation of the shelter. The board responded to our concerns by sending letters to the ex-board members thanking them for their past work. Both women continued to work in the Center.

Further, staff recommendations that all board members participate minimally in the eighteen-hour volunteer training was turned down. Board members were elected and served without prior knowledge of the Coalition's original plan for the working of the shelter. The board/staff division became sharper as fewer board members maintained contact with battered women at the shelter. This division and the fact that the more strongly feminist women had already left the original group and so did not run for the board, helped to solidify the more professional, liberal feminist block on the board. This segregation of board members from the program paved the way for what was to come.

PHASE FOUR: ADMINISTRATION AND STAFF

During this time the Center was growing in the scope of services and programming it offered women and children. The number of staff began to expand from the original two. In July 1977 we hired the first full-time counselor, and by October five staff people funded by CETA were hired. During the same month the board decided that the Center needed an administrator who would report to and make contact with the funding agencies, keep track of the finances, and oversee the Center's administration. An administrator was hired in November and the staff of eight women was divided into two work groups: those involved in funding, administration, and the running of the house, and those who came into direct contact with the women and children using the services of the Center. The latter came to be known as direct services or program staff. The direct services staff consisted of myself as director, two counselors, a childcare worker, and a lawyer/advocate. It became clear to those of us in services that the administrator's principal concern and involvement was the board. We, on the other hand, were concentrating on providing good services, training large numbers of volunteers, and expanding our funding, and felt that this focus would speak for the validity of the internal structure of the shelter.

The administrator never had been a battered woman, nor had she been through the volunteer training. She had little or no contact with women residing at the Center. In response to her approach, two groups developed. One camp, composed of the direct services staff and a large number of volunteers, was collectivist and feminist; the other, made up of the board and administrator, placed greater value on those with credentials and on a hierarchical structure. Under the influence of the administrator, the board of the Center for Battered Women was beginning to push for *one* director. The stated rationale for this was that other agencies would be better able to work with an organizational structure similar to their own, and that funding sources would be reluctant to grant funds to any group with an 'alternative' form of organization. This seemed at the least ironic, since all the funding we had received prior to this organizational change had been granted because of our demonstration of the direct relationship between a nonhierarchical structure and the power issues of violence against women. We had argued that the Center should provide a mode of cooperative, nonhierarchical work, and that the one-up, one-down model was counterproductive in working to change women's (and especially battered women's) lives. Nonetheless, in February 1978, the board voted to make the administrator the director.

PHASE FIVE: DISINTEGRATION

The first step was to demote and render powerless the staff who had been instrumental in formulating the original program and policies—in this case, the direct service staff. This was accomplished by rewriting job descriptions into jobs containing very specific and fragmented functions. Policy-making power went completely to the director. Staff meetings became little more than lectures by the director, allowing no avenue for staff input. I resigned. Three weeks later the board, with guidance from the director, fired one counselor, the childcare worker, and the lawyer. Two of them were dismissed for 'insubordination'. The Center was left with one counselor, who then resigned, leaving none of the original direct service staff. The task of ridding the Center of the original staff was complete.

There were many reactions to this upheaval. Upon resigning I wrote a letter to all volunteers stating the reasons for my resignation and listing the changes which I thought would be forthcoming. Meetings with staff, a few residents and as many as forty volunteers followed. In these meetings volunteers challenged the right of the board to make the changes. They discussed the composition of the board and the resignations of its two volunteers. Volunteers pressed for more representation on the board. The CETA workers hired lawyers and began to appeal their firing to the City of Austin. Ex-staff and volunteers approached funding sources, warning of changes in policy which would have a detrimental effect on the program. Volunteers and ex-staff began to pressure the Women's Center (which was still the parent group) to exercise its authority over the Center for Battered Women board. Joint Women's Center and CBW board meetings were held, with as many as sixty people attending. However, the Women's Center board finally opted to not exercise its control, stating that it had not entered into the internal workings of the CBW board prior to this, and would not do so now. Funding sources monitored the events, but felt it was not wise to intervene into intraorganizational disputes. Many volunteers withdrew completely, feeling the situation to be hopeless. The fired CETA staff appeals dragged on for more than a year and finally, after many hearings, the staff decided that the issues had been lost and trivialized in the process. 'Winning', they felt, would mean nothing. They dropped their cases. The board emerged stronger than ever. All the opposition staff and volunteers were gone from the Center.

PHASE SIX: DISCREDITING AND MALIGNING

The next step was to find a way to discredit the program and policies of the original staff. The most expedient way of doing this was to let it be known through the informal social service network that the director and her allies had prevented a lesbian (translated 'man-hating') takeover. This was said despite the fact that among the five staff and forty volunteers who left the Center perhaps not more than five were lesbian. With this one word—lesbian—no other explanation became necessary. The validity of the charge remained unquestioned since none of the original staff or volunteers remained. Other agencies willingly took the shelter into the social service fold.

PHASE SEVEN: THE AFTERMATH

The following is a summary of events in the Center since the transition from a collective to a hierarchical structure. The progression toward developing a model of a 'professionalized' social service institution divorced from the community it was to service is evident.

The new leadership of the Center for Battered Women has said that it is very important to separate the issue of feminism and sexism from that of battered women. With the new federal emphasis on the nuclear family, the Center chooses to look at battered women as a 'family violence problem', but refuses to consider the societal, cultural, and political implications of why women are the ones in the family so often beaten. Soon after the original staff people left the shelter, men began to be trained and to serve as volunteers working directly with the women in the house. In the past, those who felt that men should not work in the house as volunteers compromised with those who felt that positive male role-models are necessary. The result was that men were included in regular volunteer training and received additional training to work with children in the house. Now, however, men are also answering the telephone hot-line and staffing the Center.

In the view of the founders of the Center, it is not a good idea for men to work in a shelter for battered women. Their presence can reinforce old patterns for battered women. Male volunteers and/or staff can easily be cast (or cast themselves) in the role of rescuer, encouraging a dependent role. Just when they need to be developing their own strengths, battered women can focus their attention on a man as the person most likely to solve their problems. This helps to perpetuate a continued cycle of dependence and inequality—two of the causes of battering.

The Center for Battered Women has undergone the transformation to a social service agency by becoming more and more removed from its 'client' population. The feminist ideology brought insights into programming for battered women. This belief demanded that staff and volunteers not make separations between themselves and battered women. We were able to integrate an understanding of the oppression and violence against women with a concern for the individual woman. This same ideology created a shelter based on the opinion that informal worker/resident relationships, self-help and peer-support would be more effective in fulfilling some of the immediate needs of battered women than rigid, bureaucratic structures. For example, women now living at the center must make an appointment to see a counselor days ahead of time. In the past, this type of interaction between the staff and a woman could just as easily have taken place at the kitchen table as in an appointed time in a more formal office setting.

There is now a distancing of staff from women who stay at the shelter. Direct service people complement policy and procedures made by an administrator and board which is divorced from the group they are intending to serve. Little room remains for the less formal, more supportive sharing which was an original goal.

PREVENTIVE MEASURES

There are some lessons from our experience which may help insure that feminist-based shelters remain places that are responsive to the needs of battered women:

1. It is essential that women who organize shelters have an identifiable feminist analysis, which encompasses an understanding of the ways in which that analysis affects services to battered women. In addition, it is crucial that this specific analysis be part of all board orientations, volunteer training, and public education. This policy is necessary in order to make all who come in contat with the shelter understand that feminist ideology is not a tangential issue, but basic and essential. It will serve the dual purpose of informing possible shelter participants of the ideological basis of the program, as well as continually placing the issue of battered women in a feminist cultural and political context.

2. The issue of lesbianism has lost none of its volatility in recent years. Lesbians have continually taken part in all aspects of the women's movement, and the battered women's movement is no exception. It is therefore imperative that each group or collective initially acknowledge lesbians as a valuable part of their organization as one way of eliminating lesbianism as a negative issue. This can be accomplished by publicly encouraging the active participation of lesbians as staff, board, and volunteers. Further, position papers outlining the ideological framework of the shelter must include the contribution of lesbians in all aspects of the shelter program.

3. As feminists we realize how vital the inclusion of ex-battered women, working class, minority women, and volunteers is in forming a community-based governing board. Too often, these women have little money, little time, and little children! While their inclusion may not guarantee the development of a feminist analysis, it is a step toward keeping services tied to needs.

4. Those of us who have worked developing refuges for battered women know we cannot exist in a service vacuum. In order for a shelter to be effective, we must initiate and maintain working relationships with the police, courts, hospitals, welfare departments, and mental health services. We must also, however, maintain our own organizational integrity. We can work with the police or welfare, but we also must retain enough freedom to be able to be an effective and strong advocate for women who are beaten. Links are vital, but we must be cautious, and understand the tenuous line between working with existing agencies and being seduced by the 'respectability' and seeming advantages these law enforcement and social service agencies appear to offer, often at the expense of the battered women. The feminist stance and advocacy role must not be diffused.

5. Feminist shelters must join other feminist services and groups in providing a base of support for one another. The roles and functions of each group may be different, but the shared ideological base is of critical importance. This alliance will provide an alternative to the traditional social service network. It is important in terms of referrals, but even more vital because it provides a constituency which can understand the broader implications of the shelter's work. Indeed, should they be needed, other groups can be political allies as well as friends.

CONCLUSIONS

The lure of building powerful social service fiefdoms is not gender-based. The shelter movement will attract women (and men) who view these services as stepping stones to personal career goals. It is vital for us to recognize that many in local, state or federal agencies will more easily accept that which is already familiar, those who do not threaten their own beliefs. The community support needed to maintain a feminist-based shelter for battered women requires political sophistication. Self-education, our own raised consciousness, and good faith are not enough. Consensus decision-making works only if everybody is playing by and believes in the same rules. Our unhappy experience shows that battered women's shelters committed to the full empowerment of women will remain feminist in content and approach only by constant discussion, analysis, and vigilance.

Women for Sobriety*

Jean Kirkpatrick

Women for Sobriety, Inc. is located in Quakertown, Pennsylvania. Women for Sobriety (WFS) is two things: a program for alcoholic women and also an organization. The purpose of the organization is to reach as many women in this country and other countries with a program of recovery from alcoholism via self-help groups. The organization itself was incorporated in July 1975. Prior to that time the program existed in a very rough form and by 1975, it became obvious that to use the program, it was necessary to incorporate and try to become a nonprofit organization within which the WFS program would be administered and put out in some form, probably in the form of literature.

IDENTIFICATION OF NEED

It is very difficult to talk about this early part of WFS since it is so amorphous. I, Jean Kirkpatrick, am a recovered alcoholic and this organization came about through my way of recovery. My recovery period was from 1971 through 1972–

*From Dale Masi, *Organizing for Women*, Lexington, Mass.: Lexington Books (1981), pp. 185–191.

1973 and on upwards. By 1973, it occurred to me that if I could recover so well with the way I was doing it, then maybe hundreds and thousands of other women in the United States could also use this same way of recovery. It is my belief that it is not necessary for alcoholics to be tied to recovery programs for the rest of their lives within the structure of a meeting. I think it is very necessary that recovering alcoholics have a program, a systematic way of changing their lives and growing, but I do not feel it is necessary for all to be committed to weekly meetings.

Early in 1975, I began to think that the best way to show other women my recovery program was to start a group, a WFS self-help group. It was at this juncture, in mid-1975, that the organization was incorporated in our small town of Quakertown. To be incorporated in the state of Pennsylvania as a nonprofit corporation, it was necessary to draw up bylaws. This I did. Of course, there was no organization anywhere; there was nothing but what I had jotted down and which was referred to as the New Life Program. The operational facility of WFS was my bedroom.

This procedure continued even after incorporation in 1975 until the end of the year. During this time I was able to have a couple of women use the program. A few groups began to spring up: by February 1976 I had written the first newsletter. By January 1976, there happened to be some publicity on what I was doing and that this program was the first different and new program from the Alcoholics Anonymous (AA) program, which was founded in 1935. The big publicity hanger for the media was the fact that no other program had come along with anything different from AA in all those years. I believe that because the AA program is so successful, everyone felt that nothing else was needed. This simply was not true. Examination of the membership figures of AA shows that only 10 percent of all alcoholics in the United States are in the AA and that less than 4 percent of all women alcoholics are in the organization.

When I wrote my program I knew the AA program was founded by men and that, in the very beginning, women were not permitted to join. I also knew because the WFS program was administered the same way as AA, in the self-help group settings, I would get a lot of backlash about it since AA is held in the highest reverence. To come along with anything else seemed to be rather profligate. The first national publicity that WFS received in January 1976, shocked me to see the headline, Women Form Own AA. And another headline in a New Orleans paper stated that I had said AA does not work and *everyone* needs WFS. I had said AA did not work entirely for me and I felt that I needed something else.

PROGRAM DEVELOPMENT

By July 1975, WFS was incorporated in the state of Pennsylvania with a set of bylaws. I had received the corporate seal and the notification was published in the newspapers that the sole purpose of WFS was, and is, to disseminate help for women alcoholics to help them overcome their alcoholism.

I was still operating WFS from my bedroom when a United Press International story broke in some fifty-five newspapers across the country. The mail began to reach 100 to 150 letters a day; the highest number received in one day was over 200 letters. Overwhelmingly, the mail was from women who had tried AA but simply could not get sober with the program. Most asked for the WFS program and the location of the closest WFS program group to join. Up to this moment, the WFS program was not established outside the state of Pennsylvania. The first problem was to print the program and to write a brochure about it.

To answer all the letters, I simply had to get help. Everyday five of us prepared 3 × 5 cards with names and addresses of the women alcoholics and we extracted comments from the letters. We would then send the women our new brochure and explain that there was not a WFS program in her area as of yet, but she would be notified.

Following the publicity of January 1976, I realized we had a great need for money. I found out that each county in Pennsylvania has money from the state and the state gets money from the federal government. At this point I did not know that under the Department of Health and Human Services, there existed an agency known as the National Institute for Alcohol Abuse and Alcoholism. I did not even know that money could probably be had from Bucks County. I received a nasty letter from the person running alcoholism programs in the county and it said that no program would exist in his county without his being informed of it and I was to immediately come to him and explain what WFS was all about and what in the world it was doing in his county. The man has since left office. Nevertheless, I began to get very frightened and was extremely intimidated by this. I began to wonder if it is not possible for some organization to start without having approval given by a county authority. However, I continued to ignore these letters and, needless to say, the relationship with the county and the state was very poor and still is.

I next turned to private foundations, of which I knew nothing. I wrote to all the Philadelphia foundations. Luckily one of the representatives from a Philadelphia foundation got in touch with me and said they might consider funding this operation. Well, of course, there was no operation. All I had was the same thing I had before which was a piece of paper saying we were incorporated; we now had a logo, a brochure, and a single-page program printed. We also had excessive mail coming in and still no staff and no money.

In May 1976, I heard that there was a national conference sponsored by the National Council on Alcoholism and I decided I had better appear. I was still negotiating with the foundation and they informed me they were coming to meet me. I proceeded to assemble a staff. I was the president and Dr. Rapoport, a

nonalcoholic dentist, was the vice president. I asked Natalie Shifano, whose husband designed the logo, to be secretary, and Sonja Lowenfish to be treasurer. Now
we had officers. I submitted these names to the foundation and still they were not
satisfied. They continued to hold the application; they would move it from month to
month.

When I returned from the National Conference on Alcoholism I rewrote the
entire proposal. For instance, I de-emphasized the fact that Dr. Rapoport was a
leading authority as a periodontist. Instead I noted that she was the wife of a
prominent lawyer in the city of Allentown. I identified Mrs. Lowenfish as the
mother of two children and the wife of a prominent architect in New York. I
emphasized the fact that Mrs. Shifano's husband was a successful advertising
executive on Madison Avenue in New York. Finally, that of all four board members, I was the only one who was divorced, and that I would be held accountable by
them and that we would work closely together.

From the moment I put the emphasis on the husbands and that these women
were acting with three very well-established men in their lives and that they would
keep control of me, WFS immediately got the money. Although I learned that
lesson very early, it has not worked since that time. However, I think that since then
we have gotten so much stronger that I fail to use a similar approach because I have
difficulty in doing it.

PROGRAM IMPLEMENTATION

In May 1976, WFS received $40,000 in funding. This was to pay for two full-time
salaries, a secretary's and mine. We finally had some money to begin to operate.
The problem was that the money was to be used just for this area of eastern
Pennsylvania but WFS was a national organization, and of course we got as many
letters from Colorado, Washington, or Texas as Pennsylvania and keeping them
separate was difficult.

I was inexperienced in all the ways of fulfilling what I had proposed to do for
the foundation. I failed to take into account the fact that, first of all, we were dealing
with women. Second, women alcoholics are very difficult to reach and, third, it is
very hard to go against an established organization like AA and expect people to
welcome you with open arms.

In addition, months passed before I found a person who was willing to act as
field representative. It requires special qualifications to get groups started, and I
never did find the person who was exactly right for the job. The first person I hired
was a woman who was very capable and very able at self-management. She would
operate in Philadelphia and surrounding areas for the work-week, but on Friday she
was on her own. Her job was to discover effective methods of meeting women
alcoholics and setting the time and place for her to meet with them to start a group.
Then she would meet with the group until it was established enough for her to move

on to start another group. We were unable to say that X number of women had already recovered using the program. In fact, except for myself, there was no other woman who had recovered with the WFS program. In any event, the woman I hired to get the groups started encountered numerous problems. After about four months, she decided she was wasting her time.

The second person that took the job of field representative to start WFS groups was a woman I thought would work out. She was a beautiful person to see; she was bubbly and had an assertive kind of personality. She was a long-time member of AA and had wonderful sobriety. Recently widowed, she was just married to a man who was very big in AA. Immediately, she began to run into some flack as to why she wanted to be associated with WFS when it jeopardizes her with AA. She lasted one month.

We searched another eight weeks before we found a woman who was a re-covered alcoholic and a Ph.D. candidate. She also seemed exactly right and began to make some progress. With her, we began to run about three good groups in Philadelphia. I felt secure about this and thought our problems were solved only to find that she began drinking again. So it became necessary to let her go. By this time, our one year of funding had ended and we had really failed in what I had set out to do.

The thrust of the proposal that I had presented to this Philadelphia foundation was that, in one year's time, WFS would be able to put the program solidly into the city and the surrounding areas. I told the board of the foundation that I would have at least six groups started, and probably ten, and that those ten groups, at the end of the funding period would go on and on, self-perpetuating, and in time be able to take care of at least 100 women within a five-year period.

Well, we did have some women in groups, but the results were very, very disappointing. We failed because I did not know enough about how to implement it. In addition, I failed to take into account the skepticism and sometimes the absolute prejudice and criticism that came from the alcoholism community about the new WFS program.

The WFS program is now five years old and we are just beginning to be accepted in the community of alcoholism. There is still a great deal of prejudice and a lot of harassment. Many of our groups folded because of the harassment they got from some members of AA groups. I hasten to add that this is not the official AA position. I received quotations from their founder, Bill Wilson, which stated that AA is not the only way to recover, that there are many other programs, and that AA members should not criticize other programs. Unfortunately, many AA members believe that the AA program is the only way and they refuse to see that if it is not working for women, other options must be available.

We have survived the first five years and, since that initial funding, we have never had additional funding, despite having written to 500 foundations. Possibly one of the greatest barriers has been our inability to achieve funding at the federal level. I think we must have funding at the federal level because we are a national organization. The fact that we are a national organization has really worked against us. It has cut us out of funds from our county and from Pennsylvania, even though the corporation is registered here. It has hurt us in applications to foundations, because foundations are interested in local giving. A foundation like United States Steel will give money to organizations in Pittsburgh or wherever it has a large plant. If there is a plant in Gary, Indiana, they will give money in that area. There are a few foundations that give to national organizations, some of which are Ford, Rocke-feller, and Carnegie, but these particular foundations do not give to alcoholism programs. It is their assumption that alcoholism and its treatment are taken care of with funds from the federal government.

The federal government itself could be criticized for discrimination. Just in the year 1975 alone, out of the $75 million that went into alcoholism only $2,500,000 was for women's programs. Money for women's programs has been increasing but ever so slowly and certainly not to a point where it is equivalent to money for men's programs. I have failed to provide an effective proposal to the federal government.

So the program evolved into its current form, to be used in self-help groups across the country and internationally. Its conceptualization came out of my being able to examine myself, to discover my own needs for recovery.

Our income derives from the sale of literature, collections from the groups, my speaking engagements, and the profit from my book. We are beginning now to enlarge our line of literature as much as possible and we are beginning to sell books written by other persons. Prior to this, we were unable to do that because we did not have the capital funds to invest in other books.

In 1979, our fourth year of operation, we were able to produce $68,000 from these sources. Unfortunately, we need approximately $100,000 a year at the very minimum. WFS is located in a house owned by me. Because of this, WFS does not get evicted when it cannot pay its monthly rent. Luckily, we are now beginning to get some very large contributions from persons who are committed to our cause.

Perhaps one of our greatest difficulties as an organization is that we are con-stantly compared to a national organization of great prominence, one that has certain well-known traditions and establishments, and that of course is AA. AA's strength lies in the fact that it is there, that it has a continuity, and the program remains unchangeable. This is also true for WFS.

It was my belief that professional women in the community of alcoholism would welcome this program, that we women have our own national program. As an organization we have encouraged every woman to become a part of it, and emphasized that WFS is not a one-person, one-woman organization. We have encouraged women to get behind it, so that all of us can work together to bring this program to all women alcoholics in the United States. I hate to admit it, but in the five years that I have been working with women, I can honestly say that perhaps it is from our cultural training and our cultural forces that most women have many problems when it comes to working with each other, having a commitment, assuming responsibility, and even working cooperatively. We have met a lot of resistance in the fact that women do not cooperate with each other, that they continue to have feelings of jealousy and tend to stab one another in the back.

ANALYSIS

If I were to ask myself what I would have done differently if I had to do it over again, I really do not know if I would have done anything differently. Because of no funding, it has been a matter of a few of us doing everything and there has never been time to really think about what could be different. In a week's time, we receive a minimum of approximately fifty requests for help. Whenever there is a TV show or a newspaper that mentions our work, we will get as high as 500 letters a week but, unfortunately, that does not happen too often. Every woman who writes us gets a copy of our program, a sample copy of the newsletter, and always suggestions on how to use the program if she so desires. We are trying to develop new strategies to increase support for the program. I think this can only be done by our board of directors, who are becoming increasingly active in the organization.

It is most definitely an uphill fight, and I think it will continue to be for the next several years; but whenever I do a workshop, I always ask the group assembled how many in the room have heard of WFS. Now, without fail, every hand goes up. Five years ago I was very lucky if one hand was raised.

In summation, I can only say we work at it day by day, we work away at resistance to change and try hard to help women who week our help. Each day we are getting more and more women to help us and a more positive attitude from the community. It will take time, but we are prepared for this. We have been down a long and thorny path, but I feel that things are changing and I know that the WFS program is here to stay.

Symbollically the Enemy is the Pentagon

Jessica Shubow

The Women's Pentagon Action grew out of a conference at the University of Massachusetts in Amherst in 1980, which was entitled "Women for Life on Earth." People at the conference felt it was time for women to take direct action to confront the institutions that were oppressing us and threatening our lives. And so women began to meet in small groups predominantly in the New York, New England area and within an extremely short time, maybe a month or more, began to put together a unity statement. We wanted something that would allow women, wherever they were coming from, to participate in creating an action that would be a collective experience. It was important that the involvement of women in this process would be an empowering experience. We were all capable of feeling the impact of the growing reactionary attacks on women and minority people, and we needed to recognize that we had enough anger and enough sense of self-esteem and defiance to go forward and say "We've had enough. We will not be dehumanized."

The unity statement was distributed widely and women began to talk about what such an action should feel like. This meant, "What do I need to get out of an action?" It was felt to be anything from boring to debilitating to listen to speakers rant and rave endless rhetoric about a situation that already felt overwhelming. Traditionally many women felt that they had done tremendous amounts of footwork in preparing for demonstrations and actions against a whole myriad of issues and then got to that and did not feel particularly integrated in the final product. They heard often, very articulate, academic white men telling them what the problem was and what they needed to do. Demonstrations like that didn't give us the strength or the vision to change things. It was hoped the Women's Pentagon Action would feel different than other actions. Women were tired of feeling like "the Other" in movements, in their lives; they wanted to be central actors in a movement that would involve human beings fighting for liberation, fighting against oppression.

Within a short time we laid the groundwork for an action that drew three thousand women to Washington, D.C. This was November 1980. We met before the action to grow to know one another, to share our experience, to share our visions and to prepare to empower one another to confront our common enemy. Symbolically the enemy was the Pentagon, but when we talk about militarism, we understand that militarism is about domination and exploitation. It's about people believing they have a monopoly on the truth and imposing that will on others. It's been done by men to millions of women. It's been done by races against others. It's something that this system really must depend on.

There is nothing more powerful than the experience of coming together proudly as who you are. So in our unity statement we give a range of who we represented. We said we were mothers and we were lesbians, we were lesbian mothers, we were workers, and so forth, and listed what kind of work was represented in our group to show that recognition of difference does not hurt our effectiveness but gives us the strength to move forward creatively.

As we came to the Pentagon, we did a silent vigil through the Arlington National Cemetery which borders the monster building. Close by the building you'll find empty space waiting for the next group to come in. We went through the cemetery to dramatize the seriousness of what we were demonstrating about. At the Pentagon itself we engaged in four stages as a collective group.

In the first stage, we mourned the violence and death and destruction of women's lives as a result of the full range of the system of which militarism is one manifestation. We placed simulated tombstones into the ground, bearing the names of actual human beings who had died as a result of imperialist wars, as a result of domestic violence, as a result of alcoholism, as a result of violence in the streets that was condoned by a society that didn't stop it. It had a tremendous visual impact. We sat with them and we cried together. It's very unusual to see an en masse demonstration with so much of an outpouring of genuine emotion that suddenly can't be talked around. One of the ways that women have often been put down in movements is to be out-argued. But we say this is not a question of rational debate alone—our lives are not a debatable issue.

After the stage of mourning, a large puppet came through to tell us we were entering into our stage of rage. Together we experienced a sense that we have had enough. We say "No." There is such a strength in the word no, particularly when you say it simultaneously with thousands. What was important here is that we were not seen as a faceless mass but as actual human individuals with the dignity and the commitment to say "I do not have to live in a world where I'm going to be dehumanized any more." Here is an expression of our commitment to seeing that things are not going to continue as they have been.

The stage that followed was the stage of empowerment. Thousands of women surrounded the five sides of this mammoth building and shared a feeling that the human spirit could choke the horrible death-like power that comes out of this institution. Each person whose face appeared in that window was forced to confront the human demonstration of a willingness to fight—and to fight from a position of self-love and not defensiveness because we are a community.

The next stage was that of defiance. This is where we say we are willing to put our bodies on the line, and that those of us who will go as far as we need to as individuals will be backed up and supported and given the nurturance and love that has so often been left out of aggressive movements. We say that we return violence and domination—whether it's the police, or the military machine or the system in general—with our force of community, of commitment, of love, and of creativity and we say that you may not destroy, you can't destroy that spirit with violence. It goes beyond it, it overpowers violence.

At this point there are nearly fifty local groups that are loosely affiliated and that identify with the spirit of the Women's Pentagon Action. The group I'm in is called the Boston Women's Pentagon Action. We don't think that one needs to have a monopoly on the truth to be a political activist. Our most important power comes from our concrete experience in our own lives, and as women we have many instances day to day of how the system works. It was important to us that we not see political work as a macho show of power but as a process of transforming the society down to its core. We are changing ourselves, we were exposing the deep-set patriarchal, discriminatory attitudes that permeate all kinds of levels of the society. We know it's a long battle, and we don't want to see martyrs. We've seen in our experience that we hold on to more women and bring in more women because the movement that we're involved in leaves them feeling richer and stronger and not more drained.

If we are talking about the Pentagon, if we are talking about a target such as a military machine, why do it as women, why do it as a separate women's group? Why do we call ourselves Pentagon Action and yet talk about other issues? What as feminists we have held critically important is that it is in human beings that a movement has its primary focus, not just winning the battle, not showing strength as a response to repression. And to do that, we must be self-respecting and growing individuals. Putting the personal back into politics, putting the personal into our very vision of what social change means, putting private lives and analysis of society back together because there is no difference between private life and social life. We are all living in a social world in a social situation. We have been asked why do we talk about disarmament and bring up abortion rights. It's because we believe the source is the same, that a woman who's dying a slow death because she can't get her benefits is already—the war has begun already. And the first thing we need to do is keep ourselves hopeful and empowered, otherwise we will not have the strength or the clarity or creativity to make the changes. We keep ourselves empowered by recognizing that our needs are important, that our day-to-day moods and our changes deserve attention and respect. We encourage one another to find her greatest strength or find that activity or that project that touches her most deeply so that she is also growing as a part of this process. There are only so many minutes in a day and for those of us that work or study or struggle to survive, we need to get more strength and more hope and not just look at what we have not accomplished. We give one another a lot of support about having realistic expectations of what we are. In fact, when we are not calling on ourselves to be superhuman—as men have often expected of women and as some progressive groups have often expected of themselves—we accomplish more, because we are doing it from a realistic basis.

We have been criticized for talking about too many issues at once. We talk about reproductive rights, about lesbian and gay rights, about anti-sexism and anti-racism, about stopping the war machine, nuclear and conventional. What are we trying to say here? Well in fact, deliberately we are trying to promote the connections between these issues in the lives of women right now wherever they are and move on that.

Take Back the Night

Andrea Aiello

I'm a feminist who's involved in organizing around various women's issues. I also work as a health educator doing community work as an outreach person. Right now the main project that I'm involved in is organizing for Take Back the Night, which is a march to empower women to say that they will no longer tolerate being afraid to walk alone at night, no longer tolerate being battered.

One out of every three women is raped in her lifetime. Women of color are three times more likely to be raped, assaulted or murdered than a white woman is. One out of every four women are sexually abused before the age of 18. There are an estimated 28 million battered wives in the United States—more than half of all married women, and that's from Langley and Levy, *Wife-beating, the Silent Crisis.*

The Take Back the Night marches originated in England, but they spread to this country a few years ago and they've been held in cities all over the country. A lot of people say, what does this one march do, but it's not really just a one-night deal. In order to prepare for the march, we do a lot of educating along the way. Education is interviews in the media, on radio and TV, articles in newspapers, leaflets, people going out and talking about these issues. All this brings it more to the forefront instead of something that people don't want to acknowledge. A lot of times women's issues are ignored, and the only way to deal with that is to keep bringing them up. This is the fourth Take Back the Night march to be held in Boston. The march usually begins at 7 o'clock, and it's only for women.

I first got involved through a neighborhood feminist organizing group from the Boston Food Co-op. We had a block party to educate about women's safety issues. It was mainly for educational purposes but was also a fun, celebrative event. We also did cultural educational activities—demonstrations, speeches, songs, and leaflets on how to get involved in the Safehouse network, which in the Boston area is called Greenlight. There are Safehouse networks all over the country. The idea is to organize neighborhoods, blocks, and streets to have as many houses as possible be a Safehouse or a Greenlight house. If the house is a Greenlight house, they have a green light outside and if a woman is walking down the street, feeling harassed or scared, or is actually attacked, she knows she can go to the house with the green light on and people there are equipped to help her in a crisis. So originally the block party was organizing for that. From there we decided to tie into the main march of Take Back the Night and to organize and to march in the Allston-Brighton neighborhoods. This made sense to me from a personal point of view, from being scared of going out at night and at the same time being really angry about that. Also, in terms of the whole society there's so much violence in the advertising that goes on in this country, in songs, commercials, record covers. There's a big trend of child pornography, like the Brooke Shields advertising. I find it all really offensive and it hurts me. I feel that I'm being bombarded all the time. Those are some personal and political reasons why I've become involved in safety.

There are several ways that we used to organize the Allston-Brighton community. One was printed leaflets. We went to the bus stops at morning and evening rush hours and handed out leaflets to people and talked to them about the march. Mainly women, because we wanted women to be in the march. Men couldn't be in the march, but we also talked with men to educate them on our issues too. The leaflets said what the goals of the march were, the time and place, where we were leaving from. We also went to a lot of the bars in the area at night to talk with people. We had a lot of resistance from that. The bouncers didn't want to let us in, so we stood outside and talked to people as they walked in. In some of the bars, we stayed in the women's bathrooms so we wouldn't have any confrontations. It was very rewarding to talk with these women because they were so honest with us about things. Women told us stories about how they get hassled, whistled at, tackled, beaten, robbed, and so forth, just walking around. They could really relate to what we were talking about. The outreach was fantastic. I think a lot of consciousness raising went on in those bathrooms. Women started realizing that they could have some power and take some action and not only be victims. The bar scene was really worthwhile.

Last year there were about 5,000–6,000 women who came out citywide. Before that, it was raining and we had 7,000, so I think the marches are pretty successful. Last year when we were talking to individual people, they remembered and knew what we were talking about. Each year, more people hear about it and get tuned into violence issues and see. The educational process is very slow but very necessary.

One thing about organizing in the Allston-Brighton area is that we didn't concentrate enough on organizing older women. We were more familiar with the bar area and the bus stops. We also went to a black housing project. I went with another woman and that was really scary. Going there wasn't very beneficial for us or them. We were two white women coming into their neighborhood talking about violence issues and there was no trust built up at all. We were complete strangers and there was no reason for them to trust us. Also there'd been a lot of racial violence last year, and that created a lot more tension and a lot more reason for distrust. In order to reach out to a minority community, you have to build coalitions with members of that community. Like if there was a group of black women or some kind of black political group dealing with school closings or service cutbacks, and if we were working with them politically, then somebody from that group could help do outreach for Take Back the Night. Similarly with the Asian communities and with older women. It's important when you're trying to organize older women that you are in tune to their needs for transportation. We did have a car at the end of our march, as did all the other neighborhood feeder marches in the main Boston march to provide transportation for the physically handicapped. But it's real important to publicize that you're having transportation. We had a car but no one used it because they didn't know about it.

This year I'm working with the media committee of the march. I decided to do that because I think the process of education that goes along with the march is really important. We're setting up interviews on radio and TV stations, getting newspaper reporters to come and interview us so we can get our ideas out. We send psa's (public service announcements) to the radio stations and we send out press releases. We're also going to have some street theater at major areas around rush hour. We have plans in the works to have feminist theater companies do some street theater and try to get the media to come and cover that.

I'd like to talk a little about the goals that Take Back the Night has for 1981. One is to build a movement of women of all abilities, ages, classes, cultures, races, and sexual preferences—a movement that will respond to acts of violence against women and also to economic cutbacks that affect women, like in welfare programs. Another goal is to encourage women to take action who are not politically involved. And we want to maintain communication with different organizations for social change such as men who are working for feminist concerns, or women of color who are working on their different issues, or anti-nuke groups, or people opposing the Moral Majority. We want to make connections between these people and Take Back the Night, to bring all issues of violence that happen in everyone's lives together, including economic violence, sexual harassment and the lack of reproductive rights. Racial violence is very important. In Boston, thirteen black women were murdered in 1979 and the crimes still haven't been solved. We'd also like to make some specific demands to the city, though we haven't formulated those demands yet.

8

Organizers as Advocates

The advocate's role, which may take many forms, has developed considerably over the last two decades. Usually advocates are employees of human service organizations, but Larry Brown describes the experience of helping to create a new organization specifically to do advocacy—the Massachusetts Advocacy Center. His was one of the first of its kind in the country and it has been the model for other advocacy organizations. All the other cases in this section, however, involve people who were employed by established service organizations.

Unlike more traditional community organizing, advocacy involves organizing certain people on behalf of certain *other* people's rights. The cases in this section, for example, involve organizing around the needs of children, welfare recipients, undocumented workers, and nursing home residents. With the exception of welfare recipients, all of these groups involve people who have severe handicaps in pushing for their own rights.

Another contrast with traditional organizing is that advocates are more likely to work in the legislative and administrative arenas. They will seek to get new laws, to influence the interpretation of statutory language, to get new regulations issued, or to have unfavorable laws and regulations rescinded. It is not a hard-and-fast distinction, since advocates will sometimes work in other arenas and community organizers often have to deal with laws and regulations also. But as a general difference between the two types of organizing, it holds true.

Larry Brown's career as an advocate was inspired by Robert Kennedy's "Citizen's Board of Inquiry'' into hunger and its success in educating the American public. At the same time Brown saw how the Board's lack of systematic follow-up meant that the impact of its work was severely weakened. This was a lesson he sought to apply in helping to set up a new—and at the time unique—advocacy organization. He describes the way he helped put the organization together, stressing three stages of the advocacy process: (1) fact finding, (2) putting the facts in a permanent format such as a monograph, (3) making sure any legislative changes that occur as a result of the first two stages are implemented. This emphasis on implementation set Brown's organization apart from others, although it has been widely copied since then. Note the various types of implementation follow-up— legislative, administrative, and judicial. Brown also discusses case advocacy, helping people with individual problems. In this way the advocates were able to monitor the actual implementation of the law—another technique in the implementation process.

One of Brown's most important insights is the necessity of organizing and staying in touch with groups the laws are designed to benefit. For example, the Advocacy Center formed a coalition out of disparate parent groups that had been focused around specific handicaps. They then showed this group how it could monitor the law that it had helped to pass. Brown also felt an organized constituency was important to the advocacy agency, not just because of the clout it could muster but as a device for determining if the Advocacy Center was on the right track. A dramatic illustration of the importance of a constituency is the loss of a state law mandating free breakfast programs for poor Massachusetts school children. The law was rescinded because there was no organized constituency to back up the Advocacy Center's advocacy effort.

The Family Service Association of Greater Boston had made a decision to do advocacy work around issues of public welfare and AFDC families. Paula Georges and Howard Prunty were both employed by this agency to implement that decision. Howard Prunty moved into that position when Mrs. Georges left the agency. It is striking that while they each had the same mandate from their agency they chose to play very different advocacy roles. Georges was coordinator for the Massachusetts Coalition Against Workfare, an alliance of service organizations and other concerned groups. The coalition used confrontation as one of its major tactics. Prunty, on the other hand, used a collaborative approach in organizing businessmen to lobby for cost-of-living increases for public welfare recipients. It is clear that an advocate may alternate using collaborative or confrontations tactics as circumstances warrent. However, in these two cases one used predominantly collaborative tactics and the other confrontational tactics, even though both used some of the same forms such as educational outreach and the news media.

Georges originally attended a meeting called by a state agency around the issue of ''workfare,'' a scheme to coerce welfare recipients into performing unpaid labor. She attended as a representative of her agency and subsequently became the coordinator of a steering committee of a coalition of agencies. In that position she helped plan press conferences, organized hearings before HEW, educated welfare recipients as well as unions about what workfare was all about, and helped pressure social agencies not to accept workfare placements. She also helped organize pickets and leafleting.

While the Coalition was successful in stopping workfare, she reflects that its biggest weakness was that it was a coalition of advocacy groups rather than of recipient groups. She feels they should have engaged more directly in welfare rights organizing. Subsequently, the Coalition was transformed into a recipient-run organization and renamed the Coalition for Basic Human Needs. This organization has played a significant advocacy role in the state.

Georges is candid about the difficulties inherent in combining separate roles as both a staff member for the Family Service Association and a prominent leader of the Coalition Against Workfare. The agency opposed workfare but preferred a collaborative to a confrontational approach. The coalition, on the other hand, was often very militant. Georges handled this problem by explaining that when she spoke in public it was not as a staff member of the agency but as a spokesperson for the Coalition. The things she said represented the collective thinking and decisions of the Coalition. For advocates in this situation, the more they work under an umbrella of many organizations the less likely they are to be caught in the middle between the agency that pays their salary and the advocacy group they are working with.

Whereas Paula Georges helped organize social agencies on behalf of welfare recipients, Howard Prunty organized members of the business community. He enabled them to play a powerful advocacy role in securing a cost-of-living AFDC increase. His philosophy is that unconventional groups can be enlisted on behalf of welfare recipients. Rather than seeing certain groups as enemies, advocates can educate these groups on behalf of welfare recipients. He found sympathetic businessmen on the boards of service agencies and educated them through briefing sessions and fact sheets. He then arranged for them to testify before the legislative Ways and Means Committee under circumstances in which there was maximum publicity. He also arranged for them to meet with the Governor. He credits their intercession for the fact that a cost-of-living increase for AFDC recipients was approved. At the time of the interview he was embarking on reaching out to such groups as the American Legion, the VFW (Veterans of Foreign Wars), and the Masons.

If you were employed as an advocate by a Family Service Association, whom would you choose to organize? Other service agencies? The business community? Welfare recipients?

Frank Galvan, like Larry Brown, was motivated by a desire not just to educate the public about a particular social problem but to work directly on alleviating the problem. In this case the problem was that of the undocumented worker. Galvan was able to restructure the nature of his job so that while he began his work in the traditional AFSC manner of organizing a conference he was able to take the information gathered at the conference and use it to advocate for the rights of undocumented workers.

Because of language barriers and the fear of being deported, a sizable proportion of undocumented workers are either ignorant of their legal rights or afraid to assert them. Galvan served as their advocate by being a link between them and the Select Commission on Immigration and Refugee Policy, as well as the California Division of Labor Standards Enforcement and lawyers who helped with individual immigration problems. In each of these linkages there was a legal issue involved— either the drafting of a new law or the enforcement of existing laws. The major thrust of his work was a booklet informing undocumented workers about their rights as employees. This was not as innocuous as it sounds: many undocumented workers were being exploited and adherence to minimum-wage and worker's compensation laws would mean less profits for area businessmen. For this reason it was not as easy as he thought it would be to get the booklet distributed through the schools.

Note Galvan's sensitivity to Hispanic culture. In what ways did this contribute to the success of his advocacy work?

In "The Elderly Activist," Joselle Holmes describes another form of advocacy. An elderly activist group takes, as one of its tasks, the role of advocating for residents of local nursing homes. Members of the group felt a special kinship with the nursing home residents, since they knew they themselves might end up in a home in the not-too-distant future. Nursing home residents are rarely able to organize on their own behalf and their relatives seldom organize on their behalf.

Holmes describes the community context that helped make Cape United Elderly (CUE) an unusually strong organization. In examining their advocacy activities we find part of their strength came from the access they had to other activist groups on the Cape, as well as a sympathetic state representative. With widespread support and legitimacy, they had no hesitation in using confrontational techniques such as candlelight vigils and picketing when they felt it necessary.

The Good Advocate Needs Troops

Larry Brown

I'm the founder and director of the Massachusetts Advocacy Center and now I'm chairman of its board. We began the center in 1969 when I was a graduate student, and our budget for the first year was $9,400. Now it's twelve years old and the budget is over $500,000. It was the first statewide public-interest child advocacy organization of its kind, and in fact it gave birth to the National Children's Defense

Fund, the same thing on the national level. The Massachusetts special education law which we got passed in 1972 was the basis for a federal law along the same lines. We also helped pass the federal Bilingual Education Act. Other issues we deal with are child mental health, nutrition, school breakfast programs and the juvenile justice system. Of particular concern to us are two issues which cut across all the others— racism and inequality.

When we started the center we did not know where it would go. We started as the Task Force on Children Out of School. We were dealing with a very narrow issue. More generally, though, I was interested in the questions of whether and under what circumstances private citizens influence public policy. I started looking at the Citizens Board of Inquiry that existed in the late 1960s. They put out a document called "Hunger USA" and they got Bobby Kennedy to go on a Mississippi Tour. I was very interested because it had a significant impact. It gave rise to Senator McGovern's Senate Select Committee on Nutrition. I interviewed virtually all the principals, went to Washington and New York and, in fact, wrote a paper subsequently published in the *Journal of Health and Social Behavior*. I was critical of the Citizens Board because while they had a major impact, more could have been done.

I was very intrigued with the model. I know that long-term changes in this country don't come about except through organizing masses of people, but I'm not constitutionally an organizer. I cannot live on a low salary and work for long-term gains that might come years down the road. I'm the type A personality and I've got to be always fighting and have an issue to fight about. I also know that while the organizers are working on that longer-term agenda there are people who are being hurt right now. We can't change the political economy to deal with the structural aspects in the short term. But we do know that through advocacy we can intervene to make life a little bit better for a lot of people so long as it is well targeted and we stay on the case.

I really felt troubled in graduate school because I couldn't go out there and do what some do every day, organizing tenants and so on. I tried to think how I could use my skills as a professional with a degree but to do it for very progressive causes. That's why the Citizens Board idea appealed to me.

I got to know Hubie Jones while I was doing record keeping at Roxbury Multi Service Center. He said, "I wonder if you would be interested in doing some staff work on this problem of children excluded from school." So out of a month-long conversation I essentially made a proposal to him that I would be the director and put together a task force. I did it basically on the Citizens Board of Inquiry model. This meant we had to create an organization when there was none. We created one whose name told what the problem was—Task Force on Children Out of School.

We had to legitimize it. It couldn't be just some young Brandeis graduate student in a black agency. That doesn't have much legitimacy in this racist, elitist society. We went about it as the Citizens Board had done, picking a board of people whose positions or titles would legitimize the whole operation. Once we got them on board we went about holding hearings. We basically radicalized the board by looking at the data. The final report would not have had five of their names on it if they hadn't gone through this thirteen-month-long hearing. I set up hearings to create conflicts so they could see the opposing sides and views very clearly. These relatively passive professionals on our board were outraged.

Then I structured our organization around the Nader idea of struggling to get the laws that are on the books enforced and new regulations written. Nader never mentions the word "capitalism" but he addressed the economic establishment of this country, starting out with those who produce cars. Unlike mass movement organizing that's struggling to make basic changes in power relationships, advocacy organizing focuses on entitlements that have already been won. We simply say, "There's a law on the books that says children have a right to a free school breakfast. These schools aren't providing it. They are breaking the law." It's basically using society's official self-image in order to get more for people who need a bigger share of the pie.

In addition there were some other ingredients. We were consciously aware at that time that we could take advantage of three conditions. One was that the good guys were in office. While that was also the Nixon era we had just come out of the Johnson era and the War on Poverty and the Great Society and all that stuff, and there were rising expectations. The Good Guys were in office in Congress, and at the state level, too. We had a liberal Republican Governor, Frank Sargent. Second, there was an expanding economy. Everyone believed we could buy our way into Nirvana. We understood the limits of that but it led to a third thing and that was public support and interest for the kind of work we did. Now all those things have changed, every one of them. In fact the Mass. Advocacy Center had a board meeting the other day and we were asking, "Can the Center continue to operate on the same model? It's based on assumptions that are out of date." We had conceptually and strategically thought this whole thing through at the beginning. We made a lot of mistakes and there were a lot of things that we didn't know to think about. But it wasn't that it hadn't been thought out.

For example, when we decided we were only going to stick with children's issues, we had darn good reasons for going so. One, the issues are very emotive, they catch the public. Second, children can speak for themselves, just like the retarded can, but they can't speak as well as other groups. They clearly need advocates, someone to speak for them. Third, we knew that whenever there's a fight for the small share of the pie and all the disenfranchised scrambling together, kids usually get cut out. We wanted to make sure they at least had a voice. The final reason was that if we're ever going to be able to work on other social problems, early intervention and support in the lives of children is a necessity. If we were doing it all over again, instead of working directly on children's issues I'd have worked on the economic underpinning of the family—AFDC increases, Medicaid,

Medicare, nutrition programs, and even housing, since housing is the biggest fixed cost in any family's budget. We are now looking at what we can do about these issues. I wish that we had done that ten years ago, because at the state level we could have had some impact. Not enough are speaking up for AFDC kids, parents, and so on. I started out with the problem that was presented to me, kids out of school, which disproportionately impacts on kids from poor families. If I stood back and said what are the biggest problems of poor families, I'd focus probably on some of the same issues but somewhat differently, more from the economic perspective.

We found out that several different groups of children were out of school. The three main ones were the kids who didn't speak English, pregnant girls, and children who were mentally and behaviorally different—handicapped, emotionally disturbed, retarded. We wanted to document the number of kids out of school and write a strong report. Take one example. We began doing some preliminary interviews and data gathering and getting some kind of vague notion of what the problem was as to why kids were out of school. I wanted to radicalize my board and to educate them so we held hearings. We had two hearings on pregnant girls. I had school department officials come to the hearing to say what their policy was on pregnant girls and why it was important for them not to come to school. They said things like, "It's in their own interest not to come because they'll be made fun of." Or, "They need health care." Or, "It isn't good for the other students. If it looks like we condone it, pregnancy rates will go up."

I knew then what they were going to say, and let them say it. It was their position and I wanted my board to hear it. It was outrageous and they made fools of themselves. In fact, one administrator ended her presentation by saying pregnancy is an illness and ill people should stay at home. I wanted the issues to be drawn very clearly, so I had other people there. I had a lawyer who said that the policy was unconstitutional—it was like saying you can't have Jews in the school or left-handed people. I had a psychiatrist, Mary Jane England, who testified that for many girls, pregnancy is a way of dropping out and avoiding intolerable life situations; they should be encouraged to continue doing the normal things in their lives, including school, rather than being pushed out. Finally I had an obstetrician/gynecologist, a guy who said pregnant girls can do anything that any other woman can do including tennis and horseback riding. All of these people spoke on the same day. It was very clear that none of the reasons for excluding pregnant girls had any basis. My board was outraged. They even asked for another hearing on this issue. I did that. We also had hearings on special education, on bilingual education, and on attendance officers. We found a similar set of circumstances in each instance. For example, the attendance officers were really former cops, with no training. They'd gotten their jobs through a blatant patronage system and they were very abusive to the students.

After thirteen months of hearings and investigations we put out our report. In the report we said specifically who had to do what by when to deal with the situation.

There's basically three stages to the advocacy process. One is fact finding, going out and gathering either existing data or creating data where no data exists. Secondly putting that data in some kind of format where it will not go away. If you have a press conference, you get play on TV one day and maybe two and its gone. We put all of our information in sexy readable documents in lay language with photographs and the whole thing. Then it doesn't go away. When those things are in writing, they stay around forever and they grate on people's consciences and they just don't go away. That's one of the things I learned from the Citizens Board of Inquiry. The third and hardest step is implementation. How do you take what you say has to happen and make them do it? Through the legislative arena or the courts or most likely through administrative pressure.

Before I describe these means of implementation, a separate issue we ought to get to is, How do you maintain accountability? How do you know when you're not going off and doing the wrong thing or being an elitist and saying, "My constituency needs us" when you don't represent that constituency? In order to limit the likelihood of our doing something like that, in each of the areas that we worked with we put together all the known existing groups in the state. For example, in the area of special education we put together all the known existing special education parent groups in the state and created an organization called the Coalition for Special Education. We organized our constituency.

Now, let me turn to an example of legislative advocacy as a means of implementing what we documented had to be done. This involved the education of special needs children.

We found that we had a hodge podge of state laws. We had a law for the education of the blind, a law for the education of deaf kids, for retarded kids, emotionally disturbed kids, and a law for learning disabled kids. There were five separate laws and every one of them had different entitlements. What it reflected was how parents of these kids organized over the years. It's obvious people can identify with blindness, so the parents of the blind were the first to organize and they got a law passed and later another group came and got another law passed. But when we investigated we found that the laws didn't work and weren't enforced. We decided we had to wipe the slate clean, repeal all these laws and have one omnibus special education law with four or five simple concepts in it. We started having meetings with our combined parent groups and got a consensus that there did have to be an omnibus law passed. We went through a year-long process in drafting the thing. Two guys, Larry Kotin and Bob Crabtree, ended up writing it. Once the bill was filed and it came time to lobby for it we had some thirty organizations from all over the state called the Coalition for Special Education. That's how we got that through.

It's ironic that the first two things we did were to get two major state laws passed, the Bilingual Education Act and the Special Education Law, both of which subsequently had their federal counterparts which were based largely on the laws that we got through. We had started out by saying there are a lot of good laws on the books, they just aren't being implemented, and instead we got two major laws passed.

I gave you an example of *legislative advocacy,* getting a law passed. Now I'll give an example of *judicial advocacy.* When we found that pregnant girls were being excluded from school we shied away from litigation even though we had a full-time litigator. We did that because litigation perpetuates people's dependence on lawyers—specialized people who engage in ritualized advocacy. Even though sometimes it's good, it doesn't begin to enfranchise people and educate them very much. Something magical happens, they get the victory, but people never know how or what to do with it. Litigation takes a hell of a lot of time and resources. You can lose and even if you do win in litigation all you do is get the minimum that the law requires. Sometimes through advocacy you get more than the law requires. There's nothing in the laws that says public officials can only do so much, the law says the minimum they have to do. All that a lawsuit can do is to get the administrative process operating again. If we can do that by short circuiting all this process and get the administrative process operating, then it's much better.

With that caveat we decided that on the issue of pregnancy we were going to litigate, because we thought the case was so clear cut. We started looking around for a pregnant girl on whose behalf we were going to sue. We knew it shouldn't be in Boston. It shouldn't be somebody who was black because that plays on everybody's racist stereotypes about promiscuity among blacks. Finally one day I got a telephone call from a girl 16 years old. She lived in East Pepperell, Massachusetts, and was very upset. It turned out that she had all the right characteristics for a court suit. She was not ashamed of herself. She was articulate. She was an honor student. She was going to college and this was in April and she had told her counselor that she was pregnant. She wasn't even showing and they kicked her out of school and wouldn't let her graduate. She was pregnant, by the way, by the son of the superintendent in the next town. But they didn't kick him out, they only kicked her out of school. When we got in on the case and started asking questions they said, "Oh, we'll let her graduate, she just can't attend school." Well, Fay said, "No, I made a mistake but I'm not a criminal and I'm not ashamed. I want to have my baby and I want to continue to go to school and graduate with my peers." The school people would not back down.

We went into federal district court. We had some of the same witnesses who'd testified before my board several months ago. The judge handed down the ruling the same day, saying that education was a right not a privilege. When the state desires to take away that right it has to have compelling reasons, and none had been shown in this case. We got her back in school and we also got the legal principle established. On the basis of that we were able to force the State Department of Education to issue a statewide policy in keeping with the suit. Then we had to get the policy complied with. School systems were already afraid of us because of our track record on other things. They knew we would go after them in the media and even sue them if we needed to.

Now let me give you an example of *administrative advocacy*. Our whole model is built on the notion that laws are only worth the paper they are written on, that most of them aren't enforced. Probably 90 percent of what the center has done over the last decade has been behind the scenes in the administrative arena where laws have already been passed but not enforced. Let me give you an example of that: after the special education law was passed in 1972 it was to go into effect two years later. We wanted to force school systems during those two years to do what they were supposed to do. We did a number of things to focus attention on the education of handicapped children.

When the law went into effect in September a month and a half later we monitored it. We did a study in every school system in the state—a sort of superficial thing, but we sent a questionnaire out asking all of them if they had appointed a special education administrator or done the screening? They went bananas. They said, "The law just went into effect—why are you monitoring us? Who are you? What right does a private organization have to monitor us?" And so on. But what it did was to put their nose to the grindstone right away. In effect we were saying, "The law's here, baby, and you're going to have to comply with it!" Then we ranked every school system in the state as far as their compliance with the law and we published it. We released it publically in every little newspaper in the state—every one of them. There are 400 newspapers and every one of them ran the story on their own school system's rating. Well, school people were livid. What we wanted to do was to create a public presence and let them know we were on their case.

Then we began to work it politically. We put out documents showing citizens' groups how they could monitor their own school system. We also put out some books of all the state laws in lay language describing what the law says, what the problems are, and how to deal with them. At the end of the school year we ranked the schools again. Whereas the first ranking of all the school systems had more to do with structure and administrative stuff this had more to do with substantive stuff in the classroom. Administrators were angry. We released the results again and we created a greater furor.

The first year, instead of just letting everyone say, "The law is in effect and we'll take our time and we'll do it," we'd made it a major public issue in the state. It was a cross between traditional organizing and advocacy. Then we set up a case advocacy unit in the Massachusetts Advocacy Center. While the center wasn't set up as a direct service organization, we started getting all these calls from people who wanted help. It was almost immoral not to help them when nobody else could. And at the same time we realized that if we handled cases, it was also a way to test the impact of our policies and programs to see if they were being implemented. The center continues to this day in case advocacy and is manned largely by law students. We'll have ten, twelve people at any one time in cases and it's worked marvelously.

The Special Education Law has now been in effect for 10 years. What is clear is that there's got to be ongoing pressure to make public officials do what they're supposed to do. And at this point we have the law locked in. The reason I know that we have the law locked in is by a look at the special education budget and the fact that we don't get the Godawful cases we used to get before the law. What makes me know we've succeeded is that this past month an effort was made to repeal a lot of the provisions of 766. Our constituency base was there. We were able to turn them out and they packed the rooms. It turned the legislature around. One of the legislators told us that in all his years up there he had never seen such an effective presentation. Mass Advocacy didn't even bother to testify. We didn't have to speak on their behalf. They spoke for themselves.

You can't overstate the importance of staying in constant touch with your consituency. Here's an example of where we failed. It also shows the distinction between community organizing and advocacy. This is a totally different issue—nutrition, school breakfast. There is a federal law that says that any state or any local school district can volunteer to choose to participate in the federally funded school breakfast program. Massachusetts was the only state that actually passed a state law making the program mandatory in schools that have a certain proportion of low income children. The state law stipulates the program is mandatory. We didn't help get that law passed at all, but some people came to us and said, "Okay, hot shot Mass Advocacy Center, here's a critical issue. Here's a law. Go off and do your stuff." We looked into it and decided to do it. We did an investigation one summer. We wrote a report on hunger in the classroom and the school breakfast in Massachusetts. We did the usual thing. We showed who's not complying with the law, how much money is being lost to the state in federal funds, the impact on children's health, and so on. It was front page of the *Boston Globe,* all over the local TV stations. It was our usual model: investigate, put it in writing. Then we got to the implementation stage and it was just like cutting butter with a hot knife. Within five months after that report, and mainly through administrative advocacy, we were able to more than triple the number of low-income kids in the state who were able to eat school breakfast. It went from 19,000 to 71,000. We more than tripled it in five months and that felt good. We were getting food in kids' mouths.

What happened was something I would never have predicted. This was the straw that broke the camel's back. The local school officials, the town selectmen, the school committees were tired of having programs foisted on them and being told what to do. We'd gotten the bilingual law passed, the special education law passed, and desegregation was in the papers. They were feeling very put upon. Now then along comes Mass Advocacy forcing the state to make them obey this law and they'd had it. Plus it really ran into what I would never have guessed, an ideological conflict. People were saying the schools cannot be a substitute for parents. The schools cannot be the main social service agency. These people felt because I was a Brandeis graduate, I was Jewish. There was a little anti-Semitism in there too—one of the editorials in Brockton made a vague reference but it was very clear what they were saying. They editorialized that way. Along comes these hot shots telling us what to do and they are trying to destroy the town. They said we were trying to destroy the family by not letting people eat together and making the state take over and substitute for the family and have children come into the eating centers. They conjured up all their images of Russia, regimented societies and all this crap. At the local level, these people started getting angry and organized. The superintendents' association and the statewide organization of school committees started saying, "We know best what our people need. Our people don't need this. We don't have the money up front to spend to get later reimbursement from the Feds." And so on. For a whole variety of reasons—ideological, political, practical, whatever—they began to mobilize to repeal the law. The law was our only source of power. It's an advocate's source of power and we used it. They filed bills to totally repeal the school breakfast law and to make it voluntary.

We were caught totally off guard because there was no organized constituency in behalf of the nutrition programs and breakfast. There was the unorganized people out there, the poor people who had enough things going on in their lives who were never organized around this.

People who do community organizing are into mass movements; their base is there. It's their constituency. They can call on the troops. But we couldn't fight these people. We were the good guys who ended up being political eunuchs. I was up there in the legislature trying to convince people not to repeal the law. We got Governor Dukakis to veto the repeal. Then there was an effort to override his veto. Well, I had never worked in the legislative arena, direct lobbying before. But then for five, six months I did it. I sat there in the balcony of the senate, where I needed sixteen votes in order to sustain his veto. In other words they had to have a two-thirds vote of both chambers. We got one vote more than we needed, and we beat them. The law wasn't repealed. I then went off to Washington to work and the next year the thing happened all over again. Dukakis vetoed it and this time it was overridden. Massachusetts now has no school breakfast law.

The school districts that had implemented the law before it was repealed did not stop the program, because they saw how beneficial it was. They are now its strongest supporters. But we ended up losing the law. In one way we won a lot because about 77,000 kids eat breakfast and only 19,000 did before we started. But it could have been a lot more. This shows I think the classic difference between traditional advocacy and organizing, and what can happen when you don't have your base.

Coordinating a Coalition of Advocacy Groups

Paula Georges

So-called workfare schemes have been cropping up a lot in the last decade or so. The idea is that certain categories of welfare recipients will have to perform unpaid labor in order to keep getting their checks. It's basically slave labor for the recipients and a pernicious attack on organized labor and the wage levels it's managed to win over the years. When this idea first came up in Massachusetts in the mid-1970s I was involved in a campaign to defeat it. We were basically successful, and our experiences may be useful to people in other states.

When Governor Michael Dukakis first put the idea forward, he wanted all welfare recipients with children over six to work off their welfare checks. This was on the heels of a horrendous overall attack that he'd already made on the welfare programs that existed in the state at that time. He'd pushed through an end to General Relief, for example, which meant that single people were pushed off the welfare rolls altogether unless they fit some small special category. Now he wanted to push the attack further.

The first resistance centered around an obscure state agency called the Social and Economic Opportunities Council, or SEOC. It had been set up by the state with a small budget and in a sense paid to do advocacy. At the same time, they were also connected to the Community Action Program agencies around the state, some of which were represented on the SEOC board. On this particular issue they were in an ideal position to act. What was happening within the state administration was that when the Human Services Secretary and others began to compute what it would cost the state to put welfare mothers to work they quickly found that the cost/benefit ratio was ridiculous. Internal memorandums were being circulated, and because SEOC was part of the state government they were able to get hold of some of them and act as a conduit to the press. At the same time, they had ties on the outside and used them to draw in as many socially minded agencies and organizations as possible. They drew in CAP agencies and a lot of other groups too. I myself got involved when they contacted the agency I worked for, the Family Services Association of Greater Boston, and asked us to participate in a press conference. We lent our name to the press conference, then when they called a follow-up meeting I got interested and got permission from the agency to go as a representative. We'd been involved in welfare-reform activities for a long time, and it was natural for us to have some degree of involvement in this.

The press conference and the first meeting were basically called by SEOC, but we realized that we needed a broader-based organization. So we formed the Massachusetts Coalition Against Workfare with people from a lot of different groups.

Early on, it became clear that the state was going to abandon the idea of putting all welfare mothers to work. But it was quickly turning to another population, namely, welfare fathers. There was much more of a consensus that somehow able-bodied men should be working. They were a more vulnerable target than the welfare mothers were. But the principle was the same, and we still saw it as a threat. The change just meant that the plan would be a lot harder to fight.

One focus that we chose was the federal Department of Health, Education and Welfare. HEW had a lot of federal regulations concerning employing welfare recipients, and the state was eventually going to have to ask for a waiver if they wanted to make those welfare recipients work. So we felt that the regional HEW office would be a good target, because we knew they had to recommend to Washington whether to approve such a waiver. So at our first meeting the director of SEOC called up the regional office and asked for a meeting with the regional HEW director. And he said he had to know very soon, within an hour or so, because he was having a meeting with concerned groups and they wanted to meet with him. The director called back within an hour and granted an appointment for the following week, and so we had an immediate victory.

As it happened, the regional director was fairly inexperienced in dealing with community groups. He didn't ask, for example, how many people would come to the meeting, didn't really set limits on the format. So we went ahead and told people to come to Government Center the following week for this meeting. Later the regional director got wind of what was happening and tried to limit the numbers, but we were very firm. We said these were people coming from all over the state and it was important that they have the opportunity to meet with him. So what we had was a meeting in a very large meeting room, which probably held a couple of hundred people. We set up a public-hearing format where the regional director and various other people from the bureaucracy sat in front just like it was a public hearing, and one after another various people got up and spoke against the workfare scheme.

This event was extremely successful. We got a lot of press coverage. The testimony was a mix of carefully prepared analysis and spontaneous offerings where recipients got up and talked about what it is like to be on welfare and how minimal the benefits are. They said the problem with workfare wasn't that they didn't want to work, but that there weren't decent jobs out there. They could hardly survive now, and forcing them to work off a subsistence living wasn't fair. And other advocates got up and spoke against the plan as a labor issue. We didn't have a lot of ties with labor organizations at that point but we knew it was a direction we wanted to go in.

One thing that made the hearing such a big success from our point of view was that the governor was still talking about including welfare mothers as well as fathers in workfare. So we had a broader representation of welfare recipients than we might have had otherwise. After the hearing we realized that we needed to plan really carefully for the long haul. So at the next meeting we formed a steering committee for the coalition, and at that time I was one of the two people elected as coordinators. We also decided on a two-pronged strategy in which we'd continue trying to get the attention of the State House press corps, through demonstrations and press conferences, but we'd also use other methods of reaching people directly. We decided that we needed a simple slogan or logo that would capture what the issue was, and that the point we basically wanted to make was expressed by "Jobs Not Workfare." That was our key criticism of the program, and it made the connection between welfare recipients and the labor movement.

So what we started to do then was develop two important pieces of propaganda material. One was geared to welfare recipients, trying to get people to understand what workfare was all about and why it was important to hook up with local welfare rights groups. And the other was directed at labor unions, pointing out why workfare was a threat to them and especially to the public-sector unions. And we then used this material whenever we could get an audience of labor groups. We went around to executive council meetings of locals throughout the state, trying to get endorsements. When the state budget was held up in the legislature and state workers didn't get paid, and thousands of them went to the State House in protest, we prepared a flyer about workfare and went among the workers talking about why it was a threat to them. What we discovered from that was that the issue really had to be explained very carefully. A lot of people said, "Well, I work, why shouldn't they work too." But once they understood that it wasn't really a job, that there was no pay and there were no holidays and no fringe benefits, that it was basically unpaid labor, then they could see our point.

In the meantime, the state did decide that it would just be unemployed fathers that would be the target for the workfare scheme. And as more and more unions began to speak out against workfare, the state also began looking for an alternative to using state employees' slots. They came up with the idea of using nonprofit organizations as the place to put them to work. And they began to try to repackage the whole scheme as a training program. That was ridiculous, since their own statistics showed that these people did have work histories. Many of them came from other parts of Massachusetts, where they'd worked in plants that had moved out of town. The problem was lack of jobs, not lack of training. The state's figures also showed that there was a high turnover in the unemployed fathers program, so they were taking jobs as soon as they could find them. Workfare just didn't make sense.

So we kept calling press conferences to keep the issue in the public eye as much as possible, but we also did what we could to sabotage the state's new plan for where the recipients would work. The Family Service Agency, which I worked for, passed a resolution that they would not support workfare by being a placement site. And we used that as a way to contact other United Way agencies and convince them to do the same. We prepared literature geared to these agencies. The United Way itself didn't take a stand, but they didn't block us either—they gave us names and addresses. Our effort here was highly successful. A few agencies did agree to go along with workfare, mostly out of ignorance, but we got enough to oppose it that it began to have a snowball effect. Whenever we'd go on a radio talk show, which we did a lot, we were able to cite these agencies that had refused to cooperate with workfare.

In the meantime we kept the pressure on HEW. The regional office people didn't really want to see us any more, and the follow-up meetings took on a much more militant tone than the first one had. We tried to keep the press informed of all the maneuverings. We also found that we had some leverage in Washington, because this was early in the Carter administration and he'd brought in a lot of people with good labor and civil rights records. A lot of the people in the Labor Department were very sensitive to the charge that this was a union-busting scheme. So it was a hot potato for them. And one thing we did that probably helped a lot was that we crashed an employment and training conference that Ray Marshall, the secretary of labor, was the keynote speaker at. Through the auspices of AFSCME, the state and municipal workers' union, we got into the conference. They were part of the conference and by that time they were part of our Coalition Against Workfare too. So we got inside this dinner and leafletted all the people there, who were basically pro-labor types, and we also had a picket line outside.

What happened eventually was that we declared a victory. Even though the program was finally approved by HEW, it was in a drastically different form than they'd originally wanted. Not only was it only for unemployed fathers, but it was limited to a thirteen-week program. They'd wanted it to be that everyone would have to come into the program and stay on it as long as they were on the rolls. Their real objective was to discourage people from coming onto welfare. And what made it more a victory for us was that the way HEW rationalized letting them do it was by tieing it to a research project. Brandeis University was awarded some money to conduct an evaluation of whether workfare was successful or not, and when they came out with their report they in fact showed just what we'd been claiming—that it was a total waste of money.

The biggest weakness in what we did, despite our success, was that it was a coalition of advocacy groups rather than a coalition of recipient groups. There were a couple. But once it was no longer a threat to the entire welfare population, we were not able to really keep the interest of the few welfare rights groups that did exist at the time. And it was also not an issue that would allow you to start new groups. So that if we had it to do all over again, I think we wouldn't have lingered quite so long on this issue. We had won significantly much earlier on than we even realized. I think we should have broadened our tactics to get into more straight-out welfare rights organizing. And in fact what we did at the end, when we finally did kind of draw this phase of our work to a close—what we realized was that we really wanted to get into organizing welfare rights groups. And at the time the issue that emerged was a program in Massachusetts called Emergency Assistance which helped recipients get money for back rent and utility bills as well as a washing machine and a refrigerator. That was the kind of issue that affected the population more broadly, and when we got into organizing around that issue it eventually led to the formation of the Coalition of Basic Human Needs. That's an organization that is still ongoing and in fact has become really a recipient-run organization. So if you look at the history, it started off as an advocacy-run political organization and eventually led into an entirely recipient-run organization, which is probably the most difficult thing for an organizer to achieve, in the true sense of having the recipients and the people affected running it.

One difficulty that I probably should talk about was my role as both a staff member of the Family Service Association of Greater Boston and being a prominent leader of the Coalition Against Workfare. My agency's goals and philosophy are very opposed to the kind of thinking that workfare represented. But the preferred approach is much more of a collaborative than a confrontational approach. In other words, they would have liked to have met with the governor's officials, sat down at the table with them, and discussed in a fairly rational way why they were opposed to the scheme. And the Coalition Against Workfare at various times was both rude in terms of how it treated, how it characterized public officials and also at various times very militant in its actions—everything from picketing to sit-ins at offices. The way I was able to continue to keep working for the agency was that in the first place I explained to the people I worked for in the agency that when I spoke in public it was not as a staff member of the Family Services Association—it was as a spokesperson for the coalition. And that the things that I said were collective, representing the collective thinking and decisions of the coalition. So that if they didn't particularly like what I said or a particular tactic that was used that wasn't me speaking. Now this is not to say that there wasn't a lot of tension, or that people wouldn't have preferred that those kinds of tactics weren't used. I think that I would say that for organizers in this kind of situation, the more they can work under an umbrella, the more they will be able to do this kind of more militant work.

Businessmen as Welfare Advocates

Howard Prunty

Anyone who gets involved in advocacy work has to recognize their own anger and the need to control it. Often the kind of anger that gets expressed in a street demonstration may make the participants feel better, but it may not always be the wisest strategy at that time. For example, it may sometimes be more effective to try to meet privately with the mayor than to get a group of folks together to parade in front of the mayor's office. Strategic planning is absolutely important.

Some years ago the agency I'm with, the Family Service Association of Greater Boston, decided to get involved in advocacy work over issues of public welfare and aid to AFDC families. We've gone about it in different ways, but one project that I'd like to describe is one that brought in people who you might not think would be sympathetic. I'm referring to businessmen. A few years ago we worked to get them involved in lobbying for an increase in the state AFDC grant for the 126,000 AFDC families in Massachusetts. It worked very well.

This project grew out of an idea of mine that the human service community needed to stop talking to itself and begin to involve other people. I decided that there were businesspeople on the boards of social agencies, and that their help could be crucial in winning adequate support for the basic needs of the children covered by the AFDC program.

As background, it was clear that the business community of the state generally supported the conservative governor at that time, Ed King. They'd given him a lot of money during the campaign and supported the way he was trying to bring business principles into running the state government. But by the same token, a lot of businessmen also were concerned that welfare children and their families not be left without elementary safeguards in terms of shelter, food, clothing, and so on. We identified a number of businessmen from various social-welfare organizations who would be willing to come together and be briefed on the issue—be given the kind of information they would need in order to feel secure making a public stand.

We had to pull together information that could be shared with them about the AFDC program, the cost of living increase, the relation of AFDC to Medicare and Medicaid and food stamps, the whole ball of wax. We tried to give them a well-rounded picture of what the average AFDC family was like and what its income possibilities were. We brought in an expert from the Massachusetts Law Reform Institute to help deal with legal issues. We had three long briefing sessions, and these sessions were really important. We didn't have to convince these people that the issue was something they should be involved in, but we did have to make them feel secure that they'd be able to answer questions and not be embarrassed. So there was a lot of staff work that had to be done. We came up with fact sheets that they could refer to: what percentage of the state's population was on AFDC, what percentage was unemployed or underemployed, what jobs and what training programs were available, and all sorts of related issues. When these people finished the three briefing sessions they were in good shape.

At the end of those sessions the people in them decided to move forward on two things. One was to testify before the Senate Ways and Means Committee. This was the first time a business group had come before the committee as welfare advocates, and the legislators were really quite shocked to see them there. Three of them testified in support of the cost-of-living increase, and it went over quite well. It got a big TV coverage, and it was splashed in the papers for several days.

These people were quite pleased with the publicity, and the way they were able to have this kind of influence in expressing their concerns for children. As a second step to that, we made arrangements for a meeting with the governor. He resisted the meeting, because of all the publicity around the legislative hearing, but eventually they got to meet with him. They expressed their support for his effort to carry out business principles in the state government, but they also expressed their concern about what he was doing that was harmful to children and dependent families. Largely as a result of their intercession, in the committee hearing and with the governor, the cost-of-living increase was approved and it went through the budget process without any difficulty.

One of the problems I think many of us have in the human services field is that we tend to see various large groups of people as the enemy. The business community is a good example. We've seen in this instance that it's possible to get business support over a clearly defined welfare issue, where we were willing to take the time to lay the issue out very carefully. And in a preliminary way we've been finding other kinds of groups receptive also—groups like servicemen's clubs, for example, the American Legion or VFW, or like the Masons. But they have to be reached out to and they have to be educated. You have to separate out what their overall political stance may be and identify an issue that they would be willing to work on with you. Issues involving children often have an especially broad appeal. And I think we need to be a lot sharper in defining issues and looking for groups that may be able to join us on a particular issue.

Incidentally, that initial grouping of businesspeople has broadened into something we call the Family Children's Services Agency Council, which is made up of board members from a variety of agencies in the greater Boston area. They're getting involved in lobbying and testifying over a number of different human service issues, particularly around welfare at this point. There are a number of committed people, including not only businesspeople but some businessmen's wives, who are really devoting a good deal of time and effort to it. It's very encouraging.

Protecting Undocumented Workers

Frank Galvan

I've worked for the American Friends Service Committee in Los Angeles for the past five years, and under their auspices I've gotten involved with problems of undocumented workers from Latin America. What we're doing grew out of our impatience with a national AFSC program concerned with the general problems of the Third World. Basically, it was a program that was conducted in most of the regional offices across the United States and it was intended to sensitize the American public to the global imbalance of wealth and the problems that people face in the Third World.

Now the Service Committee is pretty much involved in organizing conferences, sponsoring dialogues, seminars and such. So our original approach in this region was to hold a series of conferences focusing on U.S./Mexico economic relations, since we're a border area. We had conferences in Los Angeles followed up by conferences in San Diego and Tijuana in Mexico. After that, I started to feel uncomfortable because it seemed as if we were just dealing with issues in the abstract and not working with people. So I mentioned that concern and I said if we're going to really address the problem instead of just talking about it, then we needed to deal with people who are actual victims of the imbalance between Mexico and the U.S. Most obviously, there were the undocumented workers, who are forced to leave their homeland to come here, to improve their economic livelihood, and then go back home. So, following in the A.F.S.C. tradition, we decided to hold a seminar to bring together people who were involved with this issue and see what was being done and what needed to be done. So we held the conference in September of '79 in San Diego. From there, we decided we would look for ways of involving ourselves with undocumented people, and see how we might best respond to them.

There were a couple things then that happened along this time. One was that I volunteered to serve as an English as a Second Language (ESL) teacher at a local Catholic high school in the evenings to adults. One of the purposes for that was to have direct contact with undocumented people themselves. So for a couple of months or so, I had a class of twenty-four students, half of whom came from Mexico and the other half from Central America. During the breaks and before and after class, friendships started and I got to know a number of undocumented people who told me about the problems that they encountered. At the same time, the Select Commission on Immigration and Refugee Policy, which was the commission started by President Carter to review the immigration laws, was holding meetings across the United States. They had twelve public meetings in different parts of the country, all of them dealing with issues of immigration. Their seventh meeting was to be here in Los Angeles. We had been in dialogue with them and we asked them, "Have you met with any undocumented people?" Up until this time they hadn't. We said, "Would you be open to having your commission members sit in a meeting with undocumented people if it's off the record and if it doesn't constitute any jeopardy to the participants?" And they said that they would. I organized a meeting in February of '80 with fourteen undocumented workers and members of the Select Commission on Immigration and Refugee Policy. We served as a link between those two groups that needed to be in contact with each other. But we also wanted the meeting for our own information, so that we could become more sensitized to the problems that the undocumented had.

After that meeting took place, we continued to meet with that group of undocumented workers and to ask them what were the issues that were of concern to them and how we could help. One of the big concerns was with regard to getting sound legal advice about their visas. Unfortunately, in the Spanish-speaking community, there are many people who are notary publics, who give legal advice that's beyond their capacity. The title *notario publico* in Mexico carries a lot more weight. It denotes somebody with academic training who is close to being a paralegal, as opposed to notary publics in this country who just stamp documents and such. But coming from Mexico, a lot of immigrants think that a notary public has a lot more credibility than he or she does. So, while we talked with them about those issues, we'd bring lawyers who'd volunteer their time to give free legal advice to them on their immigration problems.

At the same time that this was going on, we developed a contact with what's called the California Division of Labor Standards Enforcement, and within that division, the Concentrated Enforcement Program. Now this was started just a couple of years ago, specifically for the purpose of cleaning up those industries where undocumented people worked. There's a large amount of exploitation. For example, something like 80 percent of the garment workers in this area are not receiving the minimum wage and/or overtime pay. Most of them are undocumented workers.

In the restaurant industry, 60 percent of the lower-level employees are not receiving minimum wage and/or overtime pay. One of the big problems, of course, is that the undocumented don't know the law, and if they do know it they're afraid of being turned over to the Immigration people if they complain. The Division of Labor Standards Enforcement does not turn over names to the Immigration agencies. So talking to them, and talking to the undocumented people, it became clear that we could serve as the link in informing undocumented people of what their rights are in this society, specifically with regard to rights at their workplace. So out of that developed the idea of putting together a booklet, in comic book form, which is a very popular form of public education in Mexico and throughout Latin America.

Basically, the booklet covers the area of working rights. There are four sections. The first section deals with problems that the person may have at the workplace, such as not receiving the minimum wage or not having workers' compensation insurance or the like. And it informs them of the agencies that they can go to for assistance if they're faced with any of these difficulties. The second story deals with someone who's working in a dangerous environment, either dangerous chemicals or faulty equipment, and again it lists the agencies that they can go to for assistance. The third story deals with someone who has contracted an illness as a result of the workplace, and where they can go to for assistance. And the fourth story deals specifically with the problems of agricultural workers in Orange and San Diego counties, and where they can get help.

Now most of the agencies that we've listed here are government-affiliated but none of them will pass on information to the Immigration Service. Still, there's understandably a hesitancy to go to those agencies if you're undocumented. So at the end of the booklet we listed a number of churches and social service agencies that have offered to serve as intermediaries between the undocumented people who may be having trouble and the agencies listed in the book.

Basically then, that's been the thrust of the work; putting this booklet together and then publicizing it and then making it larger and following up on distribution. When we printed the first edition, we had 20,000 printed, primarily for Los Angeles and San Diego. Then we had another second edition of 10,000. And then we saw that we were getting a large request for these and we thought, this is going pretty good so let's make a third edition of much larger quantity. So in March of this year we printed an additional 80,000 copies. And with that third printing, we also included Orange County. So now we have the three counties in the most south-western part of California.

The booklet gives people a number of alternatives. They can call the agencies directly, they can call the intermediaries that we list in the back, or they can call us directly. We're listed in the front. As a result of the calls we get, we've been able to help a number of people assert their rights. An example of the kind of thing we do along these lines is a woman who worked in Gardena in a waterbed factory. She'd been injured on the job because of equipment that she was working with. She got severely burned and what happened was that the employer ended up firing her. Of course he didn't inform her that he, by law, was responsible for taking care of that injury. She found a copy of our booklet through her parish or wherever, and realized that there was such a thing as Workers Compensation Insurance. She called us and we put her in contact with Labor Standards Enforcement, and they provided her with a lawyer who got her the assistance she needed.

Of course not everyone likes the booklet. We had one big setback in getting it out to people. Through my having volunteered to assist in an ESL class, I realized that that would be a great avenue for reaching undocumented people citywide. So I approached the head of the ESL adult program for the L.A. City School System, and he was very enthusiastic. He said they would help us distribute 60,000 copies of the booklet, that they would put a copy in the hands of every Spanish-speaking adult ESL student in the district. In fact, that was one reason why we printed the 80,000. After we had them printed and I went to him, he said, "Okay, I'll speak to my Board and that should be no problem." Well it was a problem. They said, for one thing, that it had the overtones of being a political document. Which it isn't. It's a guide to agencies that exist, that they can make use of. But they felt that the school district should not be used as an avenue to be organizing people, to be raising certain sensitive issues—even if the issues were clearly covered under state law. At least one of the members also didn't like the fact that we used slang. We used a lot of colloquial Spanish because that's what they talk. But he felt that in the school they shouldn't be passing out anything that isn't correct grammar. So to get them distributed in schools now, we have to get permission from each of the principals, and of course that's a much slower process. None of the principals I've talked to has turned me down, but it's very time-consuming.

Incidentally, I should tell you how the funds were raised. All of the people that you see listed in the beginning of the booklet are sponsors, and they put up money for printing costs. As you can see, most of them are church affiliated. There's eight religious denominations; there's twelve Roman Catholic religious orders. They gave from $25 to $400. We didn't raise enough to have a hundred thousand copies printed of the third edition, but we got enough for 80,000.

The Elderly Activist*

Joselle Holmes

In writing this handbook, I want both to tell an exciting story about some elderly activists who couldn't (and can't) be stopped and to set forth some simple and sound principles of elderly grassroots organizing—principles that will stand you in good stead too. Any part of CUE's experience that doesn't tell our story or that was complex or technical, I have left out for reasons of space limitations or confusion of the story line.

Consumer advocates or activist organizations are as different from one another as individuals are. Yet they have much in common as well. Many such organizations have a common determination to *act* and *fight* for a just and humane society. Out of just such principles, Cape United Elderly (CUE) was formed on Cape Cod in the spring of 1979. An elderly rights organization, its primary focus has been nursing home and elderly housing reform.

I want to acknowledge here that CUE as an organization had some unique advantages and antecedents.

First, Cape Cod had an anti-poverty program (Community Action Committee of Cape Cod & the Island, Inc.) that concerned itself, as few such organizations have, with the specific problems of the elderly in our society. CAC hired me in the summer of 1974 to be its first organizer and advocate for the elderly of Cape Cod.

Second, CUE had as a parent organization the Cape Cod Health Care Coalition. The Coalition is a broadbased organization including community members and health care workers (now the Hospital Workers Union Local 767, SEIU, AFL-CIO). The goal of the Coalition was to target the local hospital and to pressure it to live up to its community obligations in the delivery of affordable and accessible health care for everyone. This successful Coalition was put together by the CAC and Union Representative and Coalition Director Bill Pastreich. I was assigned as a community organizer to work for the Coalition under Bill's supervision in 1977. In 1979, I was asked to recruit elderly people into that organization. It was from the

*Annotated from *The Elderly Activist Handbook* by Joselle Holmes, director Cape United Elderly, Inc. Published by Cape United Elderly, Inc., Box 954, 583 Main St. Hyannis, Mass. 02601.

Coalition that CUE "spun-off" a few months later to address its own specific issues.

Third, CUE was to be enriched by the elderly people of Cape Cod. Out of the Cape's total population of 160,000 people, approximately 56,000 are elderly. Thirty percent of that number of elderly are poor. The Cape, it is readily apparent, is a bellwether for the rest of the nation where the percentage of elderly is about 10% of the population as compared to the Cape's 35%. The elderly population of the Cape is increasing at the rate of 7% yearly—many times more than the national average. While this in itself should surprise no one, it does reveal the Cape as racing ahead into our collective national future. The problems that we face in the areas of sufficient nursing home and hospital beds for the elderly, the intensification of elderly housing needs, etc., proceed at a ferocious gallop on the Cape.

Cape Cod then is a natural birthplace for a grassroots elderly organization like CUE. We had clear issues and a lengthy history of strong community organizing and activism (which had preceded my coming to CAC by about 5 years). The Cape's elderly, we found, were eager for social involvement.

BEGINNINGS: GETTING THE GRASSROOTS ORGANIZATION STARTED

A nursing home aide wrestled a pack of cigarettes from fragile, feisty 70-year-old Phyllis Murphy. Phyllis was startled, humiliated and her hand was badly bruised. This incident in the late summer of 1978 led by a chain of unrelated events to the formation of a Cape Cod grassroots organization now known as Cape United Elderly.

Phyllis Murphy, undaunted by 10 years residency in a nursing home (and at that time a new member of the Cape Cod Health Care Coalition), was not one to take the violation of her civil rights lightly. She turned to Bill Pastreich, the director of the Coalition, who referred the matter to the Massachusetts' Attorney General's Office. The issue was not to become a top priority then and no action was ever taken.

A few months later, Phyllis joined a suit against the Governor of Massachusetts for failure to provide alternatives to nursing home care. Her courage was typical of the more than a dozen elderly people drawn to CUE from its inception.

Most organizations start with an issue and then doorknock, or in other ways, recruit concerned people. CUE started with people. As Community Action Program organizer assigned to the Coalition, I, Joselle Holmes, was asked, with the assistance of Coalition organizer Katie Dickie, to bring elderly people into the Coalition. From our very beginning in February of 1979, CUE's strength was its people. We had a few elderly people who had occasionally put in appearances at Coalition meetings and a few, mostly union, nursing home workers who were also active with the Coalition. Some others of our elderly had been members of the local branch of the Gray Panthers that was discontinued. The rest of the initial constituency we found by knocking on doors at elderly subsidized housing sites. We found it easy to interest elderly people and were limited only by our small staff and by the geographic isolation of the members (many do not drive and on Cape Cod there is very limited public transportation).

Katie and I discovered that many of the members were bored and lonely and that they longed to come together for some larger purpose. Elderly people everywhere find themselves in a social vacuum. Many are virtually locked into the loneliness of home or a tiny apartment with no means of relieving their need for human interaction and meaningful purpose. In spite of transportation problems, we brought elderly people to Coalition meetings even though at first there was no particular issue of concern to them. Meetings were not formatted for either their interest or their comfort. We offered them only an opportunity to socialize and the potential for developing their own serious issues.

If they are to become active enough to participate in your organization, elderly people require certain kinds of support. CUE supplied encouragement, potluck suppers, transportation and personal recognition. With a large staff, youthful volunteers, and accessible public transportation, organizing this willing constituency would be easy. Rural conditions make it more difficult.

With elderly people, you can have a permanent constituency. The needs of the elderly in a youth-centered, age-segregated society are endless and so their issues are infinite, also. An elderly organization, much like a union or a tenants' council, can continue as long as an organizer will undertake to make it last. Elderly individuals, CUE has found, unlike their younger counterparts, do not get what they want and then walk away from the organization.

Despite the multiplicity of elderly social issues, it is still necessary to zero in on an issue that will engage the total energies of your constituency as soon as possible. In late February of 1979, Ed Sparer, a distinguished health care lawyer from the Health Law Project (now defunct) in Philadelphia conducted a health care issues seminar for the Coalition. Always on the lookout for a direction for our elderly members to take, I asked him what he would have done faced with the problem of getting action on the civil rights violation of Phyllis Murphy in the "cigarette-wrestling match."

"Why not form a Nursing Home Council?" he asked. He had in mind the organizing of relatives and friends of nursing home residents. Actually, CUE has always found the first best friends of nursing home residents are front-line nursing home workers who know the facility's conditions first-hand and, second best, our own elderly members who are apprehensive of a nursing home commitment in their own future. Relatives of residents, in our experience, are too intimidated by the nursing home administration and the threat of a loss of a scarce nursing home bed for, or reprisals against, their relative. If they join us at all, they do not stay with us long.

"How about a Nursing Home Council?", I asked our members individually and collectively. There was a lengthy silence while they thought about it.

"We would visit nursing homes", I explained, "and make sure that everyone was OK. Snoop around, check 'em out. What do you think?"

The answers I received ran something like this:

"I like it; but will they let us in?"
"Something has to be done."
"Yes, let's. Myself, I'd rather die than go to a nursing home."

In a meeting of some 15 people held to discuss the issue we were asked by members, "Would they (the nursing home administration and staff) listen to us?" "What makes you think they'll pay any attention to us?" Some of those present had tried as individuals to get the attention of the administration for a friend or relative in a nursing home and had met with failure. "Of course", we replied, "often they won't listen to one person. But there are—what—15 people in this room. It gets harder to ignore a group of people who are organized, prepared to bring pressure, to go to the press and generally hang in there."

When taking on an issue, it is always necessary to do your homework: to study the laws and regulations pertaining to the issue and what the specific situation is in your community as regards the issue. CUE formed a committee of about 15 people to meet frequently and decide how we were going to begin to do our advocacy and monitoring of local nursing homes. We knew that we were taking on a quasi-medical bureaucracy, the functioning of which we were largely ignorant.

One of our group had read *Old Age: The Last Segregation,* a book written by Nader's Raiders (4). Another recent book with good up-to-date information is Bruce R. Vladeck's *Unloving Care* (5). Someone recommended we get *Nursing Homes: A Citizen's Action Guide* by Linda Horn and Elma Griesel, with an introduction by Maggie Kuhn (6). This handbook was to become our bible. We recommend it highly. It gives information for every state in the country on nursing home access and the laws and regulations pertaining to nursing homes.

It was from Horn and Griesel's book that we learned that Massachusetts was unique in a special way: its Attorney General's regulations provided for *community group access* to nursing homes.

You will probably get very wide community participation on nursing home issues involving medicaid discrimination and transfer trauma. Transfer trauma may occur when a very elderly resident is transferred from the facility, which has been home, to another one. Physical and/or psychological injury may be a consequence. Wide community participation on these issues is possible because they strike directly at the relatives of nursing home residents. They can become very vocal because of their fear of a loss of a nursing home bed or the injury, possibly even death, of their elderly relative. These are issues on which CUE got broad-based support in the cases of Fraser Nursing Home, the Cape Cod Nursing and Retirement Home and with the Cape Cod Hospital's elderly "AND" (medicaid) patients.

Fraser Nursing Home: A Classic Case of Community Organizing

In November, 1980 the Fraser Nursing Home in Hyannis (a union nursing home) was threatened with federal decertification under the medicaid program for failure to meet life safety provisions. Twenty-eight medicaid residents, including a fine old Finnish gentleman, 101-year-old Mr. Kumpenen, were faced with the prospect of having to be transferred to off-Cape nursing homes due to the on-Cape bed shortage. Such a move was virtually a death sentence for Mr. Kumpenen whose home had been the Fraser Nursing Home for more than 15 years. It would also probably have caused the death of at least one more elderly resident with Alzheimer's Disease.

In this instance, alarmed workers and relatives, who had just learned that the residents would be relocated off-Cape, began to organize on their own even before contacting CUE on the issue. Local State Representative Tom Lynch (always very responsive to elderly issues) became involved. So, also, did several churches, the local area agency on aging and the HSA's Sub-Area Health Council.

The State Welfare Medicaid Division's "relocation team" had already been in touch with the residents' relatives and were pressuring them for their cooperation in the transfer of the residents.

Here's What CUE Did

• We *coordinated* the meetings of everyone concerned, *sent signed letters and petitions* to the Department of Public Health and *pressed for a meeting with the Commissioner of Public Health.*

• Our lawyer *studied the regulations* governing our relocation of residents and looked for procedural loopholes or mistakes. They were found. Regulations regarding proper notification of transfer had been overlooked. Relatives of residents should have been given 6 months notice and had not. Our lawyer was prepared on these grounds to file for an injunction to hold up relocation. We also fought the relocation because of the very real risk of transfer trauma to the elderly people involved.

• CUE and the Coalition *dramatized the issue by picketing* the facility while the relocation team was there and invited the press to our action. We stated our intention to block the transfers, physically if necessary.

• CUE, the Coalition and union members *had a Candlelight Vigil* on the evening that the relatives were to meet with the relocation team at the nursing home.

We invited a television cameraman from a local station to attend. This event had charm as well—It was a cold November night with snow on the ground. The nursing home residents, enjoying it immensely, put on their coats and joined the demonstrators in carrying placards and candles outside of the facility to call attention to the situation.

• *CUE and our lawyer had a pre-meeting* with the relatives the same evening as the vigil and informed them of their rights in the issue. They were informed that they should have been notified 6 months before and that we would help them fight the transfer of the residents in court. CUE and the relatives together arrived at a strategy whereby the relatives would refuse to be interviewed separately by the relocation team at their meeting later that evening. By presenting a united front, the relatives could assert their rights as a group and not be co-opted by bureaucratic interests. Our lawyer (then Elder Law Project Director Wynn Gerhard) and I accompanied the group to their meeting with the relocation team. While the vigil with about 60 community members took place outside of the facility, the group of relatives inside confronted the "team" and put an end to the idea that the relatives would do anything other than block the transfer by any means at their disposal.

• CUE, with the help of Rep. Tom Lynch, *arranged for a meeting with the top officials of the Department of Public Health with a community group* comprised of relatives of residents, Rep. Lynch, some workers from Fraser Nursing Home, a member of the HSA's Sub-Area Council, Bill Pastreich in his capacity as Coalition Director and Union Representative, CUE's lawyer and me. The officials may have thought they would quickly dispose of our arguments and send us home. Our coalition of community members, however, had developed a strategy of well-orchestrated, impassioned and well-reasoned arguments. The relatives hammered at DPH's lawyers with a "What if it were *your* parents?" Our lawyer talked of challenging the relocations in court. The Sub-Area Council member talked about transfer traumas, and so forth. Everyone had a piece of the action and it was highly effective.

• *We had an alternative plan in place.* Rep. Lynch, a member of the Legislature's Committee on Health Care and Committee on State Administration, expressed his concern over the transfers. He proposed an alternative plan whereby Fraser's facility (an old wooden structure) would make some minimal renovations and be permitted to house medicaid residents until a newly planned facility would be in place in the fall. Meanwhile, Fraser Nursing Home would take no more medicaid recipients. This was agreed upon.

A celebration was held a few days later at the Fraser Nursing Home. The press came and covered the event. Relocation of those of the elderly Fraser residents who were still alive was made in the summer of 1982. Mr. Kumpenen was able to die in his home at Fraser's in familiar surroundings, among family and friends, at the age of 102.

Organizing for the Long Haul

In this chapter are three very different cases. They are all examples of successful organizing in their own right but the reason they are brought together here is that they represent different ideological orientations: community-development, populist, and socialist. The strategy and tactics that are described in each case flow from the overall political orientation. Taken together, the cases provide a good starting point for a discussion of how ideology affects organizing.

Of course, these three ideological positions are not the only ones that are possible. Cases included elsewhere in this book, in fact, represent a variety of other orientations. For example, the case ''Symbolically the Enemy Is the Pentagon'' represents a feminist approach that is very different from any of the three approaches in this chapter. These three cases are merely illustrative of the relationship between ideology and organizing.

In ''Hollow Hope: Community Development in Appalachia,'' a case reprinted from the first edition of this book, a young husband-wife organizing team helped a community develop a sense of pride in what they could accomplish with the skills that existed within the community. Their list of accomplishments was impressive. The community acquired a new school bus, got the state to repair roads and wells, built a small dam and irrigation ditch, and developed a folk craft cooperative.

The organizers had made an explicit decision not to confront the exploitation of the coal industry head-on even though they knew it to be the basic cause for the misery and poverty of the county. They understood that the future of the region was controlled by political and economic forces outside the community and that the major issue was the lack of jobs—an issue on which they were able to accomplish very little. However, when they left the community they were hopeful about its future and felt they had accomplished what they had intended. They had reactivated unused skills and had helped people develop pride in their community and the will to solve common problems.

The next case illustrates a populist mode of organizing. There are a number of other cases in this book in a populist tradition, but this one is unusually explicit about long-term goals. In this case, as is typical in populist-style organizing, grass-roots organizations composed of "the people" do battle with the private sector and government agencies to obtain rights and services. In this instance, National Peoples Action, representing neighborhood organizations in over forty states, took on the Aetna Life and Casualty Company. Through its campaign, NPA forced Aetna into helping a number of moderate income people acquire housing under terms they could afford. More generally, the campaign enabled NPA to make some headway against redlining by the insurance industry and by banks. Note that a range of tactics was used. Along with sanctions and confrontation, NPA sought to offer Aetna a way to improve its moral position and its profits by going along with NPA's demands.

The author points to the overall goal of making industry accountable to the needs of people in neighborhoods. She sees the action as one step in a process whereby community groups negotiate with industry much as a union would and then have the results of the negotiations legitimated by government legislation. The problem as she sees it is to determine when it is appropriate for the government to be responsible for people's needs and when it is appropriate for industry to be responsible for people's needs. Ultimately the goal is for the private sector to be restructured so that a redistribution of resources might take place.

This is in dramatic contrast to the socialist community organizing described in the next case. The goals of socialist organizing are for the working class to wrest power and control from the capitalist class and to restructure the major societal institutions—economic, familial, educational, cultural, and political—for the benefit of the working class.

Unlike the populists, socialists are interested in demonstrating that people's needs can never be adequately met as long as there is private ownership and control of the means of production. Despite this general orientation among socialists, the approach outlined in the case "City Life: Lessons of the First Five Years" is actually quite unusual. As the word socialism is likely to put people off, most socialists who do community organizing tend to downplay their ideology and ultimate goals. Generally organizers with a socialist ideology do not make that ideology a focal point for the organizing effort but instead work towards helping people see that no matter what gains are made they must be seen as part of a long-term process. In other words, a goal of any organizing effort is not only the specific victories but consciousness raising about the capitalist system.

While the City Life document is unusual in that it describes a community-level organization that is explicitly socialist, its sense of long-term strategy encompasses concerns that are central to a great many organizing drives undertaken by socialists. In particular, the document addresses the issues of racism and sexism and the wide range in education and class background among the members of the organization. The overall idea is to overcome obstacles to a unified effort to oppose the capitalist system.

The organizers in this case were very self-conscious about what they were doing and engaged in constant evaluation of their organizational forms.

Hollow Hope: Community Development in Appalachia

Coal miners were the first to fuel the technological and manufacturing explosion that made America the world's foremost industrial and military power. Since extraction began in Appalachia more than 100 years ago, an estimated $500 billion worth of raw resources has been hauled out of the region on rafts and barges and by trucks, railcars, and pipelines.

The region, still incredibly rich in natural resources, could not survive without social security and welfare payments. In many former mining communities, public assistance supports 60 percent or more of all local sales or exchanges.

America has been unwilling to reclaim the land and the lives that deteriorate in Appalachia. In 1963, John F. Kennedy set up the President's Appalachian Regional Commission. Its major accomplishment, the Appalachian Regional Development Act of 1965, earmarked 80 percent of its funds for highway construction. Those who have entered the region through these new roads know they are far from modern. Rather than bringing people, services, and products into the region, they serve as an escape route for the young, the disheartened, and the disabled, and as further tax supports for the already well-endowed mining companies.

Of those who are employed or who have worked, more than 125,000 Appalachian men have been permanently injured, their lungs impaired by inhaling coal and rock dust. There are only 150,000 miners in this country. U.S. Public Health research on black lung and related diseases is 25 years behind the British, who spend nearly 10 times as much on mine safety and research as do Americans. Even tiny Belgium spends more than we do.

Until recently, neither the industry, the union (UMW[1]), nor the legislatures of the states involved recognized black lung as a disease worthy of prevention, cure, or compensation. It took the aftermath of the Farmington disaster in November 1968 (strangely reminiscent in cause and description of the infamous Black Heath disaster that claimed 54 lives near Richmond, Virginia in March 1939), and a wildcat strike in February 1969 to move the West Virginia legislature to pass a law compensating workers whose lungs are permanently damaged by coal dust. The union did not support the strike, which lasted three weeks, included 40,000 miners, and closed the industry.

If the gainfully employed are poorly protected, what of the unemployed— those left behind in blind hollows, far from modern roads, jobs, and schools?

Straw Hollow was a good place to find out. We selected it as a target area precisely because it was so typical of the region and we wanted to demonstrate what could be done with community-development techniques. We were a staff of five from the State University's Institute for Regional Development: a professional community developer who taught at the University, two graduate students from the school of social work who spent their three days a week of field placement in the hollow, and my wife and myself. I have my MSW from a school in Boston where I grew up. My wife and I both wanted a rural experience of this sort. We met as volunteers in the Appalachian Summer Program two years earlier, and decided then to come back here some time to work.

Straw Hollow, along with Silver Creek, Loon's Lake, Unforeseen, Slattertown, and the whole Black Ridge area, had once flourished with mining activity. Under the leadership of John L. Lewis in the 1930s and 1940s, miners secured good wages after bitter labor wars. The region was prosperous enough during World War II. It was good times even for those mountain folk who had scratched out bare livings along the steep hillsides and stony bottoms for generations.

In the late 1960s, however, times were no longer good. The best seams had given out. Mechanization of strip mining had thrown many out of work. The union's efforts in securing high wages had never extended to securing adequate health and accident benefits. Many who had once been employed by the mines were now in ill health, disabled by accidents or with lungs impaired years earlier from inhaling coal and rock dust. Of the 93 families in Straw Hollow, only 8 men were gainfully employed. Eighty-seven families drew some form of relief. Those on the county welfare roles knew their meager checks were dependent on their good behavior, political and otherwise. The sheriff, the judge, and the welfare administration were all related, as were the principal storekeepers in Slattertown, where all local shopping was done. Hollow dwellers accepted these facts. They reacted to them as they reacted to most outsiders—with mistrust bordering on apathy.

Before going to Straw Hollow, we talked to organizers—a young couple like

[1]United Mine Workers.

ourselves—who had helped people from another county fight the strip miners. They were convinced that the only way to help the region was to confront the exploitation of the coal industry head on. They used tactics from the civil rights movement—demonstrations, sit-ins in front of the bulldozers, walk-outs, and voter registration. What happened to them scared us. They were arrested on sedition charges, thrown into jail, and investigated by the McClellan Committee. Their library was stolen, and their house was bombed. We didn't want that to happen to us. Above all, we did not want to be singled out as outside troublemakers. The University could not have withstood the political repercussions, and we felt that in the long run, we would have misused ourselves.

Bad feelings existed between hollow dwellers and school officials and teachers, each of whom represented very different cultures, and both of whom presented convincing arguments about the worthlessness of the other. Children dropped out of school before they were legally allowed. Many did not attend during the winter months, when a two-mile walk on muddy or icy roads with inadequate shoes (or no shoes at all) made the trip an excruciating hardship.

About the only social institution that attracted some following was the church, a fundamentalist, other-worldly, doctrinaire institution. There being so few involved in mining, the union had no interest in the hollow. No focal point existed for solving community problems. Bereft of the skills, the imagination, and the will to solve common problems, forgotten or defined as worthless by outsiders, the residents of Straw Hollow withdrew among kin and select neighbors.

The project director and the two social work students were the first to visit the community. They came regularly on Thursdays and Fridays, beginning in late September, trying to establish contacts and become acquainted. Although they introduced themselves as staff members and students from the University, they offered no specific program. "Whut you all goin' ta do out hyer?" was the usual question. "What can we help people do?" was the usual reply.

I suppose their wandering around, their refusal to make decisions about what to do for people's welfare, and their nondirectiveness must have been very disquieting for the residents. A preacher who had warned that they might be dangerous outside agitators could not find anything to accuse them of agitating about. Some residents must have decided that the visitors were freeloaders (they did accept invitations to meals at people's homes on two occasions), or goof-offs or goldbricks. The one thing they were not seen as were representatives of the outside community's exploitive and degrading institutions.

A month later, my wife and I came to town. We had decided that, unlike the other staff members who had part-time commitments to the project, we would live in Straw Hollow. The only available building was the school, a one-large-room affair that had been closed by the county authorities about four years earlier and that was in a state of disrepair almost beyond belief. We had secured permission from the county school board to use it. In this case our university credentials were useful.

Had we been VISTA volunteers or poverty workers, we would have been turned down as outsiders, government intruders, and meddlers or troublemakers.

The old school was in worse repair than we had imagined. It took my wife and me two days of hauling timbers from discarded machinery crates at one of the mines in Silver Creek on top of our old Saab, and three more days of sawing and hammering, just to fix the floors. We ran out of lumber when it came to patching holes in the north wall, and fell to using tar paper, old canvas, and oiled newspaper (we saw this done in an old movie once). As we worked, some of the teenagers and younger children came by to see what we were doing. Two of the boys offered to help. One girl who lived nearby said her mother wanted us to use their well until we could get our own going.

By the third week in November we were finished and feeling pretty good about things. My wife was outside splitting off cords of wood for the fireplace and I was inside fixing up some makeshift furniture out of branches and twine, when a number of our new friends came by. As we were thanking them for their help, it suddenly occurred to me that it was getting awfully close to Thanksgiving and that we might show our appreciation by organizing a Thanksgiving feast.

Well, it was really quite a blowout: turkey, squirrel, and pheasant. Of course not everyone came. The fact is, we hardly knew anyone in the hollow. We had decided not to go out aggressively to meet people, but to let it happen naturally as we met them on the road, at the Post Office, as they came by to check on who we were and what we were doing, and the like. Four families and some children from as many more came to the dinner. Some were having other dinners with kinfolk as well.

The next day about fifty people more, many of whom we had never seen, came by to look or to introduce themselves. We had them in for coffee. It was like an open house. And then we realized something that hadn't really occurred to us before. Our home was a familiar building to them. Many of the parents and the grandparents and some of the older children had gone to school there. It had been a community building. It still was the largest single room in the hollow, and it seemed natural for it to become a community building again. Had we kept it strictly to ourselves we would have been like squatters taking over something of theirs.

Our success in patching up our own living quarters suggested to us that we might be able to get a "clean-up" or "face-lift" campaign going before the winter set in and it got really cold. We failed to get any support at all. But some of the men who visited did like what I had done with the furniture. Some copied my ideas, and others offered their own. One old-timer taught me to whittle a funny little propeller stick, a children's toy. He and another old-timer and some teenagers began coming over two afternoons a week. We carved all sorts of things.

My wife had a loom of her own, different from anything that anyone in the area had seen. Between her weaving, the sewing and darning that had to be done, and the needlework that some women had almost forgotten how to do, we had a women's folk craft program going. On Saturdays, my wife started a sewing club for the school girls. To make a long story short, by spring we had a folk craft co-op going, sent some things to an exhibit at the University, and arranged for the sale of some items at Cape Cod and in Cambridge, Mass., where we had a number of friends with small shops.

Not once had we suggested to anyone that we wanted to help him seek a job, but after a while young men and older boys began coming in regularly asking for help. We found ourselves dividing up responsibilities. My wife and I were dealing with things internal to Straw Hollow. The students in field placements began to assume responsibility for negotiating in the external environment. One of them took on the employment task.

Periodically almost every male in the hollow tried to look for employment. Few were content to stay on relief. But each spurt of enthusiasm had resulted in failure and renewed lethargy.

One young man, a recent father, told us that he wouldn't go on ADC.[2] "I haven't sunk that low yit!" He had been to the Employment Office in Charleston on many occasions and filed applications. He was told once that he was due to enter a welding training program soon, but the next time he went, he was told that there was no application in the files for him. This happened twice and he was furious and desperate. We went to work on his case and, after some fifteen phone calls, managed to locate and expedite his application. The problem had been one of communication. He had no phone and his neighbors had not been home when the crucial call came through. This would have happened again except that we made our phone available as a backup and made sure he got the word. He is now in the training program and we are considered wizards at dealing with these matters.

As a result, we are in constant demand as aides in tracking down lost applications, advising on employment matters, making appointments for kids at the Department of Employment Security, and so forth. The employment people have been cooperative and spared some of our charges the psychological hazards of the bureaucratic machinery of their office by personalizing the service for them as much as possible. Three have been lined up so far for training programs and several others have received temporary employment. Many others were unable to be placed due to a sheer lack of salable skills. Contacts we established with a Job Corps camp about 30 miles away, and with a job training center for adult males in an urban community in this part of the state, made it possible to serve 11 of the unskilled.

We also started a tutorial project, encouraging some children to stay in school, helping many do better, and encouraging two dropouts to return. Based on our work with children, we were establishing some credibility with the teachers and the principal, which we were to cash in on later.

The teens were a special problem. Except for those we were able to get jobs or

[2]Aid to Dependent Children.

job training for, most were in dire straits. Relationships at home deteriorated if the teen-ager had any gumption of his own. Other teens were trapped in a cycle of interdependence. Some had delinquency and arrest records. A Saturday social we planned for New Year's Eve was the first they had had in four years.

With some of the contacts we made right after our Thanksgiving feast, we organized a turkey shoot with around 40 people participating, and netted $78.00 to go towards a Christmas program. We used the money to decorate a Christmas tree one of the men cut down for us. By this time we had a small "social" committee and were able to arrange a party at which 150 children attended. We played games, had treats, and were able to send candy home with everyone. Some of the teen-agers who were planning the New Year's party with us joined in caroling around the community.

By this time, we thought we were ready to call a general meeting. Some of our friends in the community had discouraged us. "Ain't none of them hill folks give a damn." "All y'll git is fightin' and arguin'." But we decided to try anyway. We asked people to spread the word, and put up a sign at the Center (what our house was now being called) and one at the Post Office.

I must tell you we were more than pleased at the outcome. The crowd began to arrive early. We had called the meeting for 7:30. By 6:45, twenty people were here, and by 7:30 we had nearly 80 people, about twice as many as our building could hold. We were afraid our crate-board floor might cave in.

The project director had come in from the University to give a talk. We reviewed the kinds of things that were beginning to develop in Straw Hollow. The co-op hadn't been organized yet, nor had we placed many in jobs, but all these projects had been begun. When the project director spoke about our concerns, he made it very clear that what was happening was a natural thing, and that we hoped we could be helpful in a number of ways. We needed to know what people in the community wanted, and then maybe with some of our know-how and outside connections we might be able to help them get it to happen.

The condition of the road was mentioned. Some wanted a school bus. Others encouraged us to continue with the tutorial work. One father felt that the most pressing need was some sort of teen-age center, but, in the only fight of the evening, was bitterly opposed by some church people who felt that a teen-age center would only "encourage sin."

Crowded as the meeting room was, somehow people seemed to be forming committees. Somewhat to our surprise (I suppose we had been full of preconceptions about Appalachians), people seemed to be rather sophisticated about committees and were well aware that little could be done in so large a group. One committee took on responsibility for contacting the school authorities about meeting in the public school two miles down the road and also agreed to work on the busing problem. Two men volunteered to contact the county commissioners about improving the road. The crafts committee, later to become the co-op officers, was a natural group by then. Three mothers volunteered to be a parents committee. They had children either in our tutorial program, in the crafts group, or in both.

The school officials at first were lukewarm to our request to use the school auditorium (fearing the place would be left in shambles) for our next meeting, but were convinced by a combination of our University credentials and the relationships we had made with some of the teachers who attested to the progress made by our students. The place was not left in a shambles after our first meeting, and we met there regularly once a month thereafter. It took a while, but eventually we got the school bus.

These were real victories for the hollow. The neighborhood was beginning to develop a certain sense of self. We felt it and were constantly reminded of it. "Never did think I'd live to see Clara Bolton give one hoot about anybody else." "Imagin Ned Holsger's boy helpin' fix that well." "Them school folk ain't so bad as I had them figured."

By spring we felt ready to suggest a "clean-up day" again. We had it. We hauled away five two-ton truck loads of trash. By the end of the summer we had gotten a crew of men to repair a bridge, getting so much newspaper publicity that we were able to pressure the county road commissioner to fix the rest of the road (school officials were with us on this one, if only to protect the bus from too much wear and tear).

The co-op was fully incorporated. Some of the teens had organized a newsletter that included not only news about our own hollow, but also news of happenings in other neighborhoods as well. It was run off on the mimeo donated by one of the mining companies and kept at the Center. We repaired several wells and built a small dam and an irrigation ditch and elected three permanent "water commissioners."

None of these are really tremendous accomplishments. There is still much to be done in linking the hollow to the rest of the world. We hope to bring the Boy Scouts and 4-H in. But unless the vast majority of the men get jobs, many of our accomplishments are meaningless. And we understand full well that the future of the region is controlled by political and economic forces outside it. Still, we leave our assignment this fall with some hope for the hollow, and it is not a hollow hope.

Targeting the Private Sector

Jacqueline B. Mondros*

Most organizing in the 1960s and the 1970s focused on making demands on government for goods and services. Such tactics may have been at least partially responsible for the recent backlash of less government aid and private sector reluctance to assume a role in public concern.

Today's organizing needs to shift to targeting the private sector. Our efforts should focus on three related agenda items. First, we should clarify and reaffirm the rights, services, and protection people can rationally expect from government and those we are owed by industry. That is, government should not be used as a handmaiden to industry, but indeed be supplier of the last resort. Second, we must alter the direct power relationships between industry and the people so that the people can hold the private sector accountable. Third, organizing efforts should work towards the redistribution of resources held by the private sector and that, of course, cannot be accomplished without restructuring the private sector.

Strategies used to target the private sector are similar to those used with public sectors. I have found no better way to fight anyone than to personalize the enemy, hit from many different directions at vulnerable points, use dramatic tactics, do the unexpected, and confront, confront, confront.[1] There are however some slight strategic differences that ought to be noted.

While I have said that the private sector issue needs to be couched in moral terms, strategy must be more realistic. That is, the strategy developed for the fight must very clearly think through the sanctions which can be induced by an indirect access constituency.[2] In public sector organizing, the sanctions are clear—we will withhold our votes. In private sector organizing, we cannot withhold our labor and we don't elect them so new sanctions have to be developed. Possible sanctions include proxy votes, withholding our own business or levering others to withhold theirs, using any regulations that do exist, and plain old embarrassment. The other side of the sanction question is strategy which takes into consideration what benefits the company might get out of complying with your demands. Appealing to altruism is not usually effective, but demonstrating how the industry can comply and still make a small profit is.

Similarly, leadership needs to be much more sophisticated in a battle with the private sector. When the target is government, it is sometimes enough for people to yell and scream that they pay taxes for the service, they elected the officials, and

---

*Excerpted from "Innovations in Organizing: Targeting the Private Sector" by Jacqueline B. Mondros. Presented at the Council of Social Work Education Annual Community Organization and Planning Symposium, New York, March 7, 1982.

[1]Saul Alinsky, *Rules for Radicals*, Vintage Books, New York, 1971, pp. 126–164.

[2]An indirect access constituency consists of those relationships where tasks, roles, and accountability are unspecified.

that they pay the salary of the service provider. No such direct access is available in the case of a private sector fight. Therefore, leadership must be educated and become knowledgeable about the complicated inner workings of the industry. They must be savvy about management principles, risks and profits, interest rates and lending practices, and government procedures and regulations. They must know as much about the industry as the company itself does.

Private sector strategies must also consider the question of leverage, that is, who are the organization's possible allies. Ironically, the government can sometimes be called upon to intercede, particularly if there are existing regulations or if they can see themselves benefitting from your actions. Sometimes direct constituencies such as unions or consumers can be used strategically as was the case in the lettuce boycott of migrant workers. Once one company has conceded to the organization's demands it is likely that they can be used as leverage to pull in other companies and other resources as they want nothing less than to see the project (where they have invested money) fail.

A CASE EXAMPLE: AETNA LIFE AND CASUALTY CO.

I have now said what I see to be some of the special problems of targeting the private sector. I would like to share with you an example of private sector organizing—the case of National People's Action, Kensington Action Now, and Aetna Life and Casualty Company.

National People's Action is a coalition of grassroots neighborhood organizations from over forty states. NPA is composed of state wide, city-wide, and neighborhood organizations. In the mid-seventies NPA had waged a national battle against mortgage redlining and succeeded in having two regulatory acts, the Home Mortgage Disclosure Act and the Community Reinvestment Act, passed by Congress. These acts were then used by neighborhood organizations to target individual banks to stop redlining. The next logical step was action against insurance redlining. Companies simply refused to write policies in inner city neighborhoods. The time was ripe for such organizing. The insurance industry is not federally regulated and the sanction of federal regulation was one which made the industry vulnerable to public demands.

Some initial research on insurance underwriting was done. Six local affiliates of NPA (two in Chicago, two in New York, one in Cleveland, and one in Philadelphia) recruited people who had lost their insurance and interested other leaders in the issue. They came together with NPA leadership and decided to target one company which was notorious for its discriminatory practices. The company was Aetna Life and Casualty, the second largest insurance company in the world. The moral basis for action was that the right of neighborhoods to be protected from fire and theft was greater than the company's right to profits.

In 1978, NPA and its six neighborhood affiliates met with the President of

Aetna in New York with three demands: (1) write insurance in neighborhoods on the basis of individual eligibility, (2) place Aetna agents in these six neighborhoods, and (3) disclose the policies written by zip codes so their underwriting practices could be documented. This meeting was followed up by the local affiliates in each city where the demands were repeated to regional vice presidents, and corporate presidents. Aetna agreed to write policies in these six neighborhoods and to meet with each local affiliate to establish a working contract. In Philadelphia, Kensington Action Now met with Aetna officials which resulted in the establishment of an insurance hotline installed in the KAN office, brochures printed by Aetna and distributed by KAN which outlined a new insurance writing policy, and a closer relationship between KAN and an Aetna agent who would write neighborhood policies.

The agreement with Aetna was then used by NPA to force three other insurance companies to sit down with leadership at the National Convention in 1979. The fight with Travellers Insurance was particularly colorful as leaders twirled red umbrellas (the company logo) under the nose of the company president.

At the same time, NPA began to approach Aetna about the subject of neighborhood reinvestment. Aetna agreed to meet with each of the six local affiliates. In August of 1979, the upper echelon of Aetna visited KAN in Philadelphia. KAN made a big production of the event. They rented a bus and neighborhood people took the officials on a tour, followed by a pot luck supper and gifts of hoagies and soft pretzels, two culinary symbols of Philadelphia. After the niceties, KAN leadership made their demands, again alluding to the regulation sanction. The organization asked for two million dollars for rehabilitation of vacant homes, two million dollars for new construction, and a $50,000 grant for project seed money. Aetna one could say, was taken aback by the demands.

Aetna considered the project and negotiation began around what the project would look like, what the relationships would be, who would operate the program, what kind of accountability was acceptable. KAN's leadership was educated and lead these negotiations. In November of 1979 at NPA's Convention, Aetna agreed to reinvest money in the six neighborhoods. During the next two months an advertisement appeared in such major publications as Time and Newsweek. It showed a man with a fork uncovering a platter with a dead crow on it. The headline said "Aetna eats crow," and the copy went on to describe the six projects.

Each neighborhood had different housing stock so it became necessary to negotiate each project individually. Once again it was the leaders of the organization who bargained. KAN's project was for the rehabilitation of single family homes with Aetna supplying the short term construction financing and seed money for the project. KAN agreed to garner additional funding and to set up a separate Community Development Corporation which is linked to the organizing efforts. In early 1980 Aetna signed a contract with each local affiliate, also designating expectations. The signing took place in Chicago where a KAN leader was asked by a reporter to pose for a picture shaking hands with Aetna's president. His reply was, "Why? I don't see no money in it." Leadership had obviously become quite sophisticated.

Now Aetna was used as an ally. KAN was able to leverage HUD, the City OHCD, and Pa. State Office of Community Affairs for staff and acquisition money backed by Aetna's commitment. Aetna gave the project references which were used to involve banks to lend long-term mortgages at 11% fixed rate, and Local Initiative Support Corporation (LISC) to provide a revolving home improvement loan fund in an area bank who also agreed to lend well below prime. Private foundations were approached by both KAN and Aetna to fund staff and a new arson prevention project for KAN and a home improvement loans project for the development arm of the organization.

Private sector targeting is new and not all of the kinks have been worked out yet, but some clear results can be seen from this project. The moral position of Aetna has been enhanced. Aetna is making some interest on its investment. The profit must be acceptable because they are now engaged in negotiations with a few other inner city neighborhoods. Certainly, they are gaining face. Neighborhood banks are making small interest on the project's mortgages. Public money is being used to support an industrial commitment, rather than providing the service itself which would be two and a half times more expensive. Soon those expenses will be covered by the project itself. The neighborhood organization is acquiring, rehabbing, and selling previously vacant properties for under $20,000. and is in complete control of the project. People are able to buy homes at 11% fixed interest rate who were closed out of the market by high interest rates. What's more, power relationships have been altered, redistribution of private sector resources is occurring, and the government is being used appropriately. Note, the organizations never promised not to support federal regulation of the insurance industry. The organizing continues, and new private sector targets are being selected.

CONCLUSIONS

Is what I have described what Reagan calls voluntary private sector involvement? Is targeting the private sector allowing government to renege on its responsibilities? I think not.

First, in my example the indirect access constituency, the neighborhood organization, called the shots. The organization selected the company to be involved, set the way in which they were involved, and controlled the format for their involvement. This is no noblesse oblige on behalf of business. The organization has sanctions which it is not reluctant to use, and in having these sanctions, have begun to equalize the power relationships.

Second, the organization has created access, it has developed an indirect relationship into a direct one. Just as labor once created its right to negotiate with industry, so has the neighborhood organization. Once the access was created it was soon legitimated by government legislation. Targeting the private sector may result in new regulatory legislation which would give protection and rights to indirect constituencies. If we simply focus on government, industry will not be forced to be accountable to us.

Last, the private sector will force the public sector to respond. As more constituencies make demands, as companies begin to be held accountable more often, as power relations are altered, we can be sure they will begin to complain to government to "get the people off their backs." And government will have to respond. Our efforts should be at demanding redistributive social contracts with both government and industry—each doing what they should and can do best and according to the people's determination of what needs doing.

City Life: Lessons of the First Five Years*

Kathy McAfee

The 1970s have been rough for the working class movement in the U.S. and rough, of course, for the left. But for the members of City Life, a community-based socialist organization in Boston, that movement is still very much alive. It helps to shape our lives and gives us plenty of hard work to do. It provides us with a sense of history and community, a network of personal support, and the vision of a future worth fighting for.

Until December, 1978, when we changed our name, City Life was known as the Tenants Action Group (TAG). TAG was formed in 1973 in Jamaica Plain, a racially mixed, mostly working class section of the city, and most of our work is still centered here. This work is carried out primarily through the three City Life organizing committees: Tenants, Workplace and Education. The organization also puts out a newspaper in English and Spanish called CommUnity News/Noticias de la Comunidad. *We have a variety of other activities, including social and cultural events and study groups that we offer to potential new members.*

The Tenants Action Group began as a group of five and has grown into an organization of about 35 people. This includes a "core" membership (13 at the present time) who are committed to a fairly high level of group discipline and to taking responsibility for the overall direction of the organization. Outside of the core is a larger group of people who belong to one of the organizing committees and regularly attend meetings but who have not (yet) joined the core group.

*From Radical America, Vol. No. 1 (January February, 1979), pp. 39–52.

Our goal is to build an organization with solid roots in our workplaces and neighbor-hoods. We want it to be a group in which working class people can grow and develop as socialists and as leaders in the struggle. And with City Life as a base, we want to help build a class-conscious working class movement that can resist the deterioration of living conditions in the city, and begin to pose socialism as the only plausible alternative to the "urban crisis."

Often people who hear about us question whether two of our goals—building a working class movement and promoting socialism—are compatible, at least at this time in the U.S. Apparently many people are convinced that they are not, judging by the numbers of leftists who have put their politics in the closet in order to help lead populist economic reform campaigns. No doubt there *are* ways to build a larger organization faster, such as by bringing together leftists regardless of class or community roots, or by organizing particular sectors of the working class around their short-range economic self-interest. But to us, combining "working class" and "socialist" is the whole point; the alternatives don't seem worth the effort.

Our approach has also been criticized by adherents of the "party-building" left, who cannot conceive of any means of developing revolutionary leadership except through a Bolshevik-style party structure, and who see mass organizing more in terms of struggles for "democratic rights" than in terms of building a mass base for socialism. But we in City Life believe that the task of making a revolution in a society such as ours—at least at this stage—calls for different organizational struc-tures and a different strategy, which we are trying to formulate as best we can as a small, local organization.

Since it has been our practical experience, and not just our theory that has brought us to this position, a short history and description of our group may help to explain it.

OUR HISTORY

The five original members of TAG settled in Jamaica Plain in 1972 with the intention of organizing in a working class community. All of us had come to some form of Marxism, or at least a class perspective, as a result of our experiences in the 60s. We were searching for a way to go beyond leftist speculations about how the working class "should" or "could" be reached. We wanted to find ways for ourselves and our neighbors to develop consciousness and power as working class people.

Since the Vietnam war was at its height, our first project was the production of an anti-war newsletter, the J.P. *Weekly War Bulletin,* which we handed out every Saturday at supermarkets and laundromats. The response was generally sympathe-tic, and as we met more local people through the *Bulletin,* we looked for ways to organize more directly around the material conditions of people's lives.

Housing seemed the obvious answer. Even a glance at the situation—acute shortage of apartments, worsening conditions, higher rents, replacement of home-owners by speculators, urban renewal and "gentrification" at the expense of working class residents—made it clear that the system of housing for profit was a disaster for all but the profiteers. We were also influenced by the half dozen or so tenants organizations in the Boston area, some founded by ex-student leftists, which were mobilizing to defend rent control legislation, block evictions, and promote rent strikes.

When we formed the Tenants Action Group, we saw our goal as building tenant unions that would be capable of fighting for better housing conditions, mainly through direct action (rent strikes, etc.) and that would be willing to support each other's struggles. We assumed that as the tenant unions grew, they would somehow come together to form a larger mass organization. We also thought that in the process of helping people to stop evictions and rent increases, we would be able to persuade many of them that housing was only one example of the failure of capitalism to meet our needs, and that only socialism could provide the basis for better housing and a better way of life. We also expected that some of the more highly conscious tenants would become members of TAG.

At that time we put more emphasis on direct tenant action and on forming tenant unions than on building TAG as an organization. We thought that without the direct experience of successful struggle, few people would become so convinced of the possibility of working class power, and that, conversely, working class power had to be built through action and organization at the base. We felt certain—and we still believe—that no revolutionary movement can succeed *in the name* of the working class, and that any genuinely working class movement has to be based in some type of grass-roots "struggle organizations." We saw tenant unions as one possible form of such organizations. (Worker's councils or worker-controlled unions might be other forms.)

Beyond this, our politics were vaguely defined. TAG had no written goals or principles, even for our own members, and no formal program for study. Every issue of the *CommUnity News* carried articles criticizing "the profit system" with specific examples from housing, health, sports, etc., and we tried to raise the question of socialism with the tenants we worked with. But action, and not education, remained our first priority.

Between 1973 and 1976 our efforts yielded some respectable results: several tenant unions formed, many rent increases defeated, repairs won, and evictions stopped. There were three cases in which our group, along with other local activists, helped to organize human blockades to prevent the eviction of an old woman, the demolition of a house, and the violent harassment of several Puerto Rican families by white neighbors. Less dramatic but just as important was the increased awareness in the community of tenants' rights, and of the anti-working class policies of the city and federal government and the local banks.

RE-EVALUATION

However, most of the tenant unions failed to survive during periods between crises, much less come together spontaneously in a militant working class movement. This, along with the failure of TAG to grow beyond a group of 10 "cadre", led us to review our strategy in part. We began to realize that in our attempt to avoid a top-down, overly-centralized organization, we were neglecting to provide the kind of structure and leadership that were absolutely crucial to enabling local working-class people—and ourselves, for that matter—to develop as militants and as socialists.

While many people from the community were interested in TAG, few had become full members. Looking back, it is easy to see why. TAG's structure was amorphous, with the criteria for joining and the responsibilities of membership only vaguely defined. Since we had no system for teaching people what we knew about organizing, only a highly confident and motivated person could really participate. And, such people had to make a near-total commitment, since there was no way for someone to get involved a little at a time.

We had no program for political education or group study, and we were putting little effort into collective, critical analysis of the work we were doing. As a result, our goals in organizing were often undefined. We had a hard time recognizing when we had succeeded or failed, much less learning from our mistakes and passing that knowledge on to new members.

We were also failing to provide potential new members with enough of the things that inspired and sustained *us* as revolutionaries: i.e., a sense of socialism as a historical and international movement; personal support, comradeship and honest criticism; in other words, an alternative culture and community.

From the beginning we had been open about being socialists, and this was a decision we did not regret. Far from being "scared off," many of the people we met were impressed or at least intrigued by our commitment and political ideas. But we realized that we could not expect new people to join our group and make a commitment to socialism unless we could offer a clearer picture of (1) what social-ism is and what it could mean in the U.S., (2) how we can get there from here, and (3) the specific ways that a new person can get involved, learn, and contribute.

BUILDING AN ORGANIZATIONAL STRUCTURE

It was the recognition of these needs that led us, in early 1976, to restructure the group, giving more attention to building TAG as an organization. The structure we set up then is the one we still have today. The first step in restructuring was to set up a system of separate core group meetings for internal organizational business, and committee meetings for planning our external organizing. There were several rea-sons. For one thing, there was more internal business to be dealt with: finances, relations with other groups, child care, cultural events, recruitment of new members, personal tensions, etc. Also, we had begun to branch into other areas of organizing besides housing and we needed separate committees for each area.

A third reason for setting up this kind of structure was to make a distinction between core group members, who belong to a committee and also attend internal meetings, and committee members who work on a committee without taking on responsibility for the organization as a whole. One advantage of making this distinction is that organizational policy is set by those who have the most experience with and commitment to the group. Another advantage is that when we meet someone who is interested in the group or in a particular issue, but who is not yet a socialist, or who is not used to working collectively, who is uncomfortable with big meetings and political lingo, that person can be asked to join a committee. That way the new person has a chance to get involved gradually, developing skills and confidence, while the rest of the organization gets to know the new person.

The organizing committees are semiautonomous in that they recruit their own committee members and plan their own week-to-week work. But major decisions that affect the whole organization, such as holding a demonstration or joining a coalition, must be worked out with the rest of the group. The work of each committee is also reviewed and evaluated yearly by the whole organization.

At the same time that we set up the committee structure we also adopted specific requirements for core group membership, including a commitment from each core member to take some degree of leadership responsibility in their committee and a share of the organization's bureaucratic work. Potential new core members are required to go through an orientation process that involves a six-month study series and at least three months of work on one of the committees. We also established criteria for who we want to bring into the core membership, giving priority to people who are working class both in background and in current occupation.

Another part of the new structure set up in 1976 was an elected leadership body of 4 people which coordinates the work and growth of the organization. The most important way that it does this is by planning and chairing the monthly core meetings at which we make all major policy decisions. (We expect that as City Life grows, such frequent core meetings may become unworkable, but we want to keep the principle of strong leadership plus democratic decision-making intact.) Another aspect of our new structure is a yearly autumn retreat at which we sum up the past year's work and plan for the new year.

THE IMPORTANCE OF STUDY

At the 1977 retreat we made a decision to give a more central place to collective study. We adopted a study plan which we have been following for the past year and are scheduled to complete in the spring of 1979. The plan included 10 topics, all problems that we felt we needed to work on in order to clarify our direction as an organization. We set aside two to eight sessions for each topic and established subcommittees to prepare each one, so that every member would have the experience of planning, leading, and summarizing the discussions. The topics were:

What do we mean by "socialism"?

Leninism and forms of revolutionary organization

Review of basic Marxist economics

Racism and nationalism in the U.S.

Methods of constructive criticism

The urban fiscal crisis and the tax revolt

Classes in the U.S. today

Sexism and the family

The dialectical method in study and practice

The role of reforms in a revolutionary movement.

There were several reasons why we decided to make collective study a priority. In the first place, it was clear from the way that differences were starting to crop up that we needed to clarify our organizing strategy. We needed a better sense of what we could hope to accomplish in this period, a clearer basis for deciding which projects to get involved in and how to evaluate the results. We needed a more definite idea of the type of organization we were trying to build and its relation to our broader revolutionary goals, including written summaries of our principles that could be made available to prospective new members. We needed a method for incorporating the results of experience into our theory, for revising our goals, and for working out political differences. Otherwise we were likely to grow in different directions and splits would be inevitable.

A second motivation for group study was to fill in the gaps between members with different kinds of intellectual and political backgrounds. At first some of us doubted that such an ambitious study plan would work in a group that, by this time, included both former grad students and working class people who had never been to college. Would it be irrelevant or too hard for some, and boring for others? But the study turned out to be challenging for every one of us, tapping the diverse insights and experiences of different members and sharpening our collective powers of analysis.

The study has had an equalizing effect within the group, not because our heads are now stuffed with equal amounts of information, but because it has increased the ability of each of us to analyze readings, apply them to our experience, and make political judgements based on what we *do* know. We feel the purpose of study is to learn to think for ourselves, not just absorb a line.

A third reason for the study was to articulate our group's position vis-a-vis the rest of the left. Having been called everything from anarchists through Trotskyists to revisionists, we felt a need to re-examine our relationship to the Leninist traditions, our attitude toward the current party-building groups, and our own views of the organizational stages that the revolutionary movement in the U.S. will have to go through. This is the aspect of our politics that other leftists have seemed most interested in, so we took the time to write a summary of our conclusions from the section of our study on Leninism. It is printed here as an appendix to this article.

Without a doubt our collective study—both the process of studying together and the content of what we've learned—has been the most important factor in consolidating our group and developing our organizing program in the past year. However, when the current study plan has been completed and as new people join, we plan to adopt a more decentralized and less intense program of collective study.

LIFE IN "CITY LIFE"

City Life's current structure, with its requirements for organizing and study, puts a lot of demands on individual members. As a minimum, each core member is expected to attend committee meetings (usually once a week) and participate in the committee's organizing work, to attend monthly core meetings and bi-weekly study sessions, to help prepare and lead one or more sections of the study, work on two issues of the *CommUnity News* each year, and pitch in with miscellaneous work, such as painting the office, attending a coalition meeting, or setting up a film showing. Right now we don't see any way to avoid this heavy a work load, but we try to be supportive by pairing up for tasks, helping each other with study and child care, and other means of sharing our emotional and material resources. We try to be flexible about work requirements at times of personal crises and transition.

There are times for each of us when we do feel overburdened. We also recognize that many working class people have responsibilities to work and parenting that makes it almost impossible for them to function as core members of a group this demanding. Our hope is that as we grow larger we will be able to have a broader division of labor and reduce our work requirements somewhat. Meanwhile we encourage people in this situation to work with us as committee members and to participate in other activities as much as they are able to.

In spite of these problems it is clear to all of us that the tighter structure set up in '76 has resulted in more growth and development in the group than the previous un-structure. It has made it possible for working class people who had no previous experience with the left to function as full members of the group, including as core members. While it has not eliminated all the problems and tensions that arise from the differences in our class backgrounds, it has given us a context for dealing with them. Also, several of our working class members, on their own initiative, have been meeting occasionally during the past year as a "new people's caucus" to discuss these and other problems. One of the suggestions that came out of the caucus was a "buddy system." Each new member can choose a "buddy" from among the old members, whose responsibility it is to give the newer person support in raising issues and to fill them in on political debates, the group's history, etc.

Of the five original members of our group, four were women, and women still make up the majority of our membership. A sizeable minority of our members are gay. Although it hasn't been our policy to give priority to recruiting female and gay members, we are glad it worked out this way. The influence of feminism and gay liberation has helped us in defining our goals, understanding what motivates people to change, and becoming more sensitive to each other and the people we work with as whole people. To us, questions of how people raise kids, share housework, give and accept criticism, and lend emotional support are as important as their under-standing of imperialism or the state. We can't expect to build class consciousness without confronting racism, sexism, and individualism. We include discussion of these issues in the meetings at which we evaluate our individual and collective work, and a lot of personal struggle about them goes on outside of meetings.

A great deal of our day-to-day work is with black people: tenants, parents, and workers. Although the core of our membership is all white at this stage, our goal is to become, or to become part of, a multi-racial organization. Becoming a bi-lingual organization presents an additional challenge. We now publish 7 of the 16 pages of our newspaper in Spanish. A group of Latin Americans (most of whom are from Puerto Rico) takes a large part of the responsibility for the Spanish section, includ-ing planning, layout, and writing some original articles in Spanish every issue. But, although we sometimes have meetings with tenants in Spanish, all of our internal organizational meetings are still in English. We hope to reach the point where we can have Spanish-speaking organizing committees or sub-committees and offer study groups in Spanish.

OUR PROGRAM FOR ORGANIZING: THE CONTEXT

Our experience as well as our study has shown us that both the material conditions and the quality of working class life are under attack now in Boston. Of course this is true throughout the country, but we've focused our analysis on Boston because we think the forms of resistance must be geared to the particular nature of the attacks. In this city a number of factors, including the impact of world-wide reces-sion, the decline of the industrial northeast, the fiscal crisis of state and local governments, and the nature of Boston as a center of finance, administration and research/education have combined to trap Boston's working class in a double squeeze.

Economic growth (both real and paper) in the real estate, finance, insurance, and health industries have required the transformation of the central city, inflation of rents and property value, the destruction of working class housing, and the displacement of poor and minority residents. At the same time, the replacement of moderate-wage manufacturing jobs with low-wage service and clerical jobs, combined with stiffened employer resistance to unionization, have kept average real wages from rising. In short, there's less housing, what there is costs more, and we have less money to pay for it.

Meanwhile the fiscal crisis (precipitated by recession, rising taxes, and black-mail by the banks) has resulted in government service cutbacks, speed-up of city and state workers, and a policy of urban "triage." What this means for working class communities is that hardly a dollar of public funds is spent unless it helps someone to make a profit (usually through urban "renewal" and gentrification), while areas that are not currently profitable are left to rot. Anything that gets in the way of this process, such as the Rent Control program won through tenant struggles in the late 60s, is being eliminated. Neighborhoods are further disrupted as ethnic and racial groups are played off against each other, while traditional community institutions like neighborhood schools, churches, and political machines have grown steadily weaker. (These institutions, although racist and hardly progressive, at one time gave some working class communities the means for bargaining for concessions from the city's ruling class.)

The desegregation of Boston public schools needs to be understood in this light. Although the process was begun in response to demands for equality by black people, members of the State's corporate bourgeoisie have used the school restructuring program linked to busing as a means of regaining partial control of the school system from the more openly racist locally-based politicians. Although the desegregation plan has weakened local patronage machines, it has also aided the streamlining of the school system in the interests of the corporations and the further removal of education from the control of working class parents. And the closing of many older schools in black and mixed working class neighborhoods as part of the plan has further weakened the ability of these communities to resist deterioration and displacement.

TOWARD CLASS-CONSCIOUS STRUGGLE

It is in this context that City Life has begun to formulate our plan for fighting back. The thrust of our current organizing program can be summed up by the slogan SAVE BOSTON FOR BOSTON'S WORKING CLASS. This theme developed from two directions simultaneously: from our analysis of what's happening economically and politically to Boston, and our own needs as working class people—tenants, parents, and workers—struggling to survive here. For us the battle has three main fronts, corresponding to our three organizing committees:

---

*By "triage" we mean the decision by business and government planners to apply scarce resources only to areas where it will do some good (for capitalists, of course). Thus housing subsidies, public facilities and services, and investments are channelled to neighborhoods that "could go either way," under the assumption that more prosperous neighborhoods will save themselves, while poor communities are a lost cause anyway.

(1) The fight to save working class housing and stop the destruction of minority and working class neighborhoods.

(2) The fight against racism and for working class Parent Power in the public schools.

(3) The fight for a decent standard of living for people who live and work here, through organization of lower-wage workers, and linking workers and the community in struggles for better services.

We are convinced that as conditions worsen, growing numbers of people will become involved in these struggles. We see our role as helping to build the struggles, while trying to convey to people that it is not just a particular neighborhood, or school, or ethnic group, or category of workers that is getting screwed, but the working class of the city. At the same time we need to convince people that if the city is to be saved, it is only us working class people who can do the saving. In others words, our job is to help turn existing, fragmented struggles into a united, class-conscious movement.

The following description of our three organizing committees may give a better picture of how we are trying to begin.

Tenants Committee

Although we sometimes go door-knocking in buildings owned by targetted slumlords, most of the tenants we work with are people who get in touch with us for help. We get as many as 100 calls a month from people who hear about us from friends, the *CommUnity News,* or radio ads. We give advice to everyone, but we put the most energy into helping people who are working class and who are willing to work collectively with neighbors. As we work with people, we try to persuade them that each major rent increase, eviction, or demolition of a sound house is a blow to the whole working class community, and that homeowners as well as tenants have an interest in defending working-class housing. We try to get white people to recognize the effects of racist housing policies and to understand their own interests, as working class people, in supporting black and Latin struggles.

When we give aid to a tenant, we usually ask the person to reciprocate by doing something for the group (like answer phones) or for another tenant (like help someone contact a housing inspector). This helps to counteract the idea that we are some kind of social service agency. If the new person shows some initiative and interest in the group we encourage her to come to a tenants committee meeting. The next step would be to talk to the person about City Life and invite them to actually join the committee.

We haven't given up on tenant unions; in fact, a few of the groups we helped organize still exist. But we found that functioning tenant unions are hard to sustain, especially when there is a high turnover of residents in the building or development.

We have also found that often the hardest thing to ask a new person to do as a first step is to organize her own neighbors. But by joining the committee, new people can get support in their own situations, experience in working collectively, exposure to socialism and the idea of building a working class movement, and the skills and confidence they need to go back and organize in their own buildings or neighborhoods.

Most of the other Boston area tenants groups from the early 70s have fallen apart (as TAG probably would have had we remained a single-issue organization), and thus the tenants movement has ceased to exist. But we think there is the potential to rebuild city-wide resistance on a *class* basis to gentrification and neighborhood deterioration, and so we are trying to strengthen our ties with working class people and groups in other parts of the city. We also spend some time discussing ruling class plans for housing and the city and trying to formulate a socialist alternative.

Education Committee

This committee is made up of parents of kids in Boston public schools. The impulse for starting it arose from the need to deal with our children's problems at school as well as from a desire to organize other parents. So far the committee's work has centered around the Racial-Ethnic Parents Councils, parents advisory groups set up in each school as part of the desegregation plan. By giving parents a foot in school doors, the REPCs have aided the growth of a city-wide parents movement, responding to worsening conditions and struggling over a variety of issues ranging from transportation and classroom size to racist administrators. Often immediate problems, such as the lack of basic supplies, are so pressing that it is hard to get to the more fundamental issues.

The City Life Education Committee members play an active role in these immediate struggles and in doing so, try to relate them to the broader issues of race and class. They also try to increase the participation, class consciousness and power of working class parents within the movement, such as by forming support groups of working class parent activists, and by challenging the notion that the education "experts" know what is best for our kids. Another way the committee tries to reach new parents and get its view across is by writing a regular column in the *CommUnity News*. We use the column to expose the racist, sexist, and anti-working class bias in school structures and curricula, and to give a sense of what education *could* be like if working class people were in control of it.

The Workplace Committee

The membership of this committee reflects the economic base of Boston. Some members work in manufacturing, transportation, or printing, but as many have clerical or service jobs in industries such as health and education. This is City Life's newest committee, and we are still too small to concentrate people in any one industry or to carry out a city-wide strategy. Most of the committee members, however, are rooted in organizing at their own workplaces, and the committee functions as a support group for them. The committee has also mobilized support for a variety of local workers' struggles, and is beginning to set up events and study groups to which members can invite the people they get to know at work.

But primarily, at this stage, the job of this committee is to formulate a City Life strategy for our workplace organizing in Boston. Among the questions the committee has been discussing are: What is the role of socialists in union organizing drives and union shops? What are the peculiarities of organizing in service industries? What are the boundaries of, and divisions within the U.S. and the local working class? How can we promote struggles that build the *positive* side of class consciousness, i.e., workers' desires to take pride in and have control over our own work?

WHY TALK ABOUT SOCIALISM?

Our organizing work has deepened our conviction that a class-conscious movement has to have socialism as its explicit goal. The question of socialism cannot be put off until some later stage because we have reached the stage at which only a socialist program can point the way out of the trap the cities are in. Short of eliminating profit as the basis of the housing industry, there is no way to break the cycles of disinvestment and decay, and of inflated housing costs, gentrification, and displacement. Likewise, only the socialization of investment will be able to reverse the loss of jobs and end the fiscal crisis. And nothing less can provide the material basis for the elimination of racism.

Changed political and economic conditions make this more clear today than it was in the 1960s. Then, it was possible to struggle in the name of justice for civil rights, "participation," and gains in housing and welfare for the poorest sectors of the working class. The economy was still expanding at a rate that allowed the poor to be given a piece of the pie without much being taken off the plate of anyone else. What most of these poor people's struggles, no matter how militant, boiled down to was a demand for the state to "give us more." But at that time, to an extent, they could succeed. Today this is no longer the case. The idea promoted by Piven and others that if we could only revive the mass disruptions and other tactics of the '60s, we could stop the erosion of the gains made back then ignores economic reality. U.S. capitalism can no longer afford buttered guns.

In the '60s—previous to global recession, the energy squeeze, and the balance of payments crisis—the growing rate of inflation, egged on by staggering public debt, could still be tolerated. But today inflation is becoming a threat to capitalist growth and, among other things, public spending has to be held down. An increasing proportion of the public funds that *are* spent must be spent to subsidize profit-making, directly or indirectly. The alternative (within the limits of capitalism, of course) would mean reduced incentives to invest and economic contraction.

In other words, today there is much less flexibility in the system. Even when those in power might prefer, for political reasons, to grant concessions such as urban reconstruction, welfare programs, or environmental controls, they find it hard to do so without cutting into someone's profit and undermining the economy in one way or another. Thus when something is given with one hand, it is taken away with the other (wage gains are eaten away by inflation, tax cuts to homeowners are compensated for by other, equally regressive forms of tax exploitation or by service cutbacks, and so on). Now that the American empire has passed its peak, there will be few ways that working class people in this country will be able to win *more,* in material terms,except at the expense of other sectors of the working class. Under these circumstances, there is little chance of reform movements that remain within a capitalist frame of reference winning any substantial improvements in working class living standards.

This is one reason why our strategy differs from that of the current populist reform groups. It is our view that these groups will be able to win few, if any, economic gains, and that such gains as may be won will either be illusory or, at worst, will actually increase the gap between the more advantaged sectors of the working class (whites, longer-term residents, homeowners) and the lower-income, less established sectors.

In every area of our organizing we are confronted with the ways in which working class people are in conflict with each other. The deepest divisions are along lines of race, but there are other ways that groups are pitted against each other: Tenants vs. homeowners; one neighborhood vs. another; the steadily employed vs. the marginally employed and welfare recipients; citizens vs. undocumented residents; public school parents vs. taxpayers with no kids in the school system; city vs. suburban residents; and of course women vs. men and homosexuals vs. heterosexuals. If a movement broad enough to have real power is to be built, many more of these people will have to be persuaded of the common class interests that transcend these particular divisions. The context for building this class consciousness is struggles that unite people around interests that they do have in common.

However, a movement that is limited to struggling for individual economic gains, and whose goals are defined solely in terms of "economic justice," will not be able to develop this class consciousness and class unity. For while there may be some reforms that, if won, could benefit most working class people, there are many ways in which the short-range material needs of different sectors of the working class are objectively in conflict. There can be no economic reform program—within the framework of capitalism—that addresses the needs of all of us. A movement based primarily on the promise of direct material benefits without a change in the system will either set its followers up for cynicism when the demands cannot be won, or will be dashed on the rocks of racism and interest-group politics when it becomes clear that some people's needs must be sacrificed for the benefit of others.

Does this mean we should stop fighting for economic reforms? Definitely not. But it does mean that our goal in waging these struggles must be to challenge the basic assumptions of capitalism, the constraints that stand in the way of *all* of us having fulfilling and materially secure lives. One side of this challenge involves exposing the fundamental irrationality and exploitativeness—not just the "corruption" and "injustice"—of the present system. The other aspect of it involves the development of an alternative, a socialist program that must be conveyed to people in convincingly concrete terms.

A socialist program for the U.S. isn't something we can develop simply by sitting down and writing it. Although we could sketch some of the broad outlines now, to a great extent such a program will only begin to appear plausible, winnable, or even desirable to people as the struggle develops and as people are changed in the process. For one thing, a workable socialism will require the redefinition of many of our needs away from individualized consumption and in the direction of more collective forms. Under socialism, less alienating and individualized forms of housing, transportation, and recreation could provide the basis for some of the non-material benefits—like security, increased social contact, a feeling of community—that even now people perceive as missing from their lives. But no speech or pamphlet alone will convince people that the missing dimension, a sense of community and collective purpose, can be regained and is worth fighting for. But the actual experience of collective struggle *can* convince and transform people, just as it did many of us in the '60s.

Another essential ingredient for socialism that can only be developed through mass struggles is working class leadership and the confidence among working people that we can take over and run things better. To us in City Life, socialism means that the working class is in power at all levels of society. But the power to govern is not something we can just "take"; it has to be created through struggle, mass participation and over a long period of time. This is why we say the means of struggle are as important as the ends. In any particular battle, the extent to which people are mobilized, take collective risks, break through old patterns of individualism, sexism, and racism, gain a sense of their potential power, and strengthen the skills and accountability of leadership is as important as whether the particular demand is won or lost.

This is a point on which we disagree with both the populists and with the traditionalist [Marxist-Leninist] groups, and where we think the two approaches have a lot in common. Both the populist and the current party-building groups, from what we have seen, tend to rely on hierarchical forms of organization and on methods of struggle which do little to increase the confidence, decision-making ability, and leadership potential of rank and file members.

City Life does not claim to have all the answers. While we have a lot of confidence in the politics that have been laid out here, there is clearly a lot more that we need to learn. With the support of the rest of the group, I decided to stick my neck out and publish this article in the hope that other people and organizations will respond with descriptions of their own organizing experience and their conclusions from that experience, whether they tend to support or call into question the lessons we have drawn.

APPENDIX

Interview Guide

This guide is similar to those used by the interviewers who gathered materials for this volume. It may be used by students, researchers, and practitioners interested in gathering additional illustrations of practice.

1. Can you first give me a thumbnail sketch of the project or program activities in which you have been personally involved in the last few months? (CLEARLY DISTINGUISH DISCRETE "PROJECTS" IF POSSIBLE. SHARPEN THE IDENTITY OF ONE OR TWO FOR LATER ELABORATION)

2. Are you presently involved in any of these projects? (IF THERE ARE SEVERAL, PICK THE ONE IN WHICH HE/SHE SEEMS MOST PERSONALLY INVOLVED EVEN IF RECENTLY COMPLETED. AVOID A VERY NEW ONE FOR PURPOSES OF DETAILED EXPLANATION.)
   How did the project begin?
   How did the *idea* for the project arise?
      (PROBE FOR: Individual initiation
                   Degree of information available
                   Felt need
                   Decision regarding plans to proceed
                   Decision regarding organization of formal project)

3. What was the stated project goal at that time? How was the goal determined? By whom? Were alternatives considered? Why were they rejected?

4. What were the first steps that you personally took in the project? (PROBE FOR PURPOSES THAT PROMPTED HIM/HER TO TAKE THE ACTION HE/SHE DID.)

5. What kind of things did you do in the weeks that followed to develop the project further?

   (PROBE FOR: What happened at each stage

   Developments within each stage

   Why each action was taken

   What influenced him to take such action

   What factors were involved in his decisions)

6. In what ways do you continue to be involved in the project?

   (PROBE FOR: Policy making

   Program planning

   Program implementation

   Degree of responsibility)

   (SELECT THE AREA OR EVENT OF GREATEST INTEREST TO THE RESPONDENT.) Can you tell me in detail just what happened? (PROBE FOR ACTIONS TAKEN, PURPOSES FOR ACTIONS.)

7. Where do you see the project going from here? How would you characterize the present goals of the projects? Why are they different from the original?

8. What are some of the difficulties that consistently confronted you in working on this project? How did you resolve these? Which ones did you not resolve? How satisfied are you with the way these difficulties were handled?

9. If you had a chance to work your way through the complexity of the whole project again, how would you alter your involvement? What would you do differently? What other supports would you need?